Digital Design for Print and Web

Digital Design for Print and Web

An Introduction to Theory, Principles, and Techniques

John DiMarco, Ph.D.

WILEY

John Wiley and Sons

Library of Congress Cataloging-in-Publication Data:

DiMarco, John, 1969–
Digital design for print and web : an introduction to theory and techniques / by John DiMarco.
     p. cm.
  Includes bibliographical references and index.
ISBN 978-0-470-39836-4 (pbk. : alk. paper) 1. Commercial art—Data processing. 2. Graphic arts—Data processing. 3. Web sites—Design. I. Title.
  NK1520.D56 2009
  741.6--dc22
                                  2009033990

Printed in the United States of America

10 9 8 7 6 5 4 3 2

To my partner and my love, Kimberly, and my boys, David and Jack.

Contents

Appendices and online movie lessons are available at www.wiley.com/
go/digitaldesign.

Preface

Digital Design for Print and Web: An Introduction to Theory, Principles, and Techniques was written to help people succeed with digital design. It is a learning product that incorporates both video lessons and an in-depth textbook written from two perspectives—that of a student, and that of a teacher.

First I put myself in the shoes of a new designer or design student caught up in a frenzy of information. The melding of new technology, techniques, and principles causes many inexperienced designers to default to honing their computer skills, rather than establishing their design sense. This is dangerous: it creates a backlash against the creative process, which requires us to think creatively and then produce—not the other way around. As tools and technology become increasingly accessible—and powerful—I see this problem among more and more students.

To learn design, you need to recognize it and extract its principles for use in your own work. To be a digital designer, you must marry the principles of design to software techniques. You are thus engaged in using theory in practice. That is what this book is about. It will help you discover the principles of design and understand the most vital digital design techniques used today. Along the way, you will learn by seeing real-world design examples from highly prominent designers and artists. Then you will learn by doing, using step-by-step examples and tutorial movies.

As a teacher of digital design, I have come to realize that I must deliver lessons in principles, techniques, and technology. Having only two of the three components in my lectures jeopardizes the learning experiences of my students. Finding teaching resources, especially textbooks, is difficult; most simply don't deliver the depth and breadth of coverage needed to teach both theoretically and pragmatically. When teaching digital design in the past, I have often been forced to use several books for a single course—or no book at all—simply because no one book could provide both the theory and practical application that I felt I must convey to my students. That is why I wrote this book: a text that can be used in a classroom and that can serve as a valuable professional resource after the formal learning concludes. This text covers and connects introductory theoretical design foundations and industry standard techniques for visual communication problem solving using print and Web media.

Although the text presents several different industry-standard software applications, the book is technique driven rather than software driven. The techniques are applied to digital design problem solving across software titles and versions. The book aims to provide value to small lab settings that demand hands-on instructors as well as to larger courses planned around instructor-driven lectures and demonstrations that encourage experienced students to explore software techniques on their own. Inspiration is provided through images from classic and contemporary designers.

Part One presents introductory design and graphic communication concepts and principles. Theoretical coverage includes a concise design overview surveying communication goals and fundamental design principles, using historical, professional, and student images of digital print design, Web design, Web graphics, digital imaging, and digital illustration.

Part Two introduces technical coverage, providing a primer of basic to intermediate digital design techniques for students of communication design, graphic design, computer graphics, and media graphics.

Unique Features

- Over two hundred historical and professional illustrations of design concepts, print design, Web design, Web graphics, digital imaging, and digital illustration from world-renowned designers and design firms as well as students.

- Coverage of theory and practice in one text.

- Online tutorial movies for each chapter to support classroom lectures, student assignments, and lab sessions.

- Design assignments for in-class or homework assignments.

- Illustrated, step-by-step techniques.

- A comprehensive connection between theory and practice.

- Critical terms and techniques combined with short treatments to provide a thorough primer for new learners.

- Advanced production projects online for accelerated students.

- Progression toward print and Web project development.

- Pedagogical tools including chapter objectives, key design concepts, design assignments, endnotes, and additional bibliographic resources.

Acknowledgments

This book was a team effort. Following are the people who helped make it come together.

The Team at Wiley

I am thankful to the team at John Wiley & Sons who made my vision a reality. Senior editor Margaret Cummins and her assistants Leslie Saxman and Lauren Poplawski worked hard to mold my ideas into a publication that would impact the lives of students and professionals across the world. Margaret walked me through this project, sharing her wealth of experience and expertise freely. She challenged me to develop a book that would refresh the digital design publication market and enable people who read it to learn critical principles and techniques in a way that is clear, comprehensive, and innovative. I also need to thank senior production editor David Sassian and copyeditor Andrew Miller for polishing the manuscript into a finished work.

Contributors to This Book

I was so fortunate to connect with a wealth of great creative professionals when I was writing this book. These designers, photographers, and design history icons, as busy as they are, were kind enough to respond to the requests I sent them for images of their work. Those images helped make this book beautiful and practical, and I am grateful to each one of them for their contribution to my small piece of history.

James Biber of Pentagram Design

Michael Bierut of Pentagram Design

Michael Calandra

Kristen Crawford

Hillman Curtis of Hillman Curtis Inc.

Greg D'Onofrio of Kind Company

John Fekner

Brian Fendt

Kevin Fornito

Michael Gericke of Pentagram Design

Milton Glaser of Milton Glaser Studio

Luke Hayman of Pentagram Design

Kitt Hendricks of Pentagram Design

Julia Hoffmann, Creative Director, Museum of Modern Art (MOMA)

Angus Hyland of Pentagram Design

Don Leicht

Domenic Lippa of Pentagram Design

Alvin Lustig

Elaine Lustig Cohen

Richard Kirk Mills

Justus Oehler of Pentagram Design

Susannah McDonald, Archivist at Pentagram Design

Abbot Miller of Pentagram Design

Micha Riss of Flying Machine

Stefan Sagmeister of Sagmeister Inc.

Paula Scher of Pentagram Design

Jee Won Sin

Tommy Spero of Soul Associates

DJ Stout of Pentagram Design

Lisa Strausfeld of Pentagram Design

Richard Rex Thomas

Steve Watson of Turnstyle

Special Thanks

My former student, and now my friend and colleague, Kristen Crawford provided many of the illustrations and figures in this book, working through my sometimes cryptic requests. Her tireless dedication to this project was instrumental to its success. I am thankful to have met Kristen and value her friendship.

My former students Brian Fendt, Kevin Fornito, and Michael Calandra graciously provided their photography and artwork for the in-text examples and learning movies.

Richard Rex Thomas wrote a special appendix on digital photography for the book. I am thankful to Rex for taking time out of his busy life to give my readers a chunk of his expertise.

My Mentors

Dr. Frank Brady has given me the opportunity to succeed at the institution that I love, St. John's University, and the guidance I constantly need to navigate academia and achieve my goals. I cherish my relationship with him and am honored to receive kind mentoring from such an accomplished scholar. I also need to thank Dean Kathleen Voute MacDonald of St. John's University, who has supported my professional projects and research efforts from the beginning of my journey at St. John's. Dr. Richard Smiraglia has been a foundation for learning and taught me how to perform research and write effectively. Finally, my former professors (whom I now call friends), John Fekner and Rick Mills have guided me to embrace a life of creativity—something I will cherish forever.

My Students

I am grateful to the many students who inspire me every day and allow me to pay it forward as much as I can. They make me constantly consider the clarity of my teaching and my mission in life.

My Family and Friends

Nothing happens in my life without my most important support system, my family and friends. My wife Kimberly is my partner, my love, and my life. My boys, David and Jack, bring me joy and pride, and I only hope that I can help them grow into people who find true happiness and make a difference in society.

My parents, John and Frances DiMarco, show me the love and support that has helped me to pursue my dreams. My sisters, Margaret and Roseann; my brother Jerry; Gina and Richard; Corinne, Dylan, Tristan, and Ricky; and Alexis and Joey; Aunt Marie and Uncle Billy are constant sources of support and happiness. I must sincerely thank my extended family who treat me like one of their own: Karen, whom we miss dearly; Paul and Anell; Paul and Ginger; Brianna, Tori, Justin, Uncle Richie, and Aunt Chrissie; Jill and Joe; Julia, Jay, and Chris; Peyton, Josh and Matt; Aunt Barbara and Uncle Vinny; little Vinny and William; Aunt Cynthia, Brian and Eric; the DeAngelo and Molé families; and finally, our Babci, Florence Borowski. Our best friends and the godparents to my son, Steve and Debbie Demeo, are truly special. I am truly grateful to have such caring people in my life.

PART ONE
Theory and Principles

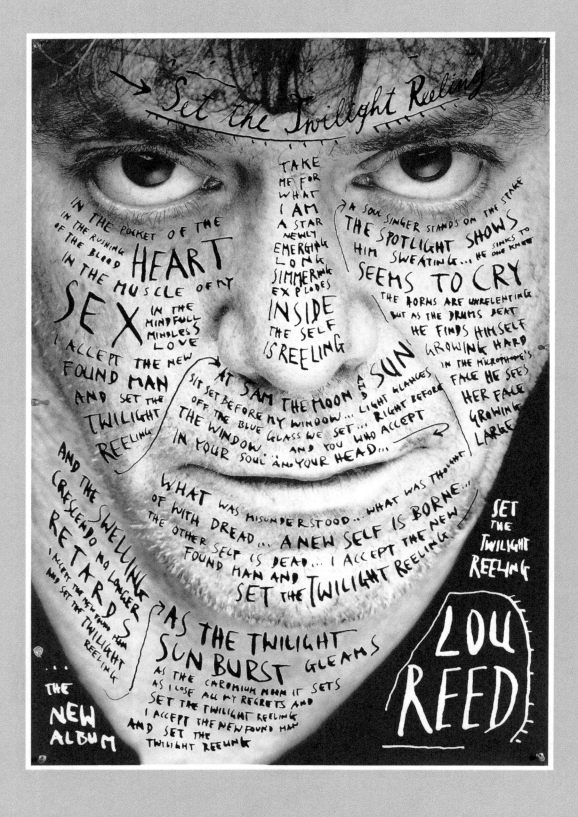

CHAPTER 1
Communication Goals

Chapter Objectives

Define graphic communication.

Identify and define communication goals: information, persuasion, education, and entertainment.

What Is Graphic Communication?

Graphic communication is the result of a long evolution of tools and techniques. That evolution was greatly accelerated by the establishment of modern, industrial societies—and graphic communication itself greatly contributed to modern social and economic development, to the extent that today visual communication is a readily identifiable force in the growth of both Western and Eastern "postindustrial" information economies.

According to historical literature, graphic communication has taken as long as 30,000 years to evolve (Meggs 1998). The role of the visual communicator—and the function of communication—developed slowly: cave paintings done between 15,000 and 10,000 B.C., the invention of writing with pictographs in Mesopotamia (3100 B.C.), the invention of paper and Chinese relief printing (second century A.D.), the rise of late medieval illuminated manuscripts (eighth century A.D.), and the breakthrough of movable type in Europe (1450 A.D.) all contributed to that development. Investigation of communication design over the last century reveals patterns of technological, economic, occupational, spatial, and cultural development that can be attributed to the creation of an information-driven economy and society that relies on communication design and technology for stability and growth.

Although enhanced and changed by modern technology, including software and computers, the basics of communication have essentially remained the same through the millennia. Communication is a process that requires a sender (the designer), a message (information or an effort to persuade), a medium (the delivery platform), and a receiver of that message (the audience). Communication comes in various forms and is delivered in various media, or platforms for communication delivery. These media include all forms of printed paper or material (books, magazines, newspapers, brochures, flyers, signage, and billboards), the Internet, mobile phones and handheld devices, television, radio, CDs and DVDs, videos, video games, and films. Media transmitted to mass audiences is called mass media; it includes television, film, recordings, mobile technology, magazines, books, the Internet, and radio. Conversely, a brochure, part of a collection of collateral material, may only be seen by a few people.

Communication and media futurist Marshall McLuhan theorized that "the medium is the message," meaning that we absorb and judge messages based on how they are delivered (Benedetti and deHart 1997). If we see an advertisement in a newspaper, we initially perceive it as factual simply because it comes to us via the mass media. Then, we step back and decipher the message to determine if it can be trusted, and to what level it can be absorbed and used by us; this process is part of media literacy. In all forms of communication, judicious design and professional production values therefore become vital to the success of a message. The final product—how it looks and performs visually—becomes a factor in the value of the communication and how it meets its goal. The content, design, and medium (output) make up the complete message, and each has an effect on the communication's perceived credibility and persuasiveness.

FIGURES 1-1, A and B (overleaf) This brochure and Web page for the Tawkin' New Yawk City Walls art exhibit combines panoramic photographs of New York City with classic graffiti stencil type that is lit up like a sign in Times Square. The copy takes a stab at the stereotypical New York accent. The exhibit's theme is that the walls of New York City are always talking to us through street art and design. Design by Jeewon Shin.

FIGURE 1-1B

Communication can be written, as with copywriting and poetry. It can be visual, as with graphic design and fine art. It can be verbal, as with speech or song, or nonverbal, as with body language, dance, or instrumental music. This book focuses on visual communication and production in print (i.e., on paper) and on the Web.

The goals of such messages are to inform, to persuade, to educate, or to entertain. These goals overlap in many instances, but ultimately we plan communication vehicles such as brochures, Web sites, advertisements, commercials, animations, posters, flyers, books, magazines, video games, films, newspapers, and presentations with one specific goal in mind. For example, a children's site could have the specific communication goal of educating children in math techniques. That central goal may be enhanced by using entertainment in the content of the site—for example, interactive games and animation that explain math techniques in a fun, engaging way. A newspaper attempts to deliver news that informs the reader quickly and efficiently by using headline text, charts, and graphs. When newspapers print sensual or shocking images, although the main goal may be to inform, the effect may be also to elicit an emotional response from readers.

Paul Martin Lester (2006, 50–51) outlined two ways that we process communication: sensually and perceptually. These differing pathways have been studied by scientists and other researchers. The sensual process, that which leads from sensation to visual communication, occurs when our eyes see visual forms and our brain takes the sensations (visual input) and makes a coherent image (also known as a gestalt). Perceptual processing occurs

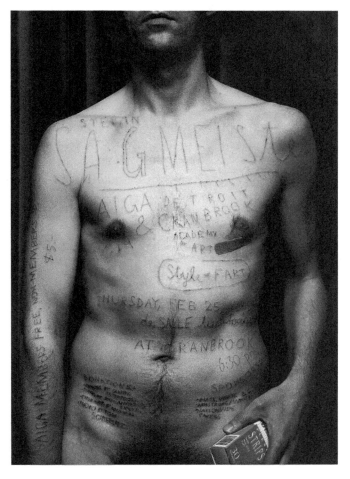

FIGURE 1-2 Sensual: American Institute of Graphic Arts (AIGA) Detroit poster designed by Stefan Sagmeister. Arresting imagery is used to convey the message that creating design can be painful. Art direction by Stefan Sagmeister.

when our brains make immediate meaning from an image we see, such as that of a traffic light. The gestalt principle states that we see the whole before we identify the parts. Our brains separate wholes into parts to establish a figure (foreground) and a ground (background). When we can visually stabilize the parts into a whole image and identify figure and ground, we can make visual sense of an image. Combining images creates new meanings from the identification of associated symbols.

Perception to visual communication occurs when we see images beyond the sensations and assign them complex meanings. An approach to understanding perception is semiotics, the study of signs. Signs have complex cultural meanings and can be seen in three ways: iconic, indexical, and symbolic (Lester 2006, 52–57). We are guided by iconic signs in everyday life: iconic signs are intended to be true representations of what they present—such as a photograph. Indexical signs have a logical connection to what they represent, such as dark clouds as a sign of stormy weather or falling snow as a sign of winter. Symbolic signs forge a cultural or social connection between an image or object and what it represents. Therefore, symbolic signs take on different meanings for different audiences—as in the case of a flag, monument, or style of dress.

As designers, we create a series of signs each time we create imagery. Our focus on the goals of a communication helps ensure that we create meaningful, simple, and understandable signs. Creating thoughtful communication requires researching the audience, recognizing its cultural and societal viewpoints, and delivering simple, clear messages that connect with its need or ability to be informed, persuaded, educated, and entertained. Indeed, using communication with the intended goal of informing, persuading, educating, or entertaining is the applied focus of digital design. The pervasive, all-encompassing power of digital information and communication technologies have given us a potent platform for gathering data, sculpting it into meaningful information, and producing designs that can be delivered via print, Web, broadcast, mobile technology, or industrial material.

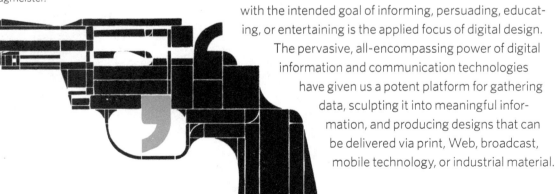

FIGURE 1-3 Perceptual: This poster for Neenah Paper uses a single punctuation mark—an apostrophe—to symbolize the gun's trigger. The deeper meaning is that the apostrophe is responsible for letter elimination. Art direction by Stefan Sagmeister.

Information

What Is Information?

Information is a raw material of—and core ingredient in—all designs and is part of all communication goals. Information is gathered in myriad ways and then adapted to fit the goal of the communication—whether to inform, persuade, educate, or entertain. We must have information in order to create a design.

Information is structured data. Data consists of random bits and pieces that can be seen all around us and can be gathered. We process data to create information that has meaning and contextualizes our reality. Numbers are a great example of data. Random numbers have little meaning to us, but when they are placed in a context, such as a birthday, on a player's uniform, or in a name (such as Louis XIV), they become information with meaning.

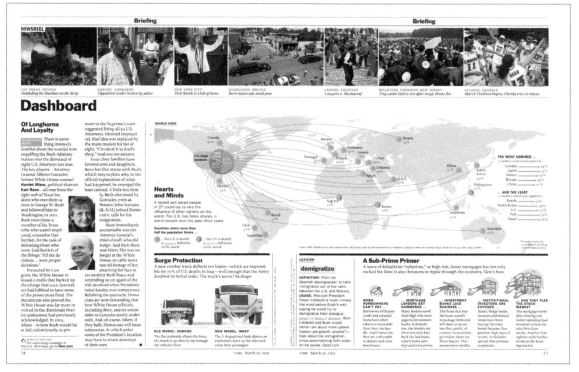

FIGURE 1-4 In this redesign of *Time* magazine, the infographic transforms data into meaningful information through thoughtful illustration and the dominance of some design elements over others. Design by Luke Hayman.

FIGURE 1-5 This Web page for Art Projects International provides small multiples of information in the form of symmetrical thumbnails to unify the visual as a whole. Design by Kind Company.

Information design arranges chunks of data and information to inform the viewer. Information-focused designs communicate to us each day as we stop at a stop sign, read a train schedule, or watch the weather report on the evening news. Information designs are seen in newspapers, newscasts, calendars, timelines, charts, corporate reports, news Web sites, and instructional materials.

The meaning attached to information design can be purposeful, as in a campus map, or it may be lifesaving, as in an emergency exit sign. Information design must have high fidelity in meaning and visual strength in execution-because it guides the viewer during action. People must navigate through a Web site in order find information (text, photos, video, and audio content). Similarly, when reading a newspaper, people must navigate through various articles and sections in order to find information (stories, box scores, and ads) meaningful to them. Although there is an element of curiosity (looking for things) and discoverability (finding things) in print and Web interactions, information design—both for print and the Web—works to guide a viewer toward meaning as quickly as possible. In print design, the message must be read, understood, and processed by the viewer so it can be acted upon. This is known as legibility. In Web design, it is known as usability. The concepts of legibility and usability are discussed further in part 2 of this book.

Principles and Goals: Design for Information

When creating designs for information, decisions related to what viewers want—and what they need to be informed—become critical to success, and smart choices must be made based on the product definition, the audience, the environment, the development tools, and available raw materials. Decisions about text, images, and technology, which are needed to develop and deliver the message, should always be planned out.

Structure is the key component in information graphics (also known as infographics); achieving the proper gestalt (unification of the parts) leads to understanding on the part of the viewer or user. Therefore, information designers frequently use fact boxes, tables, diagrams, and illustrations. In his classic text *Envisioning Information,* Edward Tufte describes the flat, two-dimensional paper or video/computer screen media used in information design as "flatland." "Escaping flatland," states Tufte, is a key goal in designing the presentation of information (Tufte 1990, 12). He promotes information density (quantity) and resolving power (clarity) in information design. He suggests the following principles to help escape flatland and build meaningful designs for information:

- Micro/macro readings represent information that is rich in detail and in overall structure. Micro refers to critical information that is read carefully to extract meaning. Macro refers to the larger whole that contains the micro components. We frequently see micro/macro readings in maps, flowcharts, blueprints, timetables, and monuments.

FIGURE 1-6 This spread from the book *100 Baseball Icons* shows how composition can be used to present a rich overall structure (macro) using detailed visual components (micro). Design by Kit Hinrichs.

• Layering and separation represent an informational structure through overlapping elements, grids, margins, and white space. We frequently see layering and separation in Web pages, charts and graphs, catalogs, ads, magazines, newspapers, books, and brochures.

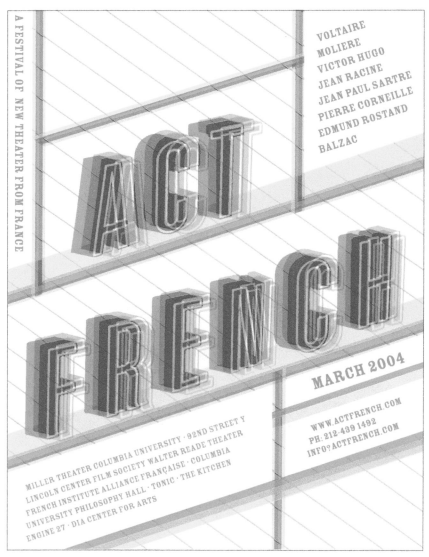

FIGURE 1-7 The Act French poster design uses layering of type and creates separation using line and space. Design by Julia Hoffmann.

- Small multiples represent information using repetition, consistency, mimicry, and iconic representation. We frequently see small multiples in instruction manuals, road maps, posters, computer interfaces, data tables, and charts.

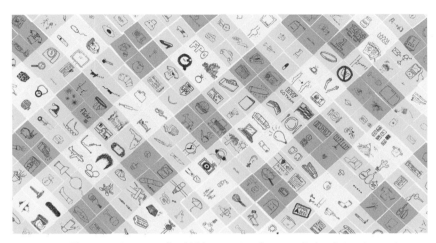

FIGURE 1-8 This wrapping paper for AIGA presents a fun overall visual structure using patterning. Smaller, detailed images create micro structures that can be viewed independently, which is also fun. Design by Julia Hoffmann.

- Color provides hierarchical value, sensation, contrast, and visual texture.[1] Color is a fundamental component of all design.

FIGURE 1-9 The Alvin Lustig history site by Kind Company uses black and white and warm colors to separate sets of visuals and information and to establish a stylized retro mood. Design by Kind Company.

FIGURE 1-10 This poster for the 2007 Shakespeare Festival uses sensual colors to evoke the feeling of love. Design by Paula Scher.

Persuasion

What Is Persuasion?

The notion of persuasion is essential to many scholars' definitions of communication. David Berlo's definition of communication states, "All communication behavior has as its purpose the eliciting of a specific response from a specific person (or group of persons)" (Berlo 1960, 16).

FIGURE 1-11 This advertising poster for the Adobe Student Design Competition depicts a designer creating an award-winning work out of paper cups (real coffee was used). This emotional approach targets the design student who identifies with carefully crafted work and caffeine, as many do. Art direction by Stefan Sagmeister. Design by Matthias Ernstberger.

Persuasion is central to all communication, especially digital design, and particularly as it is applied to advertising. Information is converted into persuasive arguments during the advertising creative process (White 2007, 11). Persuasive arguments provide controlled messages that highlight features, advantages, benefits, and a unique selling proposition to a target audience. Persuasion is attempted by delivering rational appeal (using factual argument) or emotional appeal (using values, opinions, and attitudes) to bring someone to action. Action comes in the form of buying a product or service, subscribing to an idea, donating to a public service organization, or voting for a political candidate.

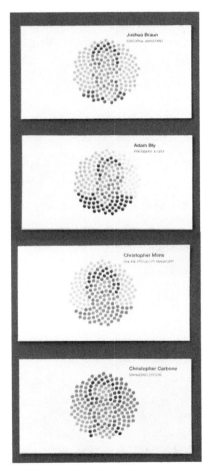

FIGURE 1-12 The pieces of a standard corporate identity package are the business card, letterhead, and envelope. This design mark uses repetition, shape, and color to convey a visualization of science and media. Art direction by Stefan Sagmeister. Design by Matthias Ernstberger.

Brands, an essential tool in persuasion, are "created in the mind," according to Walter Landor (Wheeler, 2003). Brands become the icons that customers look for when purchasing products. Built around symbolic logos, brands evolve into identities recognizable to consumers. The designer works to establish a visual icon—a logo—that represents the brand and creates a channel of persuasion built on trust and recognition. We recognize and connect to certain brands as they become iconic, indexical, or symbolic to us. The look of the corporate identity is critical in representing the company and its products and services.

FIGURE 1-14 Paula Scher quickly made visual sense of the Travelers merger with Citibank. She effortlessly mocked up the concept on a napkin during the pitch meeting. Design by Paula Scher.

FIGURE 1-15 The Citi logo. Photo by John DiMarco

Principles and Goals: Design for Persuasion

Our goal as designers who create persuasive documents is simple in theory, but quite challenging in practice. We must use type, image, and multimedia to bring the viewer to an understanding of the message and a desire to act upon it. We want the viewer to understand the feature, advantage, or benefit we are presenting. We want the viewer to agree to the unique selling proposition we are pitching through the visuals we present in our persuasive designs.

Certain elements of persuasive designs have resonance in the human mind. A design cannot be persuasive if it cannot be understood. Concentrate on one idea for each persuasive communication. Follow these suggestions in your print and Web designs to increase their persuasive value:

- Do research on the audience and the competition to put you in the viewer's situation.

- Use arresting or thought-provoking images (photos or illustrations) that act as a magnet for the viewer's eyes.

- Use display type (which is larger and more dominant than the body text) that draws the reader in. Create visually dominant attention-seeking headlines.

- Explain and clarify features, advantages, and benefits in highly legible body copy.

- Use grids to arrange elements in order of importance.

- Use size to clarify meaning and create visual hierarchy.

- Use color to attract attention, group elements, indicate meaning, and enhance aesthetics (Lidwell et al. 2003, 38).

- Keep messages and visual elements simple so recognition is quick.

- Use themes to connect with the audience.

FIGURE 1-16 A digitally created, thought-provoking visual dominates this poster, "We Are All African," which forges a persuasive message. Design by Milton Glaser.

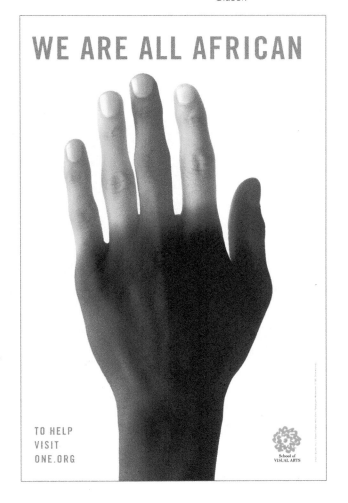

Education

What Is Education?

Simply stated, education is the process of transferring knowledge and skills. Instructional design is also known as designing for education and is also used in designing for training. The goal of education design is to translate learning objectives (lessons) into measurable outcomes for the learner. Connecting a lesson-based communication into a learning experience requires instructional design; the designer must create engaging, understandable chunks of communication that guide the viewer toward comprehension, application, criticism, and synthesis of something that is new. We see design for education in textbooks (such as this one) and children's books, online learning objects (such as interactive games and activities), educational brochures (like the one at your dentist on how to properly brush your teeth), educational television and videos (*Sesame Street* and *Blue's Clues*, for example), posters, classroom teaching materials, and e-learning courses for academic credit or corporate training.

FIGURE 1-17 E-learning is used to educate employees at Canon. This screenshot from Canon and the Imaging Industries e-learning course uses small multiples and chunks to deliver the history of the organization. Design by John DiMarco.

Principles and Goals: Design for Education

In their book *Universal Principles of Design,* Lidwell, Holden, and Butler answer the question, How can I help people learn from a design? The authors provide some fundamental sections on how a designer can enhance the learning experience for the viewer.

- Use chunks (small units) of information in designs. Chunking involves combining many units of information into smaller units, or chunks, so it is easier to remember the information (Lidwell et al. 2003, 30). Using bulleted lists, tables, and short paragraphs of text helps the learner grasp topics and avoid overload when absorbing new information.

- Use hierarchy in designs for education. Using trees, nests, and stairs in educational graphics helps the viewer make relationships to the material presented and emphasizes the importance of each element (Lidwell et al. 2003, 104).

- Pursue legibility at all costs in design for education, because it is critical to understanding. Legibility ensures that items are as clear and simple as possible so that the viewer can digest the information without questions. Using contrast, space, type, and images consistently helps build legibility in your education designs.

- Use mental models to illustrate concepts that involve user experience and how something works (Lidwell et al. 2003, 130). Use real-life models if available and appropriate, but do not use models that are not specific to the task. The design should incorporate the real event and the expected outcome in order to create scenario-based learning. Mental models are used in simulations. For

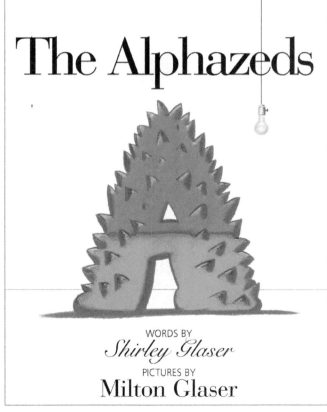

FIGURE 1-18 Children's books are educational design projects. They require the designer to focus on using communication to educate and entertain through design and, most importantly, illustration. Design and illustration by Milton Glaser.

example, flight simulators teach pilots how to use aviation instrumentation without being in planes. For the designer to understand the model and to grasp key interactions, he or she should use the model in real life first, before—as well as during—the design process, if possible.

- Use progressive disclosure in education and instructional designs to manage complex information so that it is displayed only at the necessary time (Lidwell et al. 2003, 154). Give viewers only what they need to learn at that particular moment. New, more complex information should be discovered upon request or after simpler information is digested. In print design, progressive disclosure is seen in footnotes, appendices, and instructions. Instruction manuals guide the reader toward learning about a product by revealing more complex features as the reader gets deeper into the manual's contents. In Web design, progressive disclosure is seen by clicking a button labeled More or Next. Web-based training, also known as e-learning, uses progressive disclosure to pace the learner through the materials and to give relevance to each chunk of information being presented.

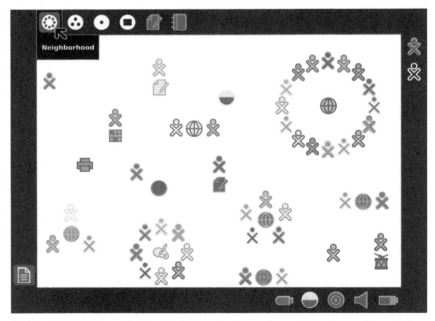

FIGURE 1-19 The Sugar interface design for the One Laptop per Child Foundation is built for intuitive operation and uses a mental model to represent neighborhoods. Design by Lisa Strausfeld.

Entertainment

What Is Entertainment?

Dictionary.com defines entertainment as "something affording pleasure, diversion, or amusement, esp. a performance of some kind."[2] Design for entertainment is seen in fine art, television programs, plays, animation (for TV, Web, and gaming), video games, films, books, magazines, movies (on television or the Web), e-books, and digital video on the Web.

Principles and Goals: Design for Entertainment

Entertainment design requires focus on creating an art form that has the ability to engage the viewer or listener to appreciate a product emotionally and intellectually (Pramaggiore and Wallis 2008, 3). The basic framework of items that you would need to focus on when designing for entertainment are:

- Narrative or documentary (the story and the writing: fiction or nonfiction)
- Cinematography (the camera work: shot setups, framing, lighting)
- Staging (the set design: stage or screen)
- Audio (dialogue and sound effects)
- Characters (the talent: actors or animations)
- Visuals (titling, images, special effects)
- Style (the look and feel of the details)
- Delivery medium (television, print vehicle, Web site, DVD, video, CD-ROM, movie theater, stage, concert hall).

FIGURE 1-20 The A&E Web site is built to entertain and persuade the viewer to explore the program offerings and visit the site's banners and links.

Entertainment design as a visual product (not a manuscript of text only) relies upon images and narrative to create connection with the viewer. The digital design of visual entertainment content is seen extensively in works with moving images, such as movies and animations. Entertainment design is also seen in the packaging of entertainment content and news, such as posters, CD and DVD covers, books, digital videos, Web sites, and magazines.

FIGURE 1-21 This poster for recording artist Lou Reed's album *Set the Twilight Reeling* uses handwritten typography over a tightly cropped photograph of the artist to transfer the personal emotions embedded in the lyrics. Art direction and design by Stefan Sagmeister.

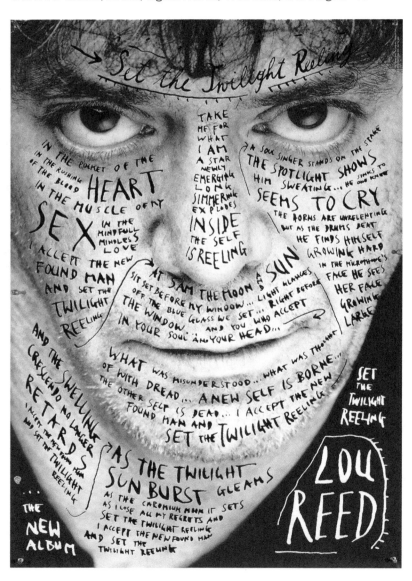

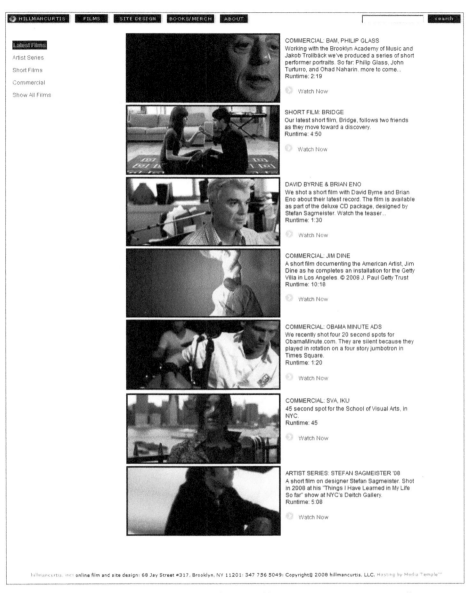

FIGURE 1-22 The Hillman Curtis Web site is a functional business promotion site as well as an entertainment portal showcasing short films shot and designed for both Web and broadcast output. Design by designer and filmmaker Hillman Curtis.

References

Benedetti, Paul, and Nancy deHart. 1997. *On McLuhan: Forward through the rearview mirror.* Cambridge: MIT Press.

Berlo, David K. 1960. *The process of communication: An introduction to theory and practice.* San Francisco: Rinehart.

Holtzschue, Linda. 2006. *Understanding color: An introduction for designers.* Hoboken, NJ: John Wiley & Sons.

Lidwell, Paul, Kritina Holden, and Jill Butler. 2003. *Universal principles of design.* Gloucester, MA: Rockport.

Lester, Paul. 2006. *Visual communication: Images with messages.* Belmont, CA: Thomson Wadsworth.

Meggs, Phillip. 1998. *A history of graphic design.* New York: John Wiley & Sons.

Pramaggiore, Maria, and Tom Wallis. 2008. *Film: A critical introduction.* London: Laurence King.

Tufte, Edward. 1990. *Envisioning information.* Cheshire, CT: Graphics Press.

Wheeler, Alina. 2003. *Designing brand identity: A complete guide to creating, building, and maintaining strong brands.* Hoboken, NJ: John Wiley & Sons.

White, Alex W. 2007. *Advertising design and typography.* New York: Allworth Press.

Notes

1. Holtzschue (2006, 30) writes that sensation is the body's response to stimulus.

2. http://dictionary.reference.com/browse/entertainment

CHAPTER 2
Design: Definition and Devices

Chapter Objectives

Define design as a
   problem-solving tool
   for communication.

Introduce basic design types.

Identify modern, functional
   influences.

Identify and integrate modern, functional design
   devices.

Explore exemplary and
   inspirational images from
   a variety of artists and
   designers.

Design as a Problem-Solving Tool

What Is Design?

A noun and a verb, *design* has a variety of meanings. As a verb, design designates an activity. To *design* something is to conceive, invent, or create to solve a problem. As a noun, *design* designates a visual or industrial composition. Connecting the two, we can define design as a visual or industrial composition that solves a problem.

Design is a process *and* a tool. We see the residual effects of design in new and improved products and technological innovation. On the industrial side of design, let's use automobiles as an example. A major automobile safety problem is the head-on car crash. A head-on crash may cause a driver or passenger to be catapulted out of the vehicle upon impact, causing serious or lethal injury. To solve this problem, industrial designers first invented lap-only seatbelts. Lives were saved as time went on. However, research showed that injuries still occurred, because passengers were getting injured from the whip of their upper bodies into the dashboard. So the seatbelt was redesigned to add a shoulder harness. The shoulder harness was better, but it still did not offer protection if the vehicle crumpled into the occupants during a crash. Recognition of that problem spawned the design of the airbag for drivers and front passengers. Still not good enough. Passengers in the front and back seats can be injured or killed when there is a side impact crash. Problems move design, and design moves innovation forward. The latest innovation in automobile safety is the side curtain airbag.

Can you see how design spirals through innovation and creation to solve problems through iterations and process? The iterations, also known as versions, help the designer build on the notion that form follows function, meaning that we must solve the problem at its core initially. This requires us to get the function and purpose clear; only then can we think about form and the aesthetic aspects of the project.

FIGURE 2-1A This cover for *Creativity* magazine shows how form is translated through clear, functional type and image. Design by Michael Bierut.

FIGURE 2-1B This Web site for Hillman Curtis Inc. shows how form is translated through clear, functional layout. Design by Hillman Curtis.

Design is not simply a final result; design is a spiraling process that is used to solve a problem and achieve a goal. So, what are the problems we work to solve as digital designers? The problems we solve, through visual communication and multimedia communication, are rooted in the communication goals of our clients. The problem could be that more products need to be sold; we therefore focus on design for persuasion. The problem could be that we need to tell the story of a great event or person; we therefore focus on design for entertainment. The problem could be that we need to guide people to a destination; we therefore focus on design for information. The problem could be that we need to transfer knowledge about how to do something; we therefore focus on design for education. Remember, the problem exists in the communication goal we are trying to achieve. We have to figure out who our audience is and how to inform, persuade, educate, or entertain them using print or Web media. In many cases, we must pursue multiple goals. We want the viewer to see the communication, read the message, and act upon it.

FIGURE 2-2 Milton Glaser's classic logo I Heart (love) NY was initially created for the New York State Department of Economic Development to promote tourism. After the September 11 attacks on New York City, the mark's design was updated to communicate a message of hope and unity. The logo is a cultural icon that is adored worldwide. Design by Milton Glaser.

FIGURE 2-3 Seattle design firm Turnstyle shows modern design influence with clear communication and legibility in BrandScents, a series of self-promotion air fresheners that focus on client brand awareness. Design by Turnstyle.

In Edward Tufte's 2003 manifesto on the evils of bad presentation design, *The Cognitive Style of PowerPoint*, he warns that "the tools are not the content...the content is the content and those who create content must care how it is presented in the form of quantity, style, pace, and most importantly, message" (Tufte 2003). The tools of design are whatever you have. We use pencils, markers, and paper to create two-dimensional designs on paper. We use cameras, scanners, computers, and digital design software to create computer graphics, printed page layouts, animations, and Web pages that move into the realm of 3-D virtual design and 4-D time-based design. But the tools do not make the designs. The designer must find the solution through knowledge of the client, source materials, and calculated methods. The next section provides broad information on modern styles.

Modern Influence

The Industrial Revolution spawned innovations in manufacturing that created an increased need for graphic communications. As the United States, England,

and most of Europe began this shift toward mass production, technologies such as photography and lithographic printing provided the production tools needed to deliver information to mass audiences. The modernism in commerce was fueled by modernism in the art and design disciplines. Modernism movements in design gave birth to functional design and challenged designers to create meaningful communications based on predetermined standards and formats, including posters, brochures, book covers, magazine designs, and advertisements (Meggs 2006).

Tools and techniques used by designers today were influenced by modernism; these techniques include montage, collage, symmetrical and asymmetrical typography, geometrics, and most importantly, function before form. Many modern movements, including futurism, Dada, and de Stijl, have influenced artists and designers. You can explore art history texts and archival Web sites to get exposure to all the movements in modern and postmodern art.

To help you grasp the styles and their characteristics, I have briefly summarized (and provided some treatment examples for) several modern styles—including cubism, constructivism, Bauhaus and New Typography, American late modern, and Swiss International—that stand out as highly influential in digital design today. I suggest that you explore each style to build your composition options. You can transfer and combine these characteristics into your design projects to help find your own approaches.

Cubism

- Cubism has aesthetic connections to modern-day digital design as it is characterized by flattened forms, overlapping and intersecting planes, and the collage of abstract forms to create a visual whole.

- The movement was pioneered by the artists Pablo Picasso (1881–1973) and Georges Braque (1882–1963) and occurred in two stages that included analytic and synthetic cubism (Golding 1994, 66–67).

- Analytic cubism moved away from traditional figure modeling and perspective-based techniques, focusing on using natural forms and then abstracting the painting to flattened shapes.

- Synthetic cubism evolved as a visual language and was defined by the technique of collage. Introduced by Picasso as a modernist approach to assembling "non-art materials" into coherent synthesized images, collage (from the French verb "to glue") techniques combined various components such as colored cut paper, cloth, wallpaper, type clippings, newspapers clippings, and textures (Arnston 2006, 6).

FIGURE 2-4 This design treatment's abstracted form and flattened shapes shows the influence of the analytic cubism style (Meggs 2006). Design by John DiMarco.

Constructivism

- Constructivism arose in the wake of the Russian revolution of 1917, and was given further impetus by the Soviet Union's New Economic Policy of 1921, as a vehicle for commercial and political communication.
- Born in the Soviet Union, it spread across Europe, leading to constructivist movements in Poland, Belgium, and Czechoslovakia.
- Constructivism presented an approach that focused on designs rich in geometric forms, photomontage (the making of a new image from two or

more photographs, an idea birthed by Dada), and utilizing type as a pictorial element (Heller and Chwast 2000, 262).

- The constructivist movement used pure line and shape and was critical to the emergence of the Bauhaus style.

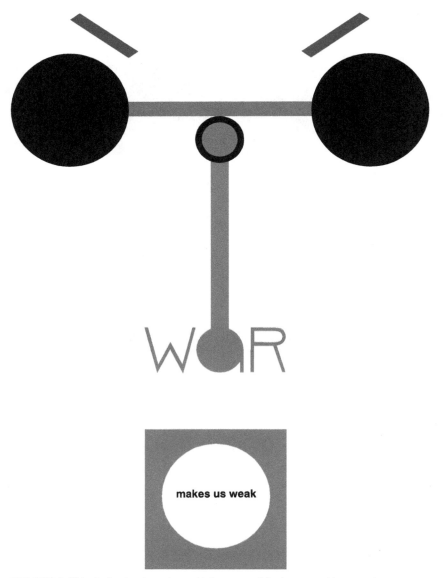

FIGURE 2-5 This design treatment, combining geometric shapes and typography, exemplifies constructivism. Design by John DiMarco.

Bauhaus and the New Typography

- Architect Walter Gropius founded the Bauhaus school when he combined the Weimar Art Academy and the Weimar Arts and Crafts School in Germany in 1919. The school was rooted in working in the real world, a rejection of the divergent approaches that were seen in art schools of the time.

- Heller and Chwast describe the Bauhaus as a place where "craftsmen and fine artists would introduce students to the mysteries of creativity and help them to achieve a formal language on their own" (2000, 113). The school combined art and craft and was the birthplace of modern architecture and design.

- The Bauhaus became a landmark for modernism in graphic and industrial design in the early twentieth century. The Bauhaus reacted to the upturn in the pace of technological and commercial development with a changed program, defining its future image under the motto, "Art and technology: a new unity." The school evolved into a workshop that focused on both the functional and aesthetic aspects of design and architecture, "producing prototypes for mass production: from a single lamp to a complete dwelling" (Bauhaus-Archiv Museum of Design, 1919).

- The concept that "form follows function" was paramount at the Bauhaus, where problem solving aesthetics. Thus, preceded concern for the Bauhaus style became the standard of functional graphic design in the late 1920s (Heller and Chwast 2000, 114). The school was shut down by the Nazis in 1933.

- The focus on functionality over aesthetics is a main standard for successful design today. Adherence to structure and fluid geometry made Bauhaus graphic work discernible and stylistic.

- The Bauhaus was an incubator for the New Typography, a style that merged the sheltered, simple ways of the Bauhaus approach with new and emerging design problems.

- The New Typography was pioneered by Jan Tschichold, a designer influenced by functional approaches who ultimately merged the Bauhaus and constructivist styles to create a new approach. The New Typography approach yielded functional designs that were blended with asymmetrical type and image compositions.

FIGURE 2-6 This design treatment borrows composition from Herbert Bayer's Kandinsky poster and uses functional information flow and type coupled with alignment and balance, which are essential influences from the Bauhaus and New Typography styles. Design by John DiMarco.

American Late Modern

- Late modern style in America emerged from the 1940s through the 1950s and was seen in the creation of wartime propaganda, as well as in posters, manuals, and news magazines during World War II (Heller and Chwast 2000, 195).

- Focus on information and education design was paramount during the war years (1941–1945) due to the government's need to publish documents used to instruct men and women in the mechanics and materials of war.

- When the war ended, graphic design work returned to focusing on using persuasive and informational communication design for selling products and ideas through advertising and publishing.

- The modern American design style incorporated illustration and photographs characterized by clarity in the expression of ideas. Short messages and vivid colors attracted attention and delivered clear messages through visuals. With the integration of abstraction and asymmetry, the style gave way to a new, refined corporate style.

FIGURE 2-7 This design treatment borrows from Lester Beall's American late modern approach and shows an elemental sign with vivid, patriotic colors combined with a simple message. Design by John DiMarco.

Swiss International

- After the war, the corporation became the main engine in society, and a new corporate style evolved in international typographic style, also known as Swiss International style.

- Stemming from Bauhaus and constructivist styles, international typographic style evolved in Switzerland and Germany during the mid-1950s through the

1960s and was characterized by "objective photography, sans serif typography, lack of ornamentation, and strict composition on the basis of the grid system" (Heller and Chwast 2000, 196).

- Images were cropped, scaled, and manipulated to create engaging, interesting designs. Grids were used to create order and clarity in delivering graphic communication. The grid has since become the standard tool for composition in digital design.

- Focusing on sans serif typefaces such as Helvetica, the Swiss International style was seen as formal and simplistic by many artists and designers of the time. The rejection of this style evolved into postmodernist approaches that melded styles and philosophies.

FIGURE 2-8 This design treatment is influenced by Swiss International style, with its symbolic form and sans serif type. Design by John DiMarco.

Design or Art?

Both design and art use design principles and elements to create content—
the story or subject matter and form—the way the story or subject matter
is presented. Artists solve their own problems with message, materials, and
aesthetic when they create paintings, sculptures, prints, or graphics. A purely
aesthetic object is an artwork that is made for adornment and visual pleasure.
Artists can define the scope and objectives for their work and pursue unbridled
visions. Designers are given a problem and must typically work within certain
specifications that present limitations to achieving that goal. Both artists and
designers create visual solutions across media and industrial solutions across
materials.

FIGURE 2-9 As an artist, John Fekner's work blurs the line between art and design. Fekner creates artwork that addresses social problems, using the environment as a medium. Design by
John Fekner.

Convergent versus Divergent

There are two main approaches to solving design problems: convergent and divergent.

Convergent thinking is linear and lends itself to solving a design problem in a commercial application. The convergent approach is systematic and rigorous, attempting to identify and define each part of the design process to meet specific goals. For example, a client requests a poster to promote its products inside a retail store. The convergent approach begins with defining the problem, then moves to research for clarification. Next, goals are established, a strategy is planned and executed, and finally the entire project is evaluated to determine its success.

The divergent approach uses a creative, nonlinear process through which the outcome is not clearly identified and the methods are exploratory. Divergent problem solving is open-ended and pays less attention to what the client wants. It works well when the problem is evolving as the process occurs, deadlines are flexible, and a sequential methodology is unnecessary. We see divergent thinking in art, where the final product is about the journey in making the artwork. Divergent thinking is a great way to generate ideas at a highly creative level due to its inherent freedom of expression and lack of specifications.

In many cases, we begin with convergent thinking but then explore divergent thinking when executing our designs. Great designs are typically a product of both approaches.

Two-, Three-, and Four-Dimensional Design

Design problems can be solved using 2-D, 3-D, and 4-D designs generated from convergent and divergent problem solving. Manipulation of assets such as text, images, messages, people, sets, lighting, materials, and moving footage are involved based on the type of design.

Two-dimensional designs have width and height. They are built with line, shape, texture, value, and color; they thereby gain influence and achieve a gestalt through unity and variety in forms and color. Two-dimensional designs consist of flat visual patterns and still image representations created to evoke a response from viewers based on sensual stimulation or rational thought. Two-dimensional designs encompass all print communications, including drawing, painting, printmaking, photography, and graphics. Even three-dimensional images created using modeling programs such as Autodesk Maya are output as two-dimensional frames that are used in animation, television, or film work.

FIGURE 2-10 The Seduction poster for the Yale School of Architecture combines beautiful, sinuous calligraphy with structured text to create design that is exquisite yet purposely functional. Design by Michael Bierut.

FIGURE 2-11 The exhibition wall of the Philip Johnson Glass House Visitors Center for the National Trust for Historic Preservation features twenty-four monitors within a space that offers a 2-D, 3-D, and 4-D visual experience. Design by James Biber.

Virtual three-dimensional designs created using computers have height, width, and depth. Three-dimensional designs that exist in reality include sculpture, product design, and architecture. These are not flat—as are screens and paper—but have mass, which requires them to occupy physical space. We connect with these designs because they share the same physical space with us. We occupy buildings and live in houses that engulf us in 3-D spaces. In her book *Launching the Imagination: A Comprehensive Guide to Basic Design*, Mary Stewart explains that in three-dimensional design, "Artists and designers must assure that form follows function in order to organize line, plane, volume, mass, and space into coherent form." Stewart reinforces this by stating "the structural integrity of a sculpture is just as important as the structural integrity of a wheelchair" (2002, 7-0). Three-dimensional design solutions present real-world problems to designers that require convergent problem solving but also benefit from divergent thinking to provide aesthetic appeal.

Four-dimensional designs are time based. They contain images with height, width, and depth that are performed over time. This means that the art and design project is not a still experience, as with print media, and not a physical experience, as with sculpture and architecture. This type of design is seen in

films, television shows and commercials, performance art (like plays and bal-
lets), animations and cartoons, and interactive Web sites. Four-dimensional
designs utilize storytelling and focus on setting (perceived location of the work),
duration (length of the work), tempo (speed and pace of the work), intensity
(level of energy), scope (the depth of intellectual engagement), and, for Web
designs, interactivity (level of interaction with the medium).

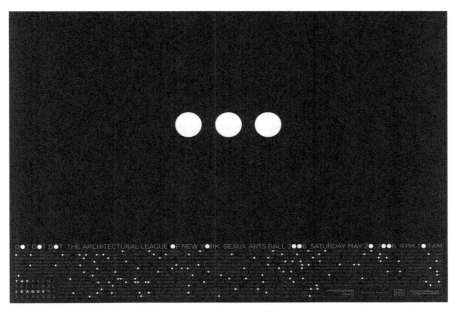

FIGURE 2-12 This poster for the Architectural League of New York is a two-dimensional design.
Design by Michael Bierut.

FIGURE 2-13 The Harley Davidson Museum is a three-dimensional architectural design.
Design by James Biber.

FIGURE 2-14 The Sugar user interface for the XO laptop provides a four-dimensional experience through virtual space. Design by Lisa Strausfeld.

Design Devices

Space, Format, and Structure

Space can be three dimensional, as with sculpture and architecture, or two dimensional, as with graphic spaces. Graphic spaces are the design areas that we use in digital design for print and the Web. Graphic space is a two-dimensional, flat plane—bounded by horizontal, vertical, or round edges—that exists on video, film, a computer screen, or a piece of paper (Meggs 1989, 69). We arrange text and images in graphic space. The graphic space creates a relationship with forms to establish a gestalt—a whole that cannot be represented by its parts—and turn separate elements into a cohesive visual communication. The space also refers to the format, which is the size and orientation of the medium that is used for the design (for example, 8.5 × 11" letter size in landscape orientation). Formats can be horizontal, vertical, or circular. They can also be customized, such as in the template for a package.

FIGURE 2-15 The poster Pasta uses scale to assert dominance and depth and uses background color and shape to create visual contrast and unity. Design by Milton Glaser.

Digital designers must use space to simulate depth. When we look at an image, we see a picture plane that represents the image as if we were looking at it through a window frame. We establish a foreground (bottom), middle ground (eye-level horizon line), and background (distance). By making foreground imagery (below the horizon line) larger and background imagery (above the horizon line) smaller, the illusion of depth can be established. Using sizing in space, the designer can create an illusion of distance. Using overlap to arrange design elements in space, the designer can create spatial depth and a stacking order. Using linear perspective, the technique of converging lines to the vanishing point, the designer can unify and create a dynamic quality of motion in a piece (Lauer and Pentak 2007, 190). Type, image, and space are the broad components in a visual design.

Negative Space

FIGURE 2-16 This two-page spread layout uses negative space to separate, as well as connect, small multiples of information. Design by Julia Hoffmann.

The empty space that exists in the established format is negative space, and using space effectively involves a careful consideration of this space. When we begin a design project, we start with negative space. A blank piece of paper or a document representing that piece of paper on the computer screen is made of negative space. We fill negative space with type and images to create a

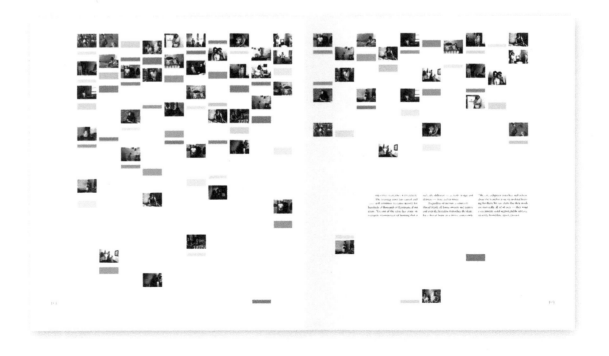

relationship between the three elements with the goal of creating a gestalt. To create the gestalt, we need to use space division efficiently and should concentrate on big pockets of negative space—not small ones. Small pockets create a tension between elements and may cause confusion due to the elements' proximity or their irrational grouping. Big pockets of space allow components to interweave to create a complete image and a communication that can be translated effectively. Using negative space effectively is critical in composition.

Composition

The way components (text, images, and space) are arranged is the composition. Compositions can be formatted for landscape (horizontal) or portrait (vertical) layouts and can contain elements that are positioned horizontally,

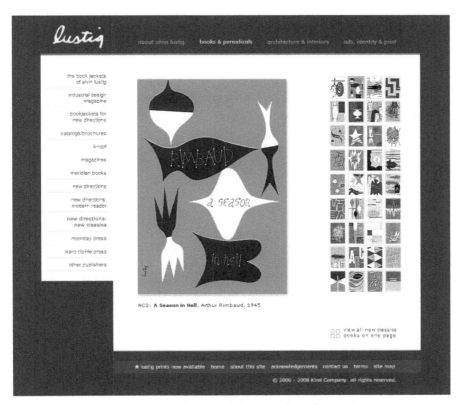

FIGURE 2-17 This Web page thoughtfully uses balance, scale, and proportion to compose navigation, text, image, and identity with simple beauty and undeniable clarity. Design by Kind Company.

vertically, and diagonally. Arrangement and rearrangement of elements changes the meaning and the gestalt of the design piece. Using various techniques—such as unity and variety, balance, scale and proportion, emphasis, repetition, alignment, grouping, overlap, collage, and proximity—contributes to the visual impact of the composition. Text and image are arranged in relationship to space using a grid.

Grids

In his book *Thinking in Type,* Alex W. White defines the grid as "a skeletal guide used to ensure design consistency. A grid should show type widths, image areas, margins and spaces to be left empty and trim size" (2005, 203). The grid is critical to digital design, because it provides the framework needed to achieve a gestalt in composition. Random placement of elements during divergent problem solving is OK, but when we use convergent approaches we must inevitably justify the elements' placement. According to grid systems guru Kimberly Elam, using a grid, particularly a 3 × 3 column grid, "provides a wide range of variation for exploration within a controlled system of organization" (2004, 7). Using the 3 × 3 grid allows you to understand the rule of thirds and use the law of thirds. The use of grids is critical to both publication and Web design.

FIGURE 2-18 The grid clearly organizes the text in this publication, which uses a three-column grid on the left side and a two-column grid on the right. Design by Turnstyle.

3 × 3 grid

composition approaches
rule of thirds / law of thirds

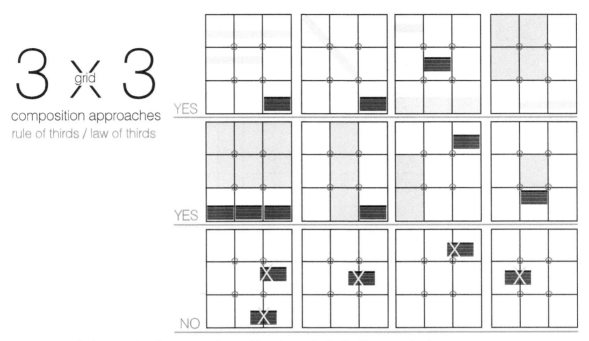

YES

YES

NO

FIGURE 2-19 Grid usage rules. Once you understand how to use the 3 × 3 grid, you can begin to break the rules and explore new approaches. Any element that is placed on the page must occupy one, two, or three full vertical, horizontal, or diagonal sections of the grid. Elements should not land in the middle of a grid square or extend across a portion of it. The circled intersections are where the eye is drawn naturally.

Rule of Thirds and Law of Thirds

The rule of thirds (also known as the golden grid rule) is a composition technique in which the medium is divided into a 3 × 3 grid of nine rectangles and four intersections. Position the primary design element at the intersections to produce an asymmetrical image and a good aesthetic. Use a secondary design element for visual balance. Positioning strong elements in the center will create a dominant visual (Lidwell et al., 168).

The law of thirds dictates that elements do not need to land directly on the four intersections, but can be placed in close proximity where attention will naturally occur (Elam 2001, 13). This allows the designer to control the compositional space by establishing acceptable places for each element and helps ensure visual consistency.

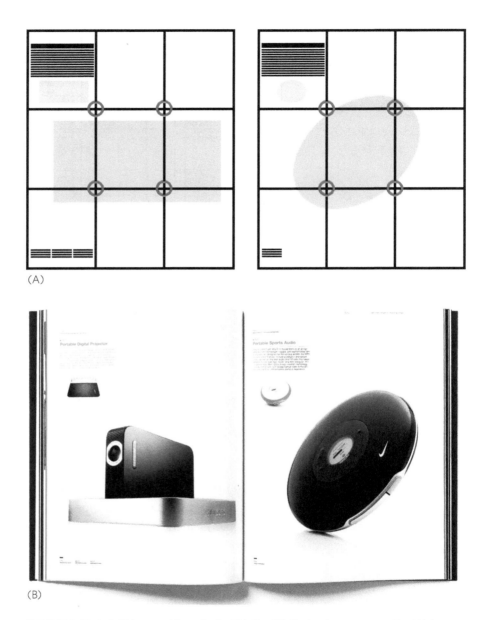

(A)

(B)

FIGURES 2-20, A, B This spread from *Design This Day* (B), the book commemorating Walter Dorwin Teague's eightieth anniversary, exemplifies the rule of thirds and the law of thirds by using a dominant element that intersects with the grid points. The placement of text and smaller elements in close proximity to the intersections are another example of the law of thirds. Notice how each piece fits into the grid (A). Design by Turnstyle.

Consistency

Consistency is a cornerstone of good design. When similar items are expressed in similar, repetitive ways, it creates consistency. There are two main forms of consistency that digital designers need to be aware of: aesthetic consistency and functional consistency.

Aesthetic consistency refers to style and appearance. A good example of this is seen in corporate identity and branding design. Companies use the same color, fonts, and icons throughout their marketing materials (brochures, packaging, signage, etc.) to create a consistent experience for the customer through recognition and association. Aesthetic consistency also needs to be evident in the images that are used. Mixing illustrations with photos in a sequence of images may hurt the consistency of the visual whole, or gestalt. Therefore, you should keep sequential items the same in style (photo vs. line art illustration) and size.

Functional consistency yields coherence in meaning and action. That is why it is a key component in Web site design, where usability (the ability of the site user to succeed) and learnability (the ability to ensure knowledge transfer) is paramount (Lidwell et al. 2003, 46). Functional consistency affects the placement of navigation buttons, the way media controls such as start and stop buttons work, and the ease of use of online forms. Functional consistency also creates implied meaning for users so that they can be transparently guided by hierarchy.

FIGURE 2-21 Keeping image types the same and creating navigation symbols that rely on recognition rather than recall are critical rules for consistent design. Design by Kind Company.

Hierarchy

Hierarchy is top-down structure. By creating a hierarchal structure with our content, we help people understand:

- What they are looking at and why it is important to them (in print)
- Where they are and where they can go (on the Web)

The invisible hand of hierarchical structure guides the user of a Web site by creating access routes to main pages (e.g., the home page, the log-in page, etc.) and links to subpages (i.e., Web site content) (Kristof and Satran 1995, 42–43). The typography's contrasting hierarchical structure—in the form of headlines, subheads, and body copy—creates a path for the reader to follow. The bigger and bolder something is, the more important it is. The smaller and lighter it is, the less important it is (White 2005, 85). The company logo is usually placed at the bottom of the page because it is the least important hierarchically. The headline—the most prominent text—typically comes first: it hooks the reader into wanting to read on (thus its ranking is above subheads and body copy).

Hierarchy is a critical component in digital design and depends on the design elements within a composition being clearly distinguishable. Hierarchy also plays an important role in the way informational components are understood. A hierarchical arrangement of informational components, called "supported alignment," facilitates an understanding of the connections between them.

FIGURE 2-22 This Web site uses hierarchy to separate primary and secondary information and links. Design by Kind Company.

Alignment

Creating cohesion and a visually effective whole (or gestalt) requires a designer to seriously consider where text and graphics are placed on a page. Alignment is the technique used for creating implied visual lines that connect elements on a page. It contributes to balance and symmetry. Design author Robin Williams wrote that "the principle of alignment states that nothing on a page should be placed on the page arbitrarily. Every item should have a visual connection with something else on a page" (1994, 27). Use left or right justified type to create clean visual lines and easy-to-follow visual connections. Avoid using centered alignment unless it is absolutely necessary or you are sure you can do it effectively.

The proper alignment of type and image creates the proper visual connections; creating meaningful connections is also achieved by proximity and grouping.

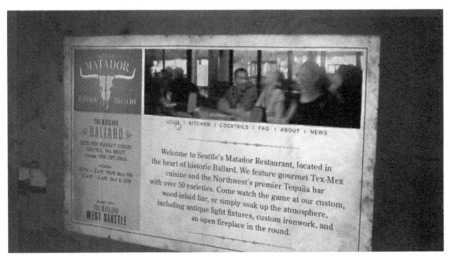

FIGURE 2-23 The use of centered alignment can be effective if well thought out, as in these business card and Web page examples. Design by Turnstyle.

Proximity and Grouping

The proximity of related items provides a visual guide for the viewer's ingestion of a page's organization and content. While proximity demonstrates importance, grouping shows connections. Placing a company's Web site address underneath its logo in an advertisement is an example of grouping. Placing the logo at the bottom of the page—far from the page's main content—is an example of proximity. The use of proximity as a design technique is also seen in the manipulation of the page's perimeter edge.

FIGURE 2-24 Proximity and grouping are critical to good communication design and creating cohesive visuals. Design by Julia Hoffmann.

Perimeter Edge

The perimeter edge is the edge of the live space for the design. The four edges of a piece of paper are perimeter edges. The four edges of a screen or monitor also create a perimeter edge. Treatment of the perimeter edge can be varied with the margins and bleeds. Margins are the spaces between text and graphics and the edges of the paper or the screen. By leaving wide margins, you create a dramatic, isolated visual. Bleeds are created by positioning text and images partially off the edge of the page, so that they appear cut off. This technique of allowing images to bleed off the page can be found in many print designs, including magazines and book covers. Bleeds give a design a dynamic look and can also evoke the feeling of motion because the type, image, or color drops off the page.

FIGURE 2-25 This corporate philosophy poster uses a perimeter edge with bleed. Design by John DiMarco.

References

Arnston, Amy E. 2006. *Digital design basics.* Belmont, CA: Thomson Wadsworth.

Barzun, Jacques, and Henry Graff. 2004. *The modern researcher.* 6th ed. Belmont, CA: Thomson Wadsworth.

Bauhaus-Archiv Museum of Design. 1919. Manifesto. http://www.bauhaus.de/english/bauhaus1919/manifest1919.htm.

Brainard, Shirl. 1991. *A design manual.* Englewood Cliffs, NJ: Prentice Hall.

Curtis, Hillman. 2000. *Flash Web design: The art of motion graphics.* Berkeley, CA: New Riders.

———. 2002. *MTIV: Process, inspiration, and practice for the new media designer.* Berkeley, CA: New Riders.

Elam, Kimberly. 2001. *Geometry of design.* New York: Princeton Architectural Press.

———. 2004. *Grid systems: Principles of organizing type.* New York: Princeton Architectural Press.

Golding, John. 1994. *Concepts of modern art.* Ed. Nikos Stangos. New York: Thames & Hudson.

Grayson, Steve. 1995. *Adobe Systems print publishing guide.* Mountain View, CA: Adobe Systems.

Heller, Steven, and Seymour Chwast. 2000. *Graphic style: From Victorian to digital.* New York: Harry Abrams.

Herman Miller. 2008. Discovering design (educational Web site). http://www.hermanmiller.com/discoveringdesign.

Hollis, Richard. 2001. *Graphic design: A concise history.* New York: Thames & Hudson.

Holtzschue, Linda. 2006. *Understanding color: An introduction for designers.* Hoboken, NJ: John Wiley & Sons.

Kristof, Ray, and Amy Satran. 1995. *Interactivity by design: Creating & communicating with new media.* Mountain View, CA: Adobe Press.

Lauer, David, and Stephen Pentak. 2007. *Design basics.* Belmont, CA: Thomson Wadsworth.

Lidwell, Paul, Kritina Holden, and Jill Butler. 2003. *Universal principles of design.* Gloucester, MA: Rockport.

Meggs, Phillip. 1989. *Type and image: The language of graphic design.* New York: Van Nostrand Reinhold,

Meggs, Phillip, and Alston Purvis. 2006. *Meggs' History of Graphic Design,* 4th ed. Hoboken, NJ: John Wiley & Sons.

Stewart, Mary. 2002. *Launching the imagination: A comprehensive guide to basic design.* New York: McGraw Hill.

Swann, Alan. 1997. *The new graphic design school.* Hoboken, NJ: John Wiley & Sons.

Tufte, Edward. 2003. *The cognitive style of PowerPoint.* Cheshire, CT: Graphics Press.

Wheeler, Alina. 2003. *Designing brand identity: A complete guide to creating, building, and maintaining strong brands.* Hoboken, NJ: John Wiley & Sons.

White, Alex W. 2005. *Thinking in type: The practical philosophy of typography.* New York: Allworth.

———. 2007. *Advertising design and typography.* New York: Allworth.

White, Jan V. 1990. *Color for the electronic age.* New York: Watson Guptill.

Williams, Robin. 1994. *The non-designer's design book.* Berkeley, CA: Peachpit.

CHAPTER 3
Design: Elements and Principles

Chapter Objectives

Identify and define visual design elements.

Introduce basic design principles.

Explore exemplary and inspirational images from a variety of artists and designers.

The Visual Pieces

Line

A line is a connected series of points that contrasts with its background. Lines can be rectilinear (straight with corners) or curvilinear (rounded), to project different visual themes. Curvilinear lines are seen in nature (plants and animals do not have absolutely straight lines) and are therefore considered organic. Rectilinear lines are associated with industry—buildings and machinery, for example. Considered mechanical, they are typically harder edged and more constraining.

FIGURE 3-1 Heavy and light variations of line are the main elements that provide value and structure in this design. Design by Richard Kirk Mills.

Lines can be used to create the contour of an object, resulting in a shape. Lines can be overlapped, or hatched, to create textures. Lines can also be used to create boundaries or to suggest motion. We create lines in digital design applications by drawing or painting and by using line tools and rules. We also create them transparently through alignment, proximity, and grouping.

Shape

A shape is an area in space created by closure. Shapes can be organic (from nature), geometric (formed according to mathematical formulas), or freely imaginary. Shapes occupy space and create a relationship between figure and ground. Shapes (figures) are image elements that contrast with the background (ground). (The ground is the "negative space.") In graphic design, by composing shape elements (type and images) using a grid, we create a gestalt. When we use the same shapes and use space as a buffer, we create an illusionary shape from the negative space. We create shape in digital design by using digital tools to draw and paint marks that connect and by using various digital design software shape tools to draw geometric and abstract shapes.

FIGURE 3-2 Shapes are drawn based on perspective to create a realistic landscape of New York City's Park Avenue South. Design by Richard Kirk Mills.

Texture

The surface quality of a shape or line is its texture. Texture can be seen and felt (tactile) in sculpture or other three-dimensional objects; it can be seen (visual) in two-dimensional artwork and design pieces. Texture is created in digital design by using overlapping images, lines, and shapes. We can also invent textures by creating different patterns (repeating elements) that simulate a textured surface (Stewart 2002, 1-15–1-17). Digital design software provides layers, so that different elements can be separated and we can then experiment with overlapping and changing their stacking order to create textures.

Value

Value is the relative lightness or darkness of a hue. A hue's value is measured by comparing it to hues of other values. These values establish an image's contrast: an image composed mainly of hues of similar values is said to have low contrast, while a high-contrast image contains hues of widely disparate values. Values can be graduated into a gradient scale (grayscale, for example) to show the difference between light and dark, as well as all the midrange values in between.

FIGURE 3-3 Texture is achieved by overlapping various marks, patterns, and materials. Design by Richard Kirk Mills.

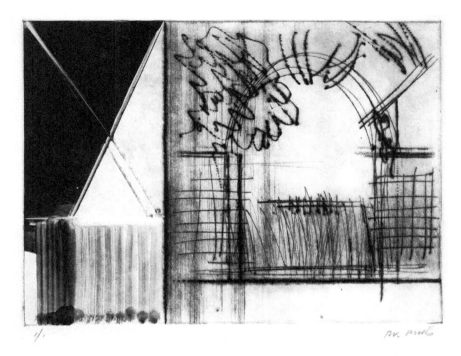

FIGURE 3-4 Value and contrast are used here to create depth and distance. Design by Richard Kirk Mills.

In illustrations, dark values are used to create depth and lighter values to create distance. Value and contrast can change the mood and visual strength of a composition. Digital design software provides color tools for manipulating values by allowing tints (lighter values) or shades (darker values) to be created from any color and used in a composition or a piece of artwork.

Color

Brief Overview of Terms

As color has become less expensive to print and the Web has allowed us to deliver our communications through a screen, color has become an increasingly important element in digital design. Color only exists in light. Light comes from many things, including the sun, lightbulbs, neon signs, projectors, and monitors. Light is energy that is transmitted in waves of varying amplitude, known as wavelengths, that correspond to various colors. A wavelength is received by the eye, and then a corresponding signal is transmitted to the brain, which recognizes the signal as a particular color (Holtzschue 2006, 13).

FIGURE 3-5 Vibrant, warm colors (red, green, and blue) make this screen-printed illustration come alive. Design by Richard Kirk Mills.

The basic terminology for describing color includes the terms **hue**, **value**, **shade**, **tint**, **saturation**, and **contrast**.

Hue refers to pure color. A hue is designated by the name of a color: Brown, red, purple, orange, green—and all the slight variations of each—are all considered hues. **Value** is the lightness or darkness of a hue. **Shade** is a hue when it is made darker (by adding black). **Tint** is a hue when it is made lighter (by adding white). We can use hues in different values to create tints or shades of that hue. **Saturation** (also called **chroma**) is the vividness or dullness of a color, which enhances or minimizes the intensity of the color. **Contrast** is the result of comparing values. Black and brown have low contrast. Black and yellow have high contrast. We choose and manipulate hue, value, shade, tint, saturation, and contrast when we create digital design compositions for print and the Web. You need to understand the basics of color to use it effectively in your design work. There are four main things you need to know about color:

1. The **color wheel (YORVBG)** is the basis for design using color. The color wheel is employed to explore color usage in order to establish color schemes (color combinations) for use in our designs.

2. The **artist's colors** are derived from the color wheel: red, yellow, and blue. These colors represent the primary colors of the color wheel,which can be combined to create secondary, and intermediate colors.

3. The **additive color model (RGB)** is based on light and is used for output to a screen or monitor (as with Web sites, film, and television). When we output Web pages, we end up with RGB and index color modes.

4. The **subtractive (CMY)** and **process (CMYK)** color models are the basis for process printing on all types of printers and printing presses. CMYK is based on pigments (inks). When we output printed pages, we end up with digital files in CMYK mode.

Your computer monitor's screen is a canvas that allows you to mix the color domains—the artist's colors of red, yellow, and blue with the additive colors of RGB. Software translates the printed output to a combination of CMYK colors.

The Artist's Color Wheel

The color wheel is a spectrum (range) of visible hues (colors) in order. The color wheel consists of six (YORVBG) or twelve colors (YORVBG + the in-between colors). The six-color wheel contains the primary colors of red (R), yellow (Y), and blue (B). Using these three primary colors, secondary colors can be made by an equal mix of two of the three primary colors. The secondary colors are green (G) (blue + yellow), orange (O) (red + yellow), and violet (V) (red + blue).

The twelve-color wheel adds another layer of colors to the visual outline, with intermediate (also known as tertiary) colors that lie between the primary and secondary colors on the wheel. They are made by mixing the three primaries in different percentages (Swann 1997, 24–25).

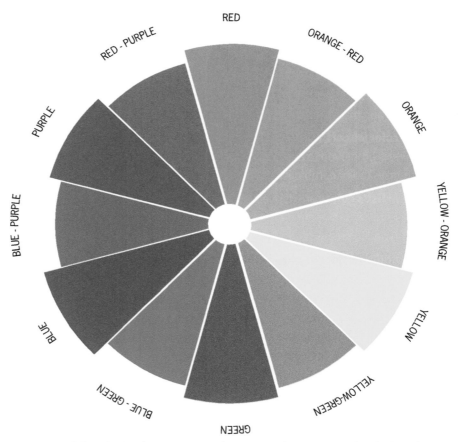

FIGURE 3-6 Color wheel with primary, secondary, intermediate, warm, and cool colors. Design by Kristen Crawford.

Additive and Subtractive Color Models

We work in RGB color mode—the additive color model—most of the time, even when we are creating work for print. Red (R), green (G), and blue (B) wavelengths can be combined to simulate a range of colors found in nature. We use RGB for our designs because it allows the widest range of color options. If our final output is going to be on the screen, in the medium of the Internet, film, or television, the final outputted files will be RGB. If we work on a print project, we can begin our project in RGB, to ensure the widest color gamut, and then convert to CMYK before outputting files to the printer or film imagesetter.

Subtracting RGB wavelengths from white light creates cyan (C), magenta (M), and yellow (Y); this is the subtractive color model (CMY). Translucent cyan, magenta, and yellow, which are based on pigments, attract, absorb, and reflect light when on a printed page. Desktop printers and printing presses add a fourth color, black (K), to create a deep black for text and lines (Grayson 1995, 8–9). CMYK is known as the process printing model because the four ink colors—cyan, magenta, yellow, and black—can be combined (processed) to create millions of printed colors.

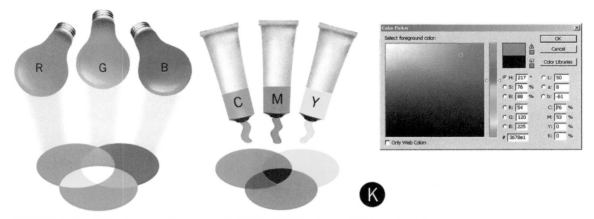

FIGURE 3-7 The RGB color model is based on light. The CMYK color model is based on ink (pigments). The color picker in Adobe Photoshop permits the use of RGB, CMYK, Web-safe, and Pantone color models.

Palettes and Swatch Books

In digital design, we use the RGB color mode for output to the screen (Web, TV, film, video). We use CMYK and spot colors (Pantone inks) for output to paper. Spot colors are solid inks that represent a single color. Using spot colors in one- or two-color jobs saves money in printing costs. But full color photographs, line art, and text cannot be printed using spot color.

There are different types of output (printing) devices, including ink-jet printers, laser printers, and printing presses made by many different manufacturers. Because CMYK colors are mixed to create millions of colors, color reproduction varies from device to device. So even though output is proofed for consistency, process color reproduction is not exact in all cases. To solve this problem,

FIGURE 3-8 Matching spot color requires the use of Pantone swatch books during conceptualization, then the use of electronic versions of those swatch books in industry-standard programs such as Adobe Illustrator, Photoshop, or InDesign.

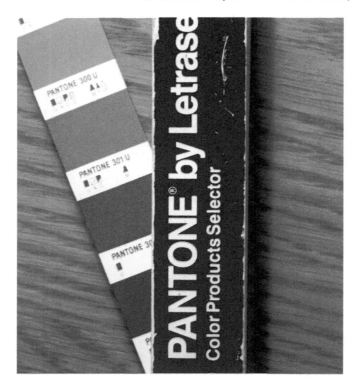

designers and printers use spot colors, also known as Pantone inks, which are solid, premixed colors that are coded to a swatch book for accuracy.

There are several Pantone swatch books; the Pantone Coated and Pantone Uncoated are the most widely used. These swatch books include color chips with small swatches of numbered colors printed on coated and uncoated paper. By looking at the swatches, a designer can get an idea of how the color will look when printed on coated or uncoated stock (paper). (The finish of the paper affects the way the color looks when printed.) Pantone colors are most widely used for one- and two-color print jobs, and also for logos. PMS, which stands for the Pantone Matching System, is the print production industry's standard term for spot color.

Companies use Pantone inks when printing their logos because doing so guarantees consistent color across the brand and the corporate identity (business cards, letterhead, brochures, etc.). For example, IBM cannot risk interrupting its brand identity with inconsistent color, so the company uses the Pantone Blue 300 (PMS 300) ink when representing its logo. When that logo is printed on business cards, it comes out exactly the same for every employee, from every print run. When IBM's ad agency creates a full-color print ad for a magazine placement, it pays extra to use a fifth color—the Pantone ink—in the ad's printing. The Pantone ink is used for the logo; the four process colors— cyan, magenta, yellow, and black—are combined to create millions of colors for the photos and line art.

For the screen (Web, TV, film, video), we use RGB colors to create millions of visible colors. However, just as color varies from printer to printer, not all monitors and video cards are the same. When standard swatches are needed for screen graphics, there are two main color palettes: the Web-safe color palette and the index color palette. These palettes use hexadecimal values for their names. The hexadecimal system is a numeral system. It uses sixteen symbols to represent a color value. The numbers 0 through 9 represent values zero to nine, and the letters A, B, C, D, E, and F represent values ten to fifteen. Color swatches using hexadecimal values are represented by six digits for each color (*hex* means six). For instance, the color black is represented by #000000. The color white is #ffffff.

The Web-safe color palette contains 216 common RGB colors that appear the same across all Web browsers and operating systems (Windows, Mac, or UNIX). We use Web-safe colors for background colors, Web-based text and lines, and for representing logos consistently on Web pages. The index color palette represents the 256 colors available in a particular operating system (Mac or Windows). I don't generally use the index color palette because it causes dithering, which is when an image's colors adapt to the system palette colors because the real color is absent. I suggest utilizing the Web-safe color palette, particularly for GIF files (flat artwork without varying tones) and color backgrounds in your Web design projects. (As you will learn in part two of this book, RGB-based JPGs are used for photographic images.)

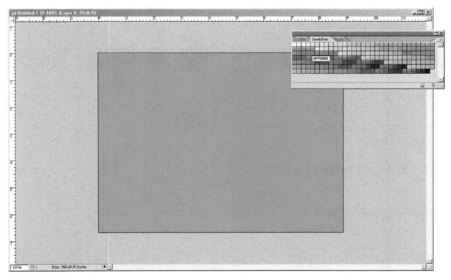

FIGURE 3-9 The Web-safe color palette in Adobe Photoshop shows the 216 common colors across computer platforms. The hexadecimal value for red is #ff000.

FIGURE 3-10 The Grayscale color slider in Adobe Photoshop provides access to a range of 256 different gray values.

The grayscale (achromatic) color palette has 256 levels (values) of gray that exist in a spectrum that runs from white to black. Grayscale color mode contains only grays and black. It can be used for black-and-white designs, such as newspaper ads. Many black-and-white publications will request—and only accept—images saved in grayscale mode, as opposed to CMYK, to keep file sizes small and to eliminate errors due to the use of stray colors in what should be a gray-only image file.

Color Schemes

Color schemes are selections or combinations of colors that we use in our design projects. Color schemes can create value contrast (variety) or harmony (unity). The main color schemes you should be aware of, and experiment with, are warm and cool colors, monochromatic, complementary, analogous, contrasting, achromatic, and black-plus.

We can describe the sensory attribute of a color residing on the color wheel by identifying it as a **warm color** or a **cool color**.

Warm primary colors: red and yellow

Cool primary color: blue

Warm secondary color: orange

Cool secondary colors: violet and green

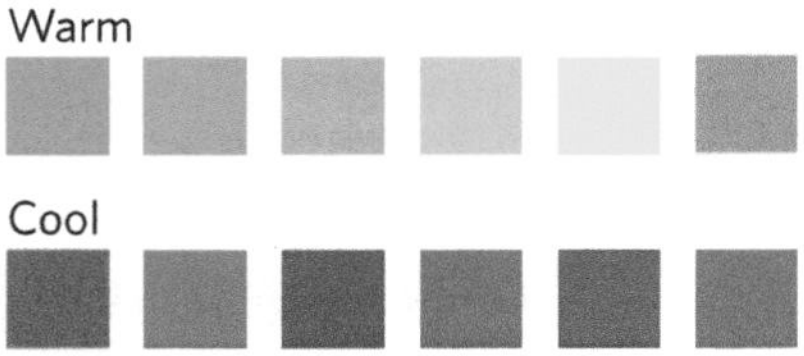

Warm

Cool

FIGURE 3-11 Warm and cool colors.

Whether intermediate colors are warmer or cooler depends on which other colors they sit closest to on the color wheel. Take a look at the color wheel (Figure 3-6) above to view the warm and cool colors in the artist's spectrum.

Monochromatic color schemes use one basic hue that may or may not contain variations in lightness (tint) or darkness (shade).

Complementary color schemes use hues that sit directly opposite each other on the color wheel. The New York Mets home uniforms, for example, use the complementary colors of blue and orange to create contrast. The blue is the quieter color; therefore, it is dominant. The orange is used as an accent color.

Analogous color schemes use hues that are located close together on the color wheel. The closeness of the hues creates harmony, but to avoid visual confusion, one color should dominate, and the others should be used as supporting colors.

Contrasting color schemes use hues that have three or more colors between them on the color wheel. These colors should contrast, not clash visually, so use bright colors as accents and less-bright colors for backgrounds and solid areas of color.

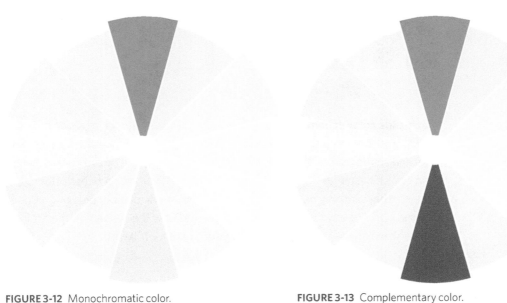

FIGURE 3-12 Monochromatic color.

FIGURE 3-13 Complementary color.

FIGURE 3-14 Analogous color.

FIGURE 3-15 Contrasting color.

Achromatic color schemes (also called grayscale color schemes) use black, white, and grays and are absent of colored hues. This is the type of scheme used when creating images in grayscale. Contrast becomes paramount, as the values of the grays, the black, and the white must create a discernable relationship between the figure and ground.

FIGURE 3-16 Grayscale scheme.

Black-plus color schemes use black, white, a palette of grays, plus one hue. In digital design using two colors, the hue is typically a Pantone color. Using tints and shades of the Pantone color, designers can create documents richer than grayscale, but at considerably less cost than four-color process printing, because they use only two colors. The classic example of black plus one color is the traditional *Yellow Pages* telephone directory (now the *Yellow Book* has color ads, too), which used only black, yellow, and grays for artwork.

FIGURE 3-17 Black plus one Pantone color.

Using Color

Color is an element of design that must be handled carefully. In his classic text *Color for the Electronic Age,* Jan V. White writes:

> *Color should not be used just because it is available. Potentially, it can do more than merely make reports, letters, and charts eye-catching. We must be discriminating and avoid acting like children with a new box of crayons. Color should not be used to dazzle but to enlighten and thus add value. (1990, 9)*

When should color be used? A few critical guidelines, paraphrased from White's text, are:

- Use color to guide the reader.

- Use color to intensify a visual message.
- Use color to speed interpretation.
- Use color to accentuate positives.
- Use color to establish mood.
- Use color to make sense and clarify ideas.
- Use color to explain and persuade.
- Use color for a certain purpose, other than "liking a color."
- Use dominant colors supported by accent colors.
- Use color schemes instead of guessing about color.

Type and Typography

Type Categories

Visuals draw the reader to look at the page, but type delivers the message and calls for action. You will get applied experience with type and typography as you progress through part two of this book, but for now, let's take a quick overview of the basics of type.

Type is used in the majority of digital design projects because most messages need words to help communicate meaning. The term *type* stands for typefaces (also known as fonts), which we use to set text (also known as letters and words). Type has a font name and then a style. Each typeface has its own styles that create a font family, the typeface's set of contrasting variations that you can choose from. Styles include roman, regular, bold, semibold, italic, book, oblique, heavy, black, condensed, thin, and bold italic. Combinations of each vary by font family: not every typeface will have a condensed or black version.

Typefaces can be broken down into six main categories:

Serif typefaces have tails (cross lines) at the top and bottom ends of the letter strokes. Serif fonts include old style fonts and slab serif fonts. Most body text (text type) is set in serif typefaces because the lines draw the eye along the type. Serif fonts include classic typefaces such as Garamond, Times New Roman, Caslon, Bodini, and Goudy. Typically used for body copy in the base style of roman (medium weight), serif fonts can be used for display (headline) type also, but they will not have the same visual strength as a sans serif font due to their flowing tails. Serifs can, however, give a composition a softer feel, due in part to the letterforms' organic curves.

Sans serif typefaces' characters without serifs have a modern, industrial style. Because sans serif fonts' geometric attributes are easily understood, they are frequently used for headlines, logos, and reverse type (white type on a dark background). Some common sans serif fonts are Helvetica, Gill Sans, Futura, Folio, Avant Garde, Swiss, Arial, and News Gothic. Sans serif fonts work well as headlines, or even as body copy in limited quantities. Because they create a heavier visual look, they are well suited to creating visual dominance through the use of type.

set in
Garamond Book
Italic Condensed
60 pt.

Bodini BT 10 pt. roman

Bodini BT 10 pt. bold condensed

Bodini BT 10 pt. book

Bodini BT 10 pt. book italic

Bodini BT 10 pt. italic

Bodini BT 10 pt. bold

Bodini BT 10 pt. bold italic

Garamond 10 pt. regular
Garamond 10 pt. italic
Garamond 10 pt. bold
Garamond 10 pt. bold italic

Times New Roman 10 pt. regular
Times New Roman 10 pt. italic
Times New Roman 10 pt. bold
Times New Roman 10 pt. bold italic

Garamond 36 pt. bold italic
Times New Roman 36 pt. bold
Bodini BT 36 pt. bold condensed

FIGURE 3-18 Serif typefaces.

set in
News Gothic
BT Bold
46.67 pt.

Futura BT 10 pt. medium
Futura BT 10 pt. medium bold italic
Futura BT 10 pt. extra black
Futura BT 10 pt. extra black condensed
Futura BT 10 pt. Extra Black Condensed Italic
Futura BT 10 pt. Extra Black Italic
Futura BT 10 pt. medium condensed italic
Futura BT 10 pt. heavy
Futura BT 10 pt. heavy italic

Avant Garde BT 10 pt. book
Avant Garde BT 10 pt. book oblique
Avant Garde BT 10 pt. medium
Avant Garde BT 10 pt. medium oblique

Gill Sans MT 10 pt. regular
Gill Sans MT 10 pt. italic
Gill Sans MT 10 pt. bold
Gill Sans MT 10 pt. bold italic

Gills Sans MT 36 pt. bold italic
Avante Garde BT 36 pt. book
Futura BT 36 pt. extra black

FIGURE 3-19 Sans serif typefaces.

Slab serif typefaces have a heavier stroke at the ends of letters. Slab serifs work well in headlines and intermediate type but not in large quantities of body copy, because the slabs clog up the spacing of smaller letters.

Script and **cursive** typefaces are designed to look like handwriting and can provide a composition with elegance if used properly. Cursive font letters do not connect; script letters do. The distinction is an important one. Script fonts are more fluid than cursive fonts and provide a more elegant option for announcements and invitations. These fonts are not, however, a first choice for corporate designs and advertising due to their low legibility. Script and cursive typefaces are best used sparingly, for small quantities of text such as headlines or intermediate text.

Black letter typefaces are also known as gothic or text letter fonts. They imitate the appearance of calligraphic letters and can give a composition some Old English style. As with scripts and cursives, use them sparingly: these typefaces do not work well at small sizes or in large quantities. Rely on these fonts to create the mood or style of antiquity. Old English and San Marco are common black letter fonts.

Decorative typefaces are fonts with abstract or elaborate letters that create a look of novelty. These fonts are rarely used by professional designers because of their inconsistency and lack of serious aesthetic value. Do not use them without examining other possibilities first. Common decorative fonts are Comic Sans, Critter, and Stop.

Symbol typefaces are geometric figures and illustrations. Symbol fonts are typically sets of objects that are drawn but can be placed in a line of text; each character can then have its attributes manipulated just as if it were a letter of the alphabet. They are useful for adding bullets and ornamental accents to text. Symbol fonts are also known as picture fonts. The font Symbol is one of the most commonly used symbol fonts.

Aachen BT Roman

Slab Serif

Aachen BT
Rockwell Extra Bold
Dynasty Black Condensed

Kunstler script Regular

Script

Edwardian Script ITC
English 157 BT
Hogarth Script D

Fette Fraktur Regular

Blackletter

Fraktur BT
Old English Text MT
Hogarth Script D

DOWNCOME

DECORATIVE

CRITTER
Croobie
Frosty

Symbols

(fts11)
(webdings)
(fts7)

FIGURE 3-20 Various typeface styles.

Type Attributes

Using type in digital design requires us to use a tool or character palette to select different fonts and then apply different attributes. The attributes that can be manipulated using digital tools include:

Font: the name of the typeface and style (italic, roman, bold, black, etc.). Not all fonts have the same style options.

Size: the height of the font in points. There are 72 points in an inch; a 72-point capital letter is approximately one inch in height. Text type sizes range from 7 point to 12 point. Type larger than 18 point is called display type.

Leading: the space between lines. Leading typically needs to be 2 points larger than font size to avoid line spacing issues. The more lines of type there are, the more space between lines is required to create visual continuity and flow from one line to the next.

Kerning: the process of adding or subtracting space between specific pairs of characters. Display type is kerned because at large sizes, certain letter combinations (an uppercase T and a lowercase o, for example) do not sit next to each other correctly in certain fonts. Kerning manipulates the space between letters by either closing gaps or adding space between letters. Kerning is measured in ems, a unit of measure proportional to type size. For instance, in a 10-point font, 1 em equals 10 points.

Tracking: the process of loosening or tightening the spacing between all the characters in an entire block of text, creating incremental spacing between letters and/or words. Tracking allows you to manipulate how much type or how many words fit in an allotted amount of space. It is also measured in ems, which are proportionate to the type size.

Baseline shift: the shifting of type above or below its standard baseline. Type sits on a baseline. Type has descenders, which go below the baseline.

Rotation: the manipulation of text or an individual letter or character from 0 to 360 degrees.

Horizontal and vertical scaling: stretching letters horizontally or vertically by percentage. The only application for this technique is to display type elements. Otherwise, it just makes type look bad, distorting the letterforms and undermining the aesthetic value of the type. Text type should never be scaled horizontally or vertically.

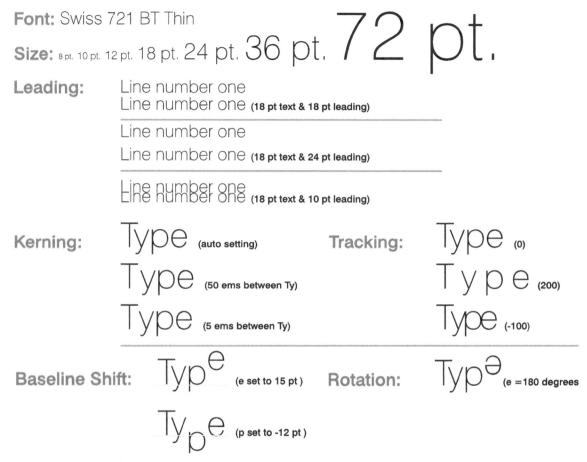

Font: Swiss 721 BT Thin

Size: 8 pt. 10 pt. 12 pt. 18 pt. 24 pt. 36 pt. 72 pt.

Leading:
Line number one
Line number one **(18 pt text & 18 pt leading)**

Line number one
Line number one **(18 pt text & 24 pt leading)**

Line number one
Line number one **(18 pt text & 10 pt leading)**

Kerning: Type **(auto setting)** **Tracking:** Type **(0)**

Type **(50 ems between Ty)** T y p e **(200)**

Type **(5 ems between Ty)** Type **(-100)**

Baseline Shift: Typᵉ **(e set to 15 pt)** **Rotation:** Typə **(e = 180 degrees**

Typₚe **(p set to -12 pt)**

FIGURE 3-21 Type attributes chart.

Getting Attention and Delivering Clarity

Typography is not simply putting text on a page, and working with typography is more than simply placing the cursor on the digital page and typing using default values. Typography is the manipulation of type and space. According to Philip Meggs, typography is "an exact art of measurement and proportion, message and form" (1989, 17–19). Readability and legibility are the cornerstones of good typography.

Typography uses visual language in the form of letters, words, sentences, and paragraphs to thoughtfully present a message within a composition.

Typography is the technique used to simplify and clarify messages so the reader can extract as much meaning as possible. This requires the designer to read and understand the message so that he or she can act as a visual translator, synthesizing the information provided into a representation using words and images.

Choosing the proper typefaces can convey the proper mood and emotion for representing a design's theme. Type is available in all digital design software packages and gives the designer many creative possibilities—illustrating with type, setting type in perfect proportion to the page, using special effects on type (such as manipulating its depth, contrast, perspective, and texture).

FIGURE 3-22 This American Institute of Graphic Arts New Orleans poster combines highly eye-catching, illustrated type wrapped around arresting and thought-provoking imagery. Art direction and illustration by Stefan Sagmeister.

READABILITY

Readability refers to type's capacity to attract and hold a reader's attention by engaging the viewer with a strong typographic visual. Readability adds aesthetic value to a design piece and makes it noticeable and interesting to the viewer. Display type (primary type), which typically includes headlines, subheads, captions, breakouts, pull quotes, and logos, must be highly readable. In addition, headlines must attract attention and draw the reader into a design. Therefore, display type is usually larger and bolder than the surrounding text type, which acts as the clarifying element for delivering the message (White 2005, 131–33). Display type should create a distinct typographical element in the composition. It may even become illegible depending on the extent to which letterforms are manipulated or spacing is manipulated, but that is OK, because the goal of display type is to grab attention and keep it (White 2007, 170–76).

FIGURE 3-23 In this poster for the 2007 London Design Festival, the type is manipulated to create an interpretation of the headline "launch." Design by Domenic Lippa.

LEGIBILITY

Legibility is type's capacity to deliver a message to the reader; text type (also known as body copy) must therefore be highly legible. Text type is considered secondary type because it comes under the display (primary) type in the hierarchy of page elements. Text type furthers the communication; it is what the viewer reads for additional explanation, facts, or details (White 2007, 182). Because it is smaller than display type, we must pay more attention to the spacing between words and lines of text type; the smaller the text becomes, the harder it is to read, process, and act upon. Intermediate type sits in between primary and secondary type—it is typically some kind of subhead. Intermediate type is usually sized and weighted to complement the display type (headline) and to have a hierarchical position over the body copy.

FIGURE 3-24 This poster featuring Nina Simone is an example of pure legibility. The composition incorporates a naturalistic serif typeface, a textured image, and a logo. Design by Milton Glaser.

Typography Considerations

The combination of display type and text type makes up most communication pieces. Display type and text type need to work together as visual elements, first to draw the reader in, and then to communicate the message. In his book *Thinking in Type: The Practical Philosophy of Typography*, typography guru, art director, and author Alex W. White suggests concentrating on the following elements to achieve both readability and legibility in typography (2005, 135); I have added some suggestions to this adapted list with the goal of providing some simple guidelines for the beginning designer.

1. **Type size.** The size of the type is critical to the visual cohesion of the composition and the clarity of the message. Headlines should be set larger than 18-point to provide hierarchy and dominance. Use 9- to 11-point type for text for maximum legibility. If the text type is too large, it hurts the gestalt and looks incorrect.

2. **Type weight.** Heavy, medium, light, and thin are all measures of type weight. Medium-weight text provides the maximum legibility, and heavy-weight type provides high visual contrast and works well for display type. Lightweight type will yield a less heavy page layout.

3. **Type posture.** This is the type's style—italic, for example, which, because it is harder to read than roman type, should be used sparingly.

4. **Line length.** To create an optimal reading experience, the length of a line should be around two alphabets (fifty-two characters) long. Longer lines impair legibility by diminishing the desire to keep reading after a few lines. Shorter line lengths create an easier, quicker read during which the viewer can recognize the message being conveyed.

5. **Letter spacing and word spacing.** Good letter spacing is transparent and eases the visual digestion of words. Use tracking to manipulate the letter spacing in a word (or the spacing between words) and kerning to manipulate the space between two specific letters to experiment with letter and word spacing in display type. Use kerning and tracking carefully, so you do not ruin the uniformity and clarity of text type. And never type two spaces after a period! There is no such thing as a double space in digital design. Never use the space bar (adding multiple spaces) in place of using tabs or indents.

6. **Line spacing.** Leading is the space between lines, also known as line spacing. For leading to be set properly it must create neutral spaces between lines that enhance legibility. Leading can also be varied to create various visual effects with display type.

7. **Justification.** Lines of text in a paragraph can either be ragged, with each line turning at a different point, or justified, with all the lines running to the same edge or margin. Ragged text is easier to read, but justification creates an engaging aesthetic by giving the type a uniform look. Use left-aligned, right-ragged type in most cases. Be sure to include at least six words per line when using justified type to avoid uneven word spacing.

8. **Case.** Type in all caps is more difficult to read than type in upper- and lowercase, so avoid using all caps in text type. You can experiment with using all caps in brief stretches of display and intermediate type, but be sure to do so sparingly.

FIGURE 3-25 All the typography considerations listed above have been utilized in these pages from *Time* magazine. Can you point them out? Design by Luke Hayman.

9. **Background.** Maintain a high contrast between text and image for maximum readability and legibility. Avoid using reversed-out text (white text on a dark background) at small point sizes. Reversed-out serifs are hard to read: when using reversed-out type, use sans serif typefaces.

10. **Serif vs. sans serif.** Serif typefaces have cross strokes (tails) at the edges of the letters. They are commonly used in text type because they are easy to read. The *New York Times* is set in Times New Roman, a serif face that has an eloquent legibility and is very easy for the eyes to digest. Serif fonts are more organic because of their flowing forms. Sans serif typefaces have sharp edges and a modern look. They work well in headlines and in reverse type. The right mix of serif and sans serif typefaces creates visual contrast and helps the eye recognize a composition's primary, secondary, and intermediate type elements.

11. **A final rule.** Never use together two typefaces that are in any way similar. For consistency, type should be exactly the same. Use the same font throughout a piece, creating contrast through size and weight. Or, for variety, use contrasting typefaces: mixing serif and sans serif faces. There are only two approaches: exactly the same or completely different.

Design Principles

To illustrate the principles and techniques of design, I have utilized the work of Alvin Lustig (1915–1955), a communication specialist who incorporated his subjective vision into graphic design. Lustig was a designer, printing expert, and researcher. He, along with Paul Rand, was influential in introducing the New York School style of design to the world. The New York style incorporated the manipulation of visual form and the skillful analysis of communication content (Meggs 2006, 374–76).

Unity is the quality of connectedness that inhabits our designs. Our task is to take different parts and create a whole image that generates a gestalt, with the different elements coexisting in harmony. In the previous section on design devices, we discussed methods for creating unity, or a gestalt, including the use of grids, the law of thirds composition, and consistency in layout. Taking these standard design devices further, listed below are design principles that can be translated into techniques for achieving visual unity.

Balance is the distribution of visual weight in the composition; it provides a sensation of comfort and stability in an image. Positioning elements on opposite sides of the page is the starting point to using balance in a composition. Balance can also be achieved with negative space—by centering an image, for example. Balance can be seen most often in horizontal space, but it can also be established in vertical space. Balance can also be created through rhythm.

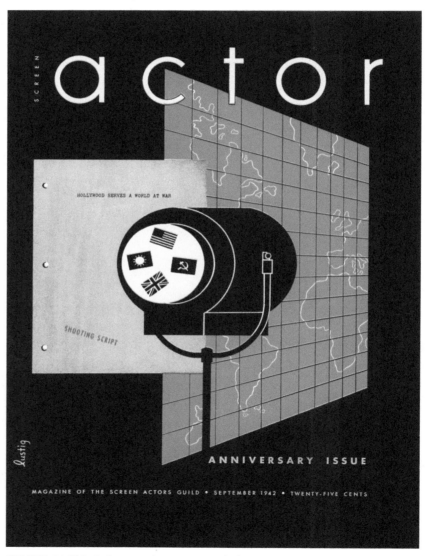

FIGURE 3-26 This design uses shapes to create balance. *Screen Actor* magazine cover designed by Alvin Lustig, September 1942.

Rhythm, which is created by repeating elements in the same or a slightly modi-fied way, establishes a pace for an image, engendering unity and visual motion. The distribution of repetitive elements arranged in a space also establishes compositional balance. Rhythm is established by using repetition.

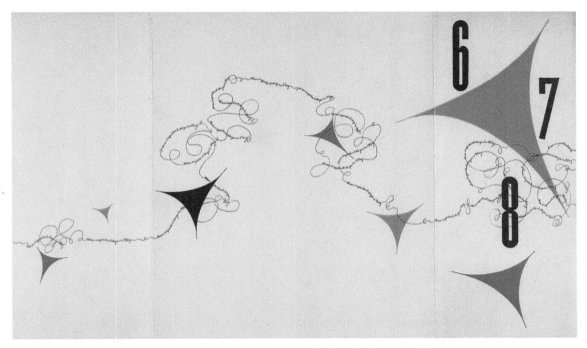

FIGURE 3-27 This design uses line, scale, and repetition to create rhythm. Conference on Art Education leaflet designed by Alvin Lustig, May 1948.

Repetition is created by repeating images and elements such as line, shape, type, space, and color. Repetition gives a design structure, consistency, and hierarchy. We see repetition in all forms of design; it is a main principle in creat-ing symmetry.

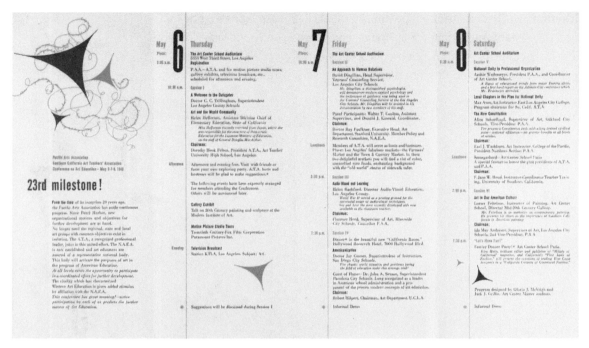

FIGURE 3-28 This design uses repetition of scale and type to create information structure. Conference on Art Education leaflet designed by Alvin Lustig, May 1948.

Symmetry is another term for mirror image. A symmetrical design has the same elements repeated proportionally to each other. This effect creates a feeling of stability and unification. We see symmetry in nature: our bodies are bilaterally symmetrical, with two arms, legs, eyes, feet, and hands. The opposite of symmetry is asymmetry. Asymmetrical forms create variety.

Variety is the range of line, shape, color, texture, and that is used in a composition. We are always striving to achieve visual impact in our designs; variety is another technique that can help us do so. Combined with other elements, such as form and line, and utilizing principles such as repetition and rhythm, unity or a gestalt can be achieved when variety is introduced into design compositions. The most straightforward way to create variety is to manipulate scale and proportion.

FIGURE 3-29 This design uses both symmetry and asymmetry to create the look of snow using geometric symbols. *Screen Actor* magazine cover designed by Alvin Lustig, December 1942.

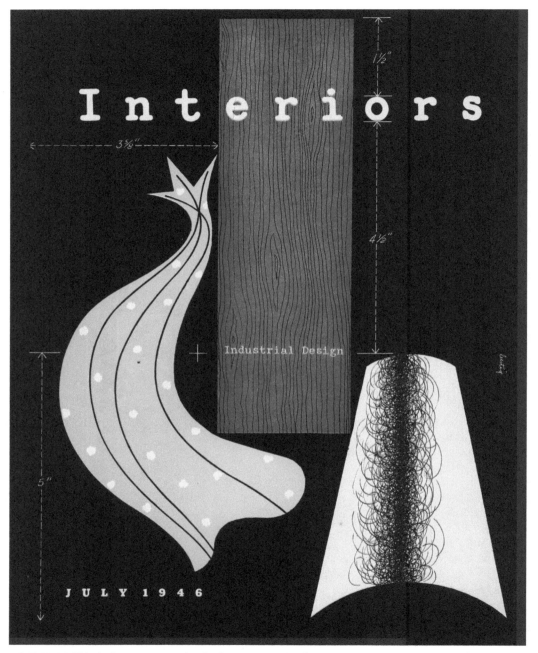

FIGURE 3-30 This design uses textural and color variety to visually represent interior design materials. Cover of *Interiors* magazine designed by Alvin Lustig, July 1946.

Scale and proportion refer to the size of objects in a composition and their relationship to one another. Scale is a technique that uses a variety of element sizes to attract attention and create emphasis. Scale is used to establish proportion among elements. (Objects with the same proportions are symmetrical, or mirror images of each other.) Scale can be used effectively to establish dominance.

FIGURE 3-31 This design uses scale, balance, proportion of white space, and dominance. The Makers of Modern Literature poster, designed by Alvin Lustig, 1949.

Dominance is critical for creating successful compositions. A composition's dominant visual element will draw the viewer in to look or read further. Attracting the reader should be the main goal of using dominant visual elements; they also help to establish hierarchy in a composition, guiding the viewer toward understanding and action. Another method of attracting attention is to use abstraction.

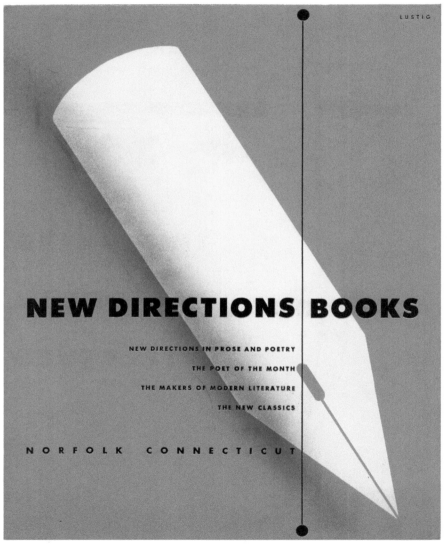

FIGURE 3-32 This design uses dominance in color and scale. New Directions Books poster designed by Alvin Lustig, 1949.

Abstraction is the manipulation of natural shapes to create simplified forms. Reducing shapes and photos through manipulation is one approach to abstraction. Digital manipulations that lead to abstractions include reducing opacity, adding effects and filters, warping, and blending imagery and text. Another approach to abstraction is to integrate elements that are not organic with others that are connected in nature. Abstraction can also be created using overlap.

FIGURE 3-33 This design uses abstract illustrations to present concrete concepts about inventors worldwide. World Inventors Exposition catalog cover designed by Alvin Lustig, 1947.

Overlap and integration is the layering of design elements (e.g., type, image, shape, line, texture) to create a new form that has depth and visual fidelity. Most digital design applications provide tools for layering objects. Overlapping (compositing) items using this layering feature is a strong method for creating abstraction. Overlapping is the main technique used to create collages (overlapped mixed media) and montages (overlapped and integrated photographs).

FIGURE 3-34 This design uses the overlap of line, shape, and image to create an integrated abstract design that maintains communication clarity. *Metropolitan Los Angeles: One Community* book cover designed by Alvin Lustig, 1949.

Evaluating and Critiquing Your Work

When we create our work for the first time, it is rarely complete. Design is a process, not a result. Critiquing your design—and its ability to create a gestalt and deliver a message—requires some sort of criteria. You must continually refine your work to get it to meet these specific criteria for good design.

There are many different ways to evaluate design work. Keeping the basics of good design in mind, I use this simple list during in-class critiques. I also use it to critique my own work during the production process. It uses the acronym BANGPP, which stands for *balance, alignment, negative space, grouping, proximity,* and *perimeter edge.* During a "crit," the students and I evaluate presented designs, identify where the design devices and principles fit into the whole composition, and determine if there is a recognizable theme. We look for strong and weak points, with the purpose of providing helpful suggestions on how to improve the work. It is a group filtering session: the group helps the designer think about decisions he or she made, helping to filter out wasted content or to enhance the composition.

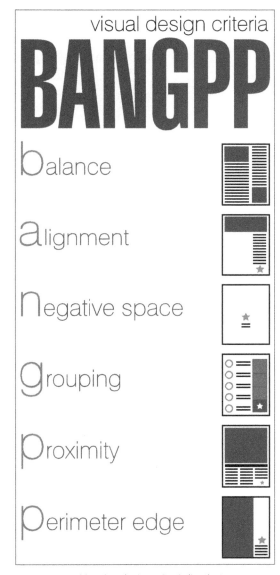

FIGURE 3-35 Here is a design criteria list that can be used when you review visual work. The acronym BANGPP stands for *balance, alignment, negative space, grouping, proximity,* and *perimeter edge.*

References

Barzun, Jacques, and Henry Graff. 2004. *The modern researcher.* 6th ed. Belmont, CA: Thomson Wadsworth.

Bauhaus-Archiv Museum of Design. 1919. Manifesto. http://www.bauhaus.de/english/bauhaus1919/manifest1919.htm.

Brainard, Shirl. 1991. *A design manual.* Englewood Cliffs, NJ: Prentice Hall.

Curtis, Hillman. 2000. *Flash Web design: The art of motion graphics.* Berkeley, CA: New Riders.

———. 2002. *MTIV: Process, inspiration, and practice for the new media designer.* Berkeley, CA: New Riders.

Elam, Kimberly. 2001. *Geometry of design.* New York: Princeton Architectural Press.

———. 2004. *Grid systems: Principles of organizing type.* New York: Princeton Architectural Press.

Golding, John. 1994. *Concepts of modern art.* Ed. Nikos Stangos. New York: Thames & Hudson.

Grayson, Steve. 1995. *Adobe Systems print publishing guide.* Mountain View, CA: Adobe Systems.

Heller, Steven, and Seymour Chwast. 2000. *Graphic style: From Victorian to digital.* New York: Harry Abrams.

Herman Miller. 2008. Discovering design (educational Web site). http://www.hermanmiller.com/discoveringdesign.

Hollis, Richard. 2001. *Graphic design: A concise history.* New York: Thames & Hudson.

Holtzschue, Linda. 2006. *Understanding color: An introduction for designers.* Hoboken, NJ: John Wiley & Sons.

Kristof, Ray, and Amy Satran. 1995. *Interactivity by design: Creating & communicating with new media.* Mountain View, CA: Adobe Press.

Lauer, David, and Stephen Pentak. 2007. *Design basics.* Belmont, CA: Thomson Wadsworth.

Lidwell, Paul, Kritina Holden, and Jill Butler. 2003. *Universal principles of design.* Gloucester, MA: Rockport.

Meggs, Phillip. 1989. *Type and image: The language of graphic design.* New York: Van Nostrand Reinhold.

Meggs, Phillip, and Alston Purvis. 2006. *Meggs' history of graphic design.* 4th ed. Hoboken, NJ: John Wiley & Sons.

Stewart, Mary. 2002. *Launching the imagination: A comprehensive guide to basic design.* New York: McGraw Hill.

Swann, Alan. 1997. *The new graphic design school.* Hoboken, NJ: John Wiley & Sons.

Tufte, Edward. 2003. *The cognitive style of PowerPoint.* Cheshire, CT: Graphics Press.

Wheeler, Alina. 2003. *Designing brand identity: A complete guide to creating, building, and maintaining strong brands.* Hoboken, NJ: John Wiley & Sons.

White, Alex W. 2005. *Thinking in type: The practical philosophy of typography.* New York: Allworth.

———. 2007. *Advertising design and typography.* New York: Allworth.

White, Jan V. 1990. *Color for the electronic age.* New York: Watson Guptill.

Williams, Robin. 1994. *The non-designer's design book.* Berkeley, CA: Peachpit.

ON THE ROAD

JACK KEROUAC

THE ORIGINAL SCROLL

FOR THE VERY FIRST TIME - READ THE UNCENSORED MANUSCRIPT OF THIS MODERN AMERICAN CLASSIC

'It changed my life like it changed everyone else's' **Bob Dylan**

CHAPTER 4
Conceptualization and Planning

Chapter Objectives

Introduce basic conceptualization techniques.

Explore exemplary and inspirational images from a variety of artists and designers.

Become familiar with various design project types.

Inspiration

Before you start the conceptualization and planning process, it helps to get inspired. One of the best ways to do that is to observe other people's work. Observe print, Web, and broadcast media in the world around you. Watching movies and television, visiting content-rich Internet sites, going to an art gallery or museum, playing a video game, and reading magazines are all ways to seek inspiration. Observe the branding, advertising, and wayfinding designs that surround you. Look at billboards and signage to interpret the intended theme and then analyze type, color, image, rhythm, style, and the possible reasons behind the (good or bad) choices. Ask yourself, What were those designers thinking when they made those design decisions? Look at design annuals from magazines, including *ID*, *Communication Arts*, *Graphic Design*, and *Print*, to find styles and trends. Once you are inspired, you can begin using a design process to help achieve your communication goal.

Seven-Step Design Process

I have isolated all the important considerations for solving a communication design problem and fused them into a seven-step design process. It is best to use a design process that works well for you, so feel free to manipulate my process to find your own. Some people are less formal in their decision making and use divergent approaches whenever possible. Other designers need a calculated approach and find it is necessary to follow a series of steps. To help my students find their own path, I based this seven-step method on both convergent and divergent approaches.

This process does not assume that you are working in a vacuum (without possibilities), but rather that you are working with a client (even if that is your teacher or your own company) to find a vision to solve the communication problem.

Seven-Step Design Process for Communication Problems

1. **Identify** the audience, problem, and communication goal(s) by creating a scope document that specifies goals, audience, concept, message, image, style, and theme.

2. **Research** the audience and medium to clarify themes and output specifications. Gather information to be used in the conceptualization and creation of the work.

3. **Target** the emotional center using concentric circles to find keywords from which themes may emerge. These themes will lead to the emotional center of the product or idea. Ask your client, research subjects, and yourself, What will make people respond?

4. **Conceptualize** on paper using outlines, flowcharts, sketches, storyboards, and integrated site maps to connect the concept and theme. Brainstorm divergent (nonlinear) thinking for creative solutions first and then convergent (linear) thinking for process. Use thumbnails to rough out possible creative directions.

5. **Create** simple solutions in the form of visual comps, prototypes, and treatments using digital design tools.

6. **Revise** by filtering, simplifying, and justifying the work through revision.0

7. **Evaluate** the design against the communication goals and scope document to measure your success and make recommendations for future updates.

   See the online Appendix I for an example of this seven-step process in action (www.wiley.com/go/digitaldesign).

Identify

As discussed in chapter 1, we create digital designs to reach a communication goal that solves a problem. Identifying the audience, the problem, and the goals are the first orders of business in the design process. The more we think about identifying these critical facts up front, the better our solution will emerge during the rest of the design process.

   The deliverable for this step is the scope document. I learned about the importance of scope documents when I worked as a curriculum development specialist, creating new media–based instructional design products. Scope documents vary depending on the project type and the client policies. These documents have two purposes: they help get a new project on track, and they provide a project framework—the "big picture"—for managers and clients, helping them understand the project's creative direction so they can provide initial approvals. In many cases, a budget is attached to the scope document to illustrate potential costs for outside services such as copywriting, photography, illustration, or postproduction work.

Figuring out the scope of a project helps you to move forward by outlining the broad content and important facts needed to begin the creation process. Remember, the identification process evolves as you learn more about the client, the goal, and the available resources. It's OK if you don't have a complete scope document at first, but continue to update it as the project progresses to help you maintain a working blueprint of what you need to accomplish. Once the scope of the project is identified, then you can move to research.

Project Scope

Project title: _____

Medium: Print, Web, or broadcast?

Goal: What is the purpose of this communication?

  Entertainment (TV and film)

  Persuasion (advertising and public relations)

  Information (news)

  Education (corporate training, academic instruction, and public service announcement)

Audience: To whom is this communication directed?

Concept: What is the big idea here—the unique selling proposition (USP), the emotional center?

Messages: What headlines and copy support the concept?

Images: What visuals support the concept?

Style: What is the visual, musical, vocal, and/or rhythmic appearance being sought?

Theme: What is the story here?

FIGURE 4-1 Sample Scope Document

Research

Research is critical to design. It provides answers to questions that guide us in the design process. The outcome of research is to discover something new. We may start with some information on the topic, but research extends the meaning of the communication goals.

When we perform research, we are using our senses to observe, record, analyze, and report data. We perform informal design research by talking to clients about their business and problems and also by looking at documents and Web sites. Formal research is performed by scientists, scholars, market researchers, and corporations. If we need historical or contemporary facts, we might utilize published research studies from conferences and journals.

There are two types of research data: quantitative (numerical) and qualitative (conceptual or narrative). Statistics are factual; they are examples of quantitative data, which is measurable, numerical data gathered through surveys, polling, and experiments. Qualitative data, which is humanistic and describes experiences, uses words to explain data findings from observations, content analyses of historical documents, results from focus groups, and interviews with people.

Both quantitative and qualitative methods have their place in the design process. The process of research requires you to look, listen, think, and record what you see, hear, and discover about the audience and the themes that will support your designs. In her book *Everyone's Guide to Successful Publications*, Elizabeth Adler offers a list of questions that can be used to tailor a piece to an audience (1993, 73–79). Answering these questions (some or all) will help you design for communication by focusing on the information you gain during the research process, rather than simply guessing or catering the piece to what you expect instead of what your target audience expects.

TABLE 4-1 Twenty Questions to Help You Target Your Audience.

> **1.** Who is your target audience? (You cannot answer "everyone.")
>
> **2.** Are there more men or women? (Find statistics to support your answer.)
>
> **3.** How old are they? Are they children, teens, adults, or seniors?
>
> *(continues)*

TABLE 4-1 (cont.).

4. Where do they live? In what city, town, state, or country?

5. What is their income level? Are they wealthy? Upper- or middle-class? Or is their income low or poverty level?

6. What is their education level? Do they have a high school education? A degree from a two- or four-year college? An advanced degree?

7. What is their knowledge level? What is their level of sophistication with the product, service, or idea?

8. How are they different from you (be specific)?

9. How are they similar to you (be specific)?

10. What is their current attitude toward the product or service?

11. What is their background in relationship to the topic? What about the product or service have they experienced so far?

12. What are their values—their ethical stance on various societal issues?

13. What are their tastes? Are they refined? Middle-class? Workaday?

14. How do they spend their leisure time? Are they introverted or extroverted?

15. Do they read magazines, books, and/or newspapers?

16. What makes them unique? Are there any special features of the group?

17. When can you get their attention most easily? At what time of day? In what environment? At what time of year?

18. In what format and media will they read or interact with the communication piece?

19. What effect do you want to have on them? How should this communication make them feel?

20. What do you want them to do? What action do you ultimately want them to take?

Adapted from Adler 1993

Target

Targeting the emotional center is an important step in the design process, as has been discussed by designer Hillman Curtis (2000, 01:09–10), who uses a three-ring circle to help target themes before and during client meetings. Each of the three rings gets filled with key words that describe what needs to be communicated in order to establish a theme and a story within the design. The closer to the center the word lies, the more important and valuable the theme. Less important, supporting themes lie in the outer circles. The keywords are determined during research, client meetings, and thematic conceptualization. Identifying important keywords that describe the project's themes gives the design team a basis for launching a concept.

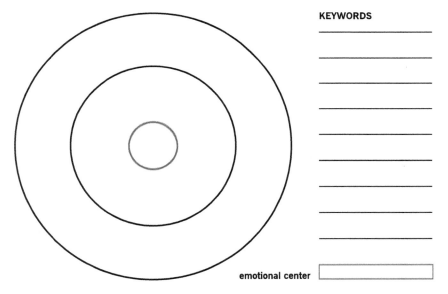

FIGURE 4-2 In his client work, new media designer Hillman Curtis uses a three-ring circle for targeting the emotional center—a term that describes just what will persuade and communicate the message best. The most important words (in relation to the theme) are placed closest to the center of the circle. During this process, ask yourself how the words you are writing down connect with the target audience's emotions.

Conceptualize

Conceptualization is exploring visual options on paper. The conceptualization process drives the digital design process by providing a skeletal representation of what our composition will look like or how our Web site or animation will work.

Conceptualizing allows you and your client to see your vision of the potential composition. It also helps you see your potential design options before beginning to use digital tools. I frequently see inexperienced designers attempt to start working on a project on the computer instead of on paper. Inevitably, the design suffers and the person ends up confused, asking the same question over and over again: What should I do? Eventually, the designer will go back to paper conceptualization to clear up the confusion and get a grip on the communication goals and how to tailor the message to the audience.

To conceptualize compositions for print, we use sketches and thumbnails. To conceptualize interactive media (Web sites) and time-based media (video, film, motion graphics, and animation), we use content outlines, flowcharts (interactive pieces), and storyboards.

Print Projects (Static)

Conceptual sketches are quickly executed freehand drawings using a multitude of overlapping lines. These sketches are used to create initial roadmaps for visual concepts. A sketch is not meant be an illustration, but it should represent the visual elements and explore composition.

Sketches are a necessary starting point for work if strong compositions are to emerge during the design process. Sketches are done on paper, preferably from a sketch pad—don't use lined composition paper. Realistic forms are not needed for sketches. Geometric forms can also be used to represent elements on the page: a line can represent a line of text, a heavier line can represent a headline, and a rectangle, square, or triangle can be used to represent images.

Thumbnail sketches are just small sketches. Thumbnails are used by art directors and designers because their smaller size allows ideas to be explored more quickly. In fact, thumbnails are very often done before full sketches so many different compositions can be studied. Using thumbnails helps determine which ideas should be further developed into sketches. Designers typically then complete a series of rough sketches that present different approaches to the final composition; these lead to a determination of which ideas should be further developed in digital format.

FIGURE 4-3, A–C Thumbnail (A), full-page sketch (B), and final design (C) for a student poster project. Design by Kristen Crawford.

Web and Motion Projects (Dynamic)

Motion and Web projects require multiple levels of conceptualization. We first must go through a process of organization to determine the content. To do this we create a content outline, a list of what assets we need (text, images, video footage, etc.) to begin digital production. The content outline should be specific, listing each piece of content by name and kind. It is a container for all content categories, which will then be refined and moved into the structure of a three-column script.

The three-column script provides a written, sequential version of what text, images, audio, video, and animation need to be included in a Web page. It is an intermediate step between the content outline and the flowchart, which allows the designer to verify the content that must go in each Web page (or, if the work is broadcast based, each animation, video, or film). The three columns break down into Web page or scene; text, images, audio, and video; and link to (for Web) or cut to (for broadcast). The script is critical for identifying your production challenges and organizing your schedule, and for ensuring that you have isolated the critical elements that exist in each section.

For interactive products such as Web sites and DVDs, a flowchart is needed to show where the links take the viewer. The flowchart allows the designer to become the gatekeeper of content. Your job as gatekeeper is to provide access to your audience, using structure to create functionality. The content, usability, and simplicity of a DVD or Web-based product are presented in a diagram using boxes to represent pages or DVD chapters and lines to represent links, which are connections from one piece of content to another.

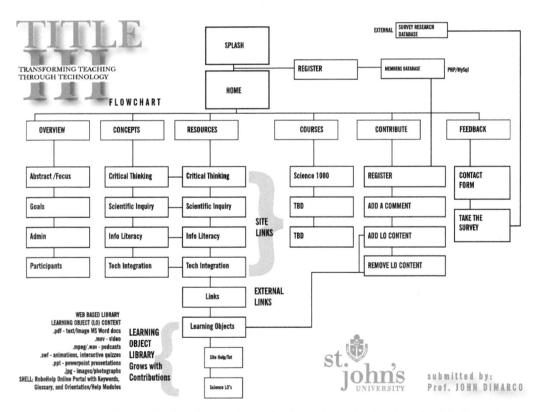

FIGURE 4-4 A flowchart provides a visual overview of the structure of a Web site or other multimedia project. A flowchart also gives the designer and client an overview of the project's scope. Design by John DiMarco.

Flowcharts come in various styles: no one style is standard. However, the flowchart must create a clear map for your digital design project. You must include hierarchical levels and links to make the flowchart easy to understand and to provide a discernable structure for the design of the content—each link represents an access control that must be designed in the final Web pages (Kristof and Satran 1995, 27–33). After creating the flowchart, the next step is to conceptualize the visuals using storyboards.

Storyboards organize visual content into a sequence for the purpose of visualizing a time-based project, such as a Web site, motion graphics movie, animation, video, or film. Essentially high-quality illustrations rather than rough representations (like sketches), storyboards for film, video, and animation are typically highly detailed, but their main goal is to show the sequence of images as it might play out in the final production piece.

Storyboards help designers and directors create work that has a proverbial "beginning, middle, and end," which insures that the sequential content makes sense, and has a comprehensible aesthetic flow. Because you are trying to illustrate the *sequence* of shots or screens, the storyboard for Web projects and motion graphics work can in some cases be very rough—as long as it is logical. For broadcast and motion productions, the designer should create a storyboard of key frames (places that define the beginning and end of a smooth transition). For Web sites, the designer should present the sequence of pages by level (the top level is always the home page), including pop-ups, to show the interactive connections between visuals.

We have done the grunt work in the design process up to this point. We have identified our communication goals, fortified our message with research, and concepetualized various ideas. Now we are ready to identify visual solutions. Development of design projects involves creation, revision, and evaluation.

Create

Digital design creation is covered in part two of this book, where we actually make stuff using digital design tools. That is definitely the fun part. After creation comes revision.

FIGURE 4-5 Storyboards provide a visual of actions for time-based and Web productions key frame by key frame. Design Micha Riss and Steve Tozzi.

Shot # 5

Shot # 6

Shot # 7

Shot # 8

Revise

We evaluate near-finished work for revisions as a comp (comprehensive), which gives the client a close approximation of the final design piece. The work may be a high- or low-quality print or, in the case of a Web site, printed screen shots or a live site to navigate through.

This is part of the process, and the designer should pick the best way to communicate with and receive comments from the client. In most cases, you will have to edit the work, not just for mistakes but also to find a better solution. Revising to enhance the design typically includes filtering and justification, to simplify the work.

Design pieces always start at a complex level; the goal is to massage the results into the simplest solution. Filtering is the process of simplifying your work for superfluous information. Justifying the design helps validate each decision as the designer asks questions like, Why did I design this layout this way? Why did I include this graphic in this Web site? Justification throughout the design process is an important method of filtering out elements and items that do not support the theme (story) and have no value to the concept (idea).

Evaluate

Evaluating our designs for aesthetic qualities requires visual critique as discussed in chapter 2. Gauging success may also encompass formal market research or communication audits; both generate quantitative data (numerical and statistical) that provide a broad view of the results. We can also use qualitative methods such as focus groups, observations, and document analysis to gather the personal views of clients and audience members in order to get a feel for the perceived essence of the works we create. In Web design, usability testing is the most popular method for assessing the feelings and habits of end users and measuring the Web site's functionality (or lack thereof).

Digital Design Project Types

Possibilities

Now that we have discussed the process, let's identify the many categories of possible digital design projects you can explore. Design is a universal function that transcends disciplines and subjects; it allows us to explore problem-solving possibilities. In chapter 1, we discussed how creating communication design requires us to identify the problem and audience, and then identify the goal, which could be to inform, persuade, educate, or entertain—or even some combination thereof. To achieve these goals, we must seek out the emotional center of the idea or product to establish a theme or story, and then deliver the story using a strong concept, professional-level production techniques, and efficient delivery systems.

We take these steps to solve communication problems using the design process. We actually solve problems through projects. Projects themselves may have multiple purposes: the item "brochure" could be used for any number of communication goals and could provide a solution in publishing, advertising, packaging, signage, news media, corporate identity, branding, or broadcast. To help navigate the possibilities, a list of design project types is provided below.

TABLE 4-2 Digital Design Project Types

Annual reports and business reports

Announcements, invitations, and postcards

Advertising

Books

Brochures and collateral materials

Calendars

Catalogs

Direct mail and direct response

Environmental graphics

Internet design (including Web sites, Web animations, and online ads)

Letterhead and stationery (corporate identity)

Logos

Newsletters

Packaging

Point-of-purchase (POP), signs, and billboards

Posters

Newspapers

Magazines

Annual Reports and Business Reports

Annual reports and business reports are a formal way for a company or charitable organization to present its constituency with relevant financial information and inform it about the organization's mission. These documents typically contain a combination of charts, graphs, text, and images.

Typical sizes:

Annual reports: 8.5 × 11″ perfect bound (glued spine)

Business reports: 8.5 × 14″ or 8.5 × 11″ (stapled or spiral bound)

FIGURE 4-6 Steelcase annual report. Design by Turnstyle.

Announcements, Invitations, and Postcards

Announcements and invitations are used to notify an audience about an event and typically contain mostly text and few (or no) images. Postcards are used for several communication goals, including persuasion (related to new products or events, usually by direct mail), information (about public events), and entertainment (as in the classic vacation postcard). Postcards have one dominant image and sometimes a headline on the front. The back of the card presents subheads with body copy accompanied by a mailing address panel.

Typical sizes:

Postcards: 4 × 6″, 5 × 7″, 6 × 9″

Announcements and invitations: 8.5 × 11″ folded down to 5.5 × 8.5″ (or smaller)

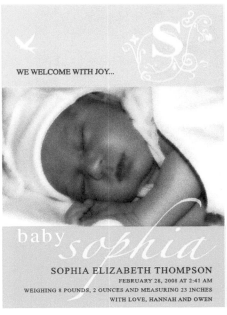

FIGURE 4-7 Announcement and invitation. Design by Kristen Krawford.

Advertising

Advertising comes in many forms, including print (magazine, newspaper, and direct response), Internet (banner and online ads), and broadcast (television commercials). Print and Internet advertisements come in a wide range of sizes, depending on the publication or Web site specifications.

The goal of advertising is always persuasion. Advertising falls into three categories: consumer (which targets the end user); institutional (which targets investors or employees, or carries public relations messages); and business-to-business (targeting the trade and business customers).

Advertising uses dominant visual elements—either type or images—to draw attention. In many cases, an image is used to enhance the visual impact and to help illustrate the theme or the story being told in the ad. Imageless advertising utilizes type as an image to attract attention, draw the reader in, and commit to action.

FIGURES 4-8 Dry soda consumer print ad and banner ad. Design by Turnstyle.

Books

Books are printed containers of information. Book design incorporates text and images into a sequence that creates a coherent whole. The focus of book design—providing a personal experience to the reader—is achieved through attention to the structure of common elements and to legibility (the clarity of the typography). Highly legible designs that are easy to read are created using type that allows the eyes to glide across the page without ambiguity or difficulty.

Books cover all communication goals: to inform, persuade, educate, and entertain. This book's goal, for example, is to educate. Book covers and spines, page layouts and spreads, and interior illustrations and photography are all components that digital designers conceptualize, plan, and produce when they design books. Manuals, handbooks, and directories are also types of books.

Typical sizes:

Perfect bound (glued spine) books: 4 × 6", 5 × 7", 7.5 × 9.25", 7 × 10", 8 × 10", 8.5 × 11"

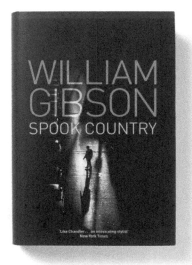
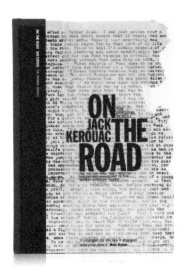

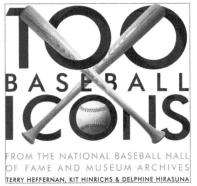

FIGURE 4-9 Various book jackets designed by Angus Hyland (top) and a book cover and spread designed by Kit Hinrichs (bottom).

Brochures and Collateral

Brochures and collateral materials present information in one to several pages and include folded brochures, booklets (little books), and flyers (small posters). Brochures are used by organizations to describe who they are, what they do, and how they do it. They are most often used to persuade or inform. For example, a flyer might be used to announce an event location or to sell a product. A brochure must have high readability: it should be attractive and hook the reader with strong type and/or thought-provoking images.

Typical sizes:

Brochures:

Classic: 8.5 × 11″ or 8.5 × 14″, folded to fit in a No. 10 business envelope

Flyers: 8.5 × 11″

Booklets:

Full size: 11 × 17″ folded to 8.5 × 11″ saddle stitched (stapled)

Half size: 8.5 × 11″ folded to 5.5 × 8.5″ saddle stitched

Any size using a spiral or comb binding

FIGURE 4-10. Portfolio brochure in the form of a small booklet with spiral binding. Design by Kristen Crawford.

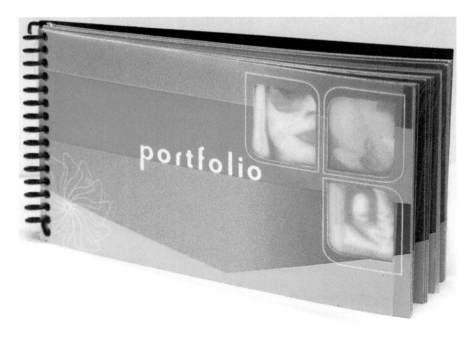

Calendars

Calendar creation combines text styles and (usually) images to generate a useful tool that has a perceived shelf life. The calendar is used for persuasion in advertising and also for entertainment, as with thematic products such as swimsuit calendars or dog breed calendars. Calendars must have both high readability and high legibility in order to attract consumers and provide an accurate table of days in each month. Grids are a main feature of calendar design.

Typical sizes:

Wall calendars: 11 × 8.5″

Desk calendars: various sizes

FIGURE 4-11 Pop-up desk calendars. Design by Turnstyle.

Catalogs

Catalogs are tools whose focus is selling products. The catalog uses grids to arrange products by categories and provide indexes and images that allow readers to skim the catalog to find what they want more quickly. Although used for persuasion, catalogs rely on strong information design to organize and present large quantities of product data.

Typical size:

8.5 × 11″, with multiple pages saddle stitched, or perfect or spiral bound

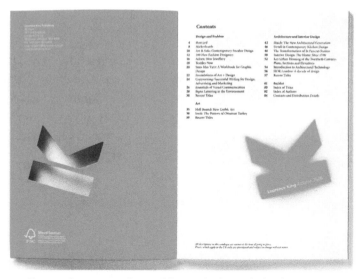

FIGURE 4-12   Laurence King catalog cover and spread. Design by Angus Hyland.

Direct Mail and Direct Response

Direct mail pieces are brochures of varying sizes, sometimes sent with a sales letter. They always contain a panel for the customer's address. Direct response pieces are a form of direct mail that includes business reply cards or tear-off panels. The goal of direct mail and direct response pieces is persuasion; they are used frequently for sales, advertising, and promotions.

Environmental Graphics

Environmental graphics provide the visual aspects of wayfinding, using information design to communicate brand identity or to shape a sense of place. Environmental graphic designers create exhibits and themed environments, architectural graphics, signage, entertainment environments, retail and store design, and information design, including maps (Society for Environmental Graphic Design 2009). Environmental graphics are used to inform (wayfinding signs), persuade (retail stores), educate (museums), and entertain (casinos and stadiums).

FIGURE 4-13 Halloween direct mail piece promoting Turnstyle, a Seattle-based graphic design firm. Design by Turnstyle.

FIGURE 4-14 Seattle University Redhawks environmental graphics. Design by Turnstyle.

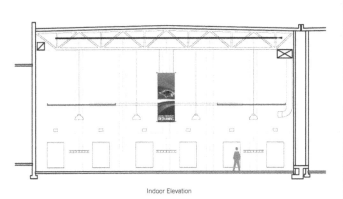

Indoor Elevation

Internet Design

The Internet is an interconnected network of computers that forms the World Wide Web, which enables all users of the Internet to share information digitally. Web designers create Web pages that are linked to form Web sites, as well as online advertisements and banners and animation and motion graphics. The Web's technical specifications present possibilities—and limitations—different from those of print design. Web design is used in achieving all types of communication goals.

Typical sizes:

Web pages: 800 × 600 pixels, 1024 × 768 pixels, or a custom size.

Animations: 320 × 240 pixels, 640 × 480 pixels, 720 × 486 pixels

Online advertisements: 728 × 90 pixels (leaderboard), 300 × 250 pixels (square), 160 × 600 pixels Skyscraper, 120 × 240 (small skyscraper)

Web pages, animations, and online ads can be various sizes.

FIGURE 4-15A Singer Kelly Rowland's Web site. Design by Tommy Spero.

FIGURE 4-15B AIGA Web site page. Design by Kind Company.

Letterhead and Stationery (Corporate Identity)

A company's or a person's letterhead consists of a logo, name, address, telephone number, fax number, e-mail address, and Web site address, or URL (universal or uniform resource locator). Stationery includes envelopes and business cards. Because consistency is critical to corporate identity, which is the visual representation of the organization driven by design, all pieces share the same concept. The letterhead and stationery are used to inform.

Typical sizes:

Letterhead: 8.5 × 11″

Business card: 3.5 × 2″

No. 10 envelopes: 4.125 × 9.75″

Mailing envelopes: 6 × 9″ or 9 × 12″

FIGURE 4-16 Turnstyle letterhead and stationery. Design by Turnstyle.

Logos

Logos are symbols that represent a company or brand. They are vehicles of persuasion created by designers using illustration and typography techniques. Designer Milton Glaser said "a logo is an entry point to the brand" (Wheeler 2003, 4–6). A logo is a symbol with distinctive visual form that triggers sensual or rational perception and encourages meaning in the consumer. Simplicity is the key to logo design, so that recognition is effortless. The brand is the meaning of the organization and provides the nucleus for all communication designs within an organization.

A logo should be able to fit comfortably on both a 3.5 × 2″ business card and (scaled up to a much larger size) on the side of a building. Put another way, logos must be clearly visible at 1 × 1″ *and* at 100 × 100′. They are typically designed in a vector application such as Adobe Illustrator so the file is scalable to any size.

FIGURES 4-17, A–K
Logos. Designs by Milton Glaser (a, b), John DiMarco (c, g), Turnstyle Studio (d), Stefan Sagmeister (e), Tommy Spero (f), Michael Gericke (h), Paula Scher (i, k), Justus Oehler (j).

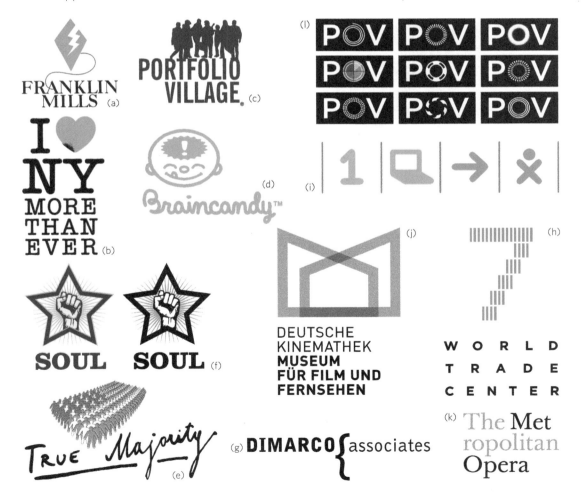

Newsletters

Newsletters cover a variety of topics and carry information to special reader-ships, such as employees, customers, or members of an association. A newsletter is usually eight pages or fewer and combines text and graphics in a format that can be read quickly. Newsletters can also be electronic and distributed on the Web. E-newsletters are comprised mostly of text and also use an easy-to-read format, with short articles and bullet lists. The newsletter is used for information, education, and persuasion.

Typical size:

11 × 17″ folded to 8.5 × 11″

A multiple-page newsletter would usually be saddle stitched.

FIGURE 4-18 Alumni newsletter. Design by John DiMarco

Packaging

Consumer goods are sold in packaging that is created by a digital designer. The package is the silent salesperson for a retail product. Packaging includes: bags, boxes, CD and DVD jackets, tags, labels, poly bags, containers, film, and foil. Packaging is critical for selling a product because it draws attention to the product and persuades the consumer to trust the brand. Package designers perform typography, create product trademarks, shoot photos, and illustrate icons. The size of the package design varies with the product.

FIGURE 4-19A Package design project. Design by Kristen Crawford.

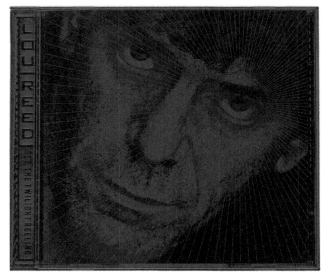

FIGURES 4-19B Lou Reed CD package. Design by Stefan Sagmeister.

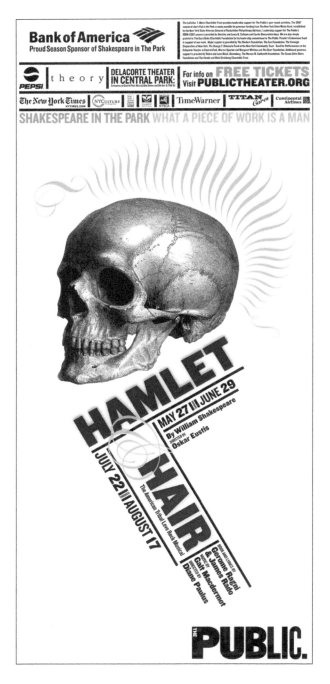

POP, Signs, and Billboards

POP, or point-of-purchase displays, are filled with merchandise. Such countertop and free-standing displays, which are encountered by consumers in retail stores, are designed to lend persuasive appeal to products and are used to organize products throughout the retail space. Signs and billboards are public communications that are used to inform, persuade, and educate audiences. We see signs everywhere in public places: for advertising (product billboards), wayfinding (location, direction, and traffic signs), and branding (corporate logos on buildings).

Posters

Posters are used for the communication goals of persuasion, education, and entertainment. In retail stores, posters persuade us by depicting models using products. Illustrated posters in doctors' offices educate us about the parts of the body. Posters with images of favorite athletes, celebrities, or musicians drape the walls of teenagers' rooms.

Typical sizes:

11 × 17", 17 × 22", 24 × 36", 36 × 48"

FIGURE 4-20 New York Shakespeare Festival billboard, 2008. Design by Paula Sher.

FIGURE 4-21 Poster for Guggenheim exhibition in Japan. Design by Stefan Sagmeister.

FIGURE 4-22 "This is a poster" poster. Design by Angus Hyland and Fabian Herrmann.

Publication Design

Publication design focuses on magazines and newspapers, which are typically used for all four communication goals. Publication design requires a digital designer to scan and retouch photos, create illustrations, perform page layout and typography, and create an information container with structure. Magazine and newspaper designers create master pages (pages that stay consistent) by building digital templates and style sheets to ensure column widths and grids are treated consistently from page to page.

FIGURE 4-23 *Dairy Today* magazine cover. Design by DJ Stout and Daniella Boebel.

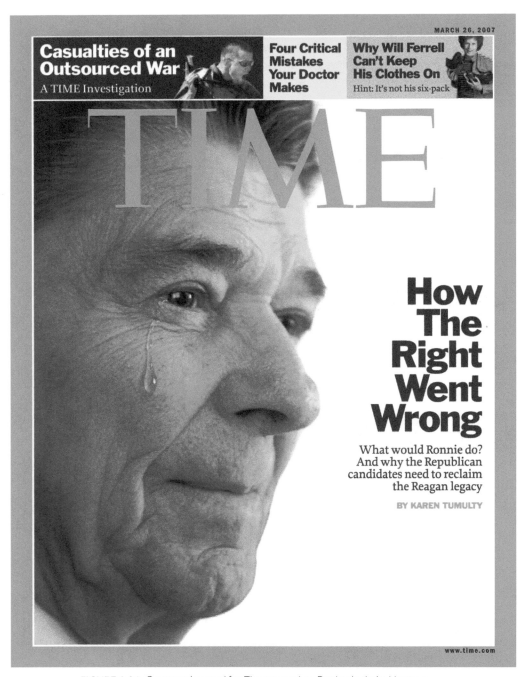

FIGURE 4-24 Cover and spread for *Time* magazine. Design by Luke Hayman.

References

Adler, Elizabeth. 1993. *Everyone's guide to successful publications: How to produce powerful brochures, newsletters, flyers, and business communications, start to finish.* Berkeley, CA: Peachpit.

Curtis, Hillman. 2000. *Flash Web design: The art of motion graphics.* Berkeley, CA: New Riders.

———. 2002. MTIV: *Process, inspiration, and practice for the new media designer.* Berkeley, CA: New Riders.

Kristof, Ray, and Amy Satran. 1995. *Interactivity by design: Creating & communicating with new media.* Mountain View, CA: Adobe Press.

Society for Environmental Graphic Design. 2009. What is environmental graphic design. http://www.segd.org/#/about-us/what-is-egd.html

Wheeler, Alina. 2003. *Designing brand identity: A complete guide to creating, building, and maintaining strong brands.* Hoboken, NJ: John Wiley & Sons.

PART TWO
Techniques

YOUR SPACE HAS BEEN INVADED

CHAPTER 5
Raster Graphics

Chapter Objectives

Identify and define raster graphics.

Identify and define the differences between raster graphics for print and Web.

Introduce basic raster graphics techniques.

Digital Imaging and Raster Graphics

Digital imaging refers to the manipulation of bitmapped images, also known as raster graphics, which are made up of small rectangles called pixels. *Pixels*, a word that is a shortened version of "picture elements," are bits of data mapped to a color and arranged in rows and columns within a digital document. The small rectangles form a complete image when viewed together. The size of the rows and columns (i.e., their height and width) represents the page size. The amount of pixels per inch (ppi) in relationship to the page size is used in raster imaging programs to represent resolution output on a screen. The number of dots printed in a linear inch (dpi) is the resolution output on a printer.

FIGURES 5-1, A, B
Close-up of image pixels in a raster graphic. Bitmapped images are formed by rectangular squares called pixels.

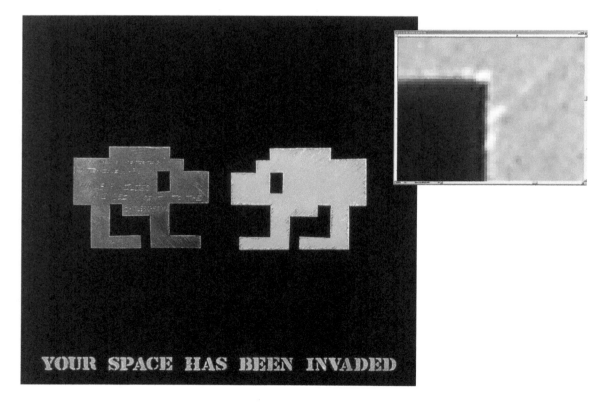

The main difference between the final output of print and Web projects is resolution. High resolution—generally 300 to 350 ppi at 100 percent of the image size—is used for all print output, whether to paper or another material, across all print output devices. Low resolution is used for Web and broadcast applications (e.g., images on a screen); these files are usually 72 dpi at 100 percent. High resolution is needed for print because it is a high-fidelity media looked at closely by the viewer, making image resolution quality paramount. Broadcast and Web images are viewed on a screen, and at a distance; fidelity is increased by adding to the screen's size, thus delivering more pixels across the screen, even as the resolution stays the same. For example, high-definition television is 72 dpi, but has a larger, denser arrangement of rows and columns in its grid. Scanned images and digital camera photos are also raster graphics that can be opened and manipulated in a digital imaging application.

Resolutions to remember for raster graphics:

Print resolution: 300 to 350 ppi

Web page and screen resolution: 72 ppi

Raster Graphics for Print and Web

Adobe Photoshop is the industry standard digital imaging tool for print, Web, and broadcast projects. Adobe Fireworks is a standard tool for digital imaging for Web output. These applications can be used for individual graphics or to create entire page layouts. Both programs do mostly the same things and have the same tools; however, Photoshop is a better program for manipulating images, retouching, and adding effects. It is also great for designing single page elements with minimal type for either print or the Web. Adobe Fireworks is a superior tool for creating Web page layouts, slicing Web graphics, and outputting Web pages. Adobe Fireworks is tightly integrated with Adobe Dreamweaver, a Web page design application, and Adobe Flash, a motion graphics program. This allows for more facile workflows.

Here are some concepts critical to outputting print and Web raster images:

- Raster images are resolution dependent.

- Raster images for print projects need to be created at 300 to 350 dpi to scale, which means to the exact size of the final output.

- Raster images for Web projects need to be created at 72 dpi to scale. As a general rule, create images at print resolution if scaling needs to be done for a Web or broadcast image. You work at a higher resolution so that quality will not be lost if your assets need to be scaled.

- Print images are output direct to printing press or a device such as an imagesetter or a desktop printer. Desktop machines output in low and medium resolutions. Imagesetters and direct-to-press devices output high-resolution negatives that are used for printing plates.

- Scaling raster images above 100 percent in page layout programs and digital illustration programs is inadvisable: it causes the images to degrade (i.e., become jagged and lose detail) when output to the screen or to paper. Create images at the size needed for final output (or larger, in case the image needs to be scaled up in the future).

- Print projects are created in RGB mode and then converted to CMYK before imagesetter output or placement on a printing press.

- RGB color is always used for Web and broadcast output. Never use CMYK for Web or broadcast graphics.

- The correct final output file formats for raster graphics are .tif and .eps for print and .jpg and .gif for Web graphics.

- The native, layered file format for Photoshop is .psd.

- The native, layered file format for Fireworks is .png.

Raster Graphics Techniques

Digital production projects are the culmination of a series of techniques that require familiarity with the various tools, palettes, and menus in the software application you use. There are thousands of techniques and a variety of digital imaging applications: all of them cannot be covered in a multisubject text such as this one. This chapter covers some of the most important techniques in order to help you get started creating layered designs in digital imaging programs.

Most of the techniques below are shown using Adobe Photoshop, but many apply to Fireworks, too. Some techniques are not executed identically in the two programs; most are, however, and with a bit of exploration, you'll be able to perform the technique in either application. (PS) will indicate a technique for Photoshop, and (FW) will indicate a technique for Fireworks. The names of menu commands, tools, panels, and palettes are printed in ALL CAPS. Dialog boxes refer to boxes that appear after selecting tools, palettes, or menu items. They provide fine-tuning controls for executing techniques. Most menu items have dialog boxes associated with them.

You will eventually find your own comfort zone with raster tools and use them accordingly when developing projects. In print workflows, Photoshop can be used for preparing images for other applications or as a standalone tool for single-page final design projects with a limited amount of text. In Web work-flows, you can use Photoshop for digital imaging and Web page screen design and then open the .psd file in Fireworks to perform optimization, slicing, and exporting. Fireworks can be used for print, but it is really geared toward Web graphics and Web page (screen) design. Web workflows with Fireworks are explored further in chapter 8.

The techniques below are presented in steps with corresponding sample project images that exemplify the techniques. You should explore various com-binations of techniques in your work to discover divergent approaches to digital imaging. You can test yourself and explore these techniques by creating addi-tional projects guided by the corresponding online movie lessons listed at the end of each technique lesson in this chapter. View these online tutorial lesson movies at www.wiley.com/go/digitaldesign.

Document Setup

Adobe Photoshop and Fireworks allow you to create raster image documents for digital design projects. Setting up a new document requires the designer to make some choices about size, resolution, and color.

Technique Lesson 5.1: Creating a New Document

This is the first step in creating a digital design project on a computer. Adobe Photoshop provides media-specific document setups for print, Web, photogra-phy, broadcast, and film. These setups provide the size and resolution settings automatically. Letter, legal, and tabloid, along with 4×6, 5×7, and 8×10, refer to paper and photo print sizes measured in inches; the pixels dimensions 640×480, 800×600, and 1024×768 refer to web pages. The presets are available to help you get started quickly, but you can also create a custom-size document. The Fireworks document setup does not have presets. You can create a new docu-ment at any size you like (a Web banner, for example, is 720×90 pixels).

TIP

Create a new final document or an image for placement in another application.

QUICK STEPS (PS & FW):

Creating a New Document (Final Receptacle Document)

1. Go to FILE > NEW.

2. Choose a preset setup from the drop-down menu (choose 8.5 × 11″). Use RGB color.

3. Use a transparent background.

4. Click OK.

   You will see a new document with a gray checkerboard, which represents a transparent background.

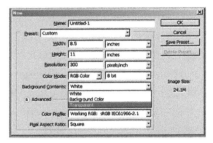

FIGURE 5-2A New document dialog box.

FIGURE 5-2B New document with a transparent background.

Technique Lesson 5.2: Guides and Grids

Guides and grids are critical to arranging items on the page. All digital design programs have guides and grids functions. In Photoshop, setting up a 3 × 3 grid for layouts will help you adhere to the rule of thirds and the law of thirds in your compositions.

QUICK STEPS (PS):

A 3 × 3 Grid

1. Go to EDIT > PREFERENCES.
2. Choose GUIDES, GRIDS & SLICES.
3. For the 3 × 3 grid, set the guides area to 33% with 3 subdivisions.
4. Click OK.

Guides

1. Go to VIEW > RULERS.
2. With rulers showing, place the cursor within the vertical or horizontal ruler and drag down guides as needed.

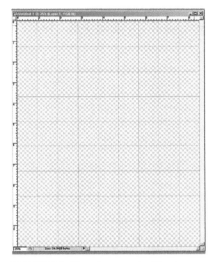

FIGURE 5-3 New document with a transparent background and 3 × 3 grid.

TIP

Set up your grid first to help with project composition decisions. Arrange objects in your composition based on the grid.

Technique Lesson 5.3: Placing Artwork (Raster or Vector)

Photoshop is typically used as a tool for assembling individual images, such as in photomontage or layered design. Always create a final document (receptacle) and place or drag images into it, rather than working from the image file. This preserves the image in case it is needed in its original form.

You can use FILE > OPEN to open raster or vector images in Photoshop. You can then drag them into a receptacle document using selections (this is covered on page 151). Or, using the PLACE command, you can import images (in a variety of popular graphical file formats) into a Photoshop document. Placed images each appear on their own layer.

TIP

Place external images into documents.

QUICK STEPS (PS):

Placing an External File

1. Go to FILE > PLACE.
   In Fireworks (FW), the command is FILE > IMPORT.

2. Choose the image file you want to place (.tif, .jpg, .psd, .png, .eps, .bmp, and .gif files will all work) and open it.

3. The image will appear with resize handles. Fit it to the document (be sure to hold down the SHIFT key while resizing it), then hit ENTER to complete the placement. The image is now on its own layer in your Photoshop document.

4. The image has been imported as a "smart object," which means that if you edit it in another program, those edits automatically appear in Photoshop. To remove the smart object properties, go to LAYER > SMART OBJECTS > CONVERT TO LAYER. This will rasterize the layer and allow you to work on it as if it were a native layer.

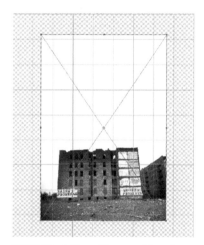

FIGURE 5-4 Placed image with resize handles.

Layers and Compositing

Images and text can be stacked on individual layers with transparent backgrounds. By manipulating these layers you can change the stacking order of objects, create overlay effects, and isolate image forms from their backgrounds, recombining them to create visuals called composites that are rich in detail and depth.

Using layers provides a digital designer the flexibility to move, rotate, scale, lower opacity, and delete individual objects within a composition without affecting the other elements. In fact, all digital design applications rely on layers. In Photoshop, .psd is the most useful layered file format. In Fireworks, .psd and .png both work as layered files, although the latter is preferable.

When a file is saved for final inclusion in a page layout program or Web site design program as an .eps, .tif, .jpg, or .gif, it is flattened, and all the individual layers become one layer known as a background layer. The individual layers then become inaccessible, making editing difficult. Therefore, always remember to save a .psd in Photoshop or a .png in Fireworks so you will have a layered file to refer back to.

Technique Lesson 5.4: Using Transparent Documents

Transparency is the ability to see through something. By using transparent backgrounds in digital design, you can composite existing images to create new images. Both images with backgrounds and images that lie on transparent backgrounds and separate layers are used, making it possible to overlap and integrate them.

QUICK STEPS (PS):

A New Document

1. Create a new document (FILE > NEW).

2. Choose TRANSPARENT for BACKGROUND CONTENTS.

    The transparent background is represented by a gray checkerboard.

Making an Existing Background Transparent

1. Double click on the background layer and rename it.

2. Once it is renamed, the absolute bottom layer of the image will be transparent, and all new layers will be transparent. If you select a group of pixels and delete them, the gray checkerboard will show through.

Technique Lesson 5.5: Using Layers for Composite Design

Layers are needed to create composite designs, which utilize overlapping elements. You can create images that take pictorial pieces from one image and lay them over another image—a background, for example—thereby creating a completely new image. Always use layers in a Photoshop or Fireworks document and save a layered file. The final output files for your project will ultimately be saved or exported in either .tif or .eps format for print or .jpg or .gif for the Web. Keep layers neat and name them according to their content.

TIP

Set up your final composite documents with transparent backgrounds. You can leave image documents with background (color) layers or select the parts that you need and drag them into your final receptacle document.

QUICK STEPS (PS & FW):

Adding Layers

1. Create a new document (FILE > NEW).

2. Choose LAYER > NEW LAYER (PS) or, using the LAYERS palette, click on the NEW LAYER icon at the bottom. Double-click on the layer name to change it to something specific.

    A new transparent layer will appear in the palette, represented by a gray checkerboard. Use EDIT > FILL to fill the layer with white. Use the FILL slider to toggle between the checkerboard and the white fill color (just to facilitate seeing the design).

Deleting Layers

1. Choose LAYER > DELETE > LAYER or, using the LAYERS palette, click on the layer you want to delete and then click on the TRASH CAN icon at the bottom of the LAYERS palette.

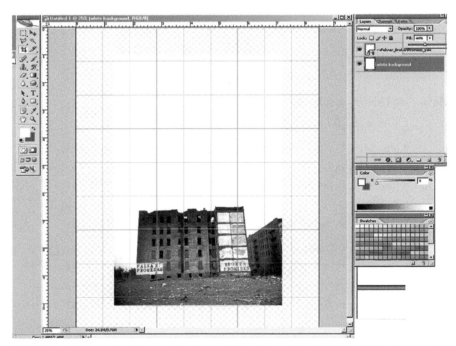

FIGURE 5-5 The opacity sliders and buttons at the bottom of the LAYERS palette allow you to add, delete, and attach special effects to items on layers.

Technique Lesson 5.6: Layer Opacity

The LAYERS palette gives you control over each layer's opacity, which is the capacity to see through an image (100 percent opacity is solid). You can manipulate the opacity of each layer separately to lower percentages, which allow any images below to show through to some degree.

QUICK STEPS (PS & FW):

Manipulating Opacity Lower Than 100 Percent

1. Open the LAYERS palette (WINDOW > LAYERS or hit F7).

2. Choose a layer in the LAYERS palette, then click on the OPACITY slider at the top. Type in a percentage or drag the slider to reveal the lowered opacity.

> **TIP**
>
> Create softness as well as tonal and image effects with overlaid images, which yield beautifully layered compositions.

Technique Lesson 5.7: Scale, Rotate, and Free Transform

After importing an external image, dragging in an image selection, creating a shape, or painting a stroke in a digital imaging program, these elements can then be transformed (manipulated) in a variety of ways, the most common being to scale or rotate them. While SCALE and ROTATE are two separate commands, the FREE TRANSFORM command allows you to do both simultaneously.

QUICK STEPS (PS & FW):

Transforming Using Menu Items

1. Choose the layer with the element you want to scale or rotate. If you have each item placed on its own transparent layer, you will be able to manipulate each layer without affecting the other layers.

2. Go to EDIT > TRANSFORM and choose what you would like to do (scale, rotate, warp, etc.). Handles will appear around the object on the layer. To scale height and width together, grab a corner and drag. Holding down the SHIFT key while you do so will keep the image in proper proportion. (You'll want to use the SHIFT key in most cases; otherwise, your images will not appear true to life.)

3. Press ENTER when the manipulation is complete.

Free Transform

1. Choose the layer with the element you want to scale or rotate.

2. PRESS CTRL + T (Windows) or CMD + T (Macintosh); manipulation handles will appear. Grab a corner handle and drag (remember to hold the SHIFT key) to scale the object on the layer. To rotate the object, place the cursor directly outside of the handles, and a curved rotation arrow will appear. Rotate the element right or left.

3. Press ENTER to complete the transformation.

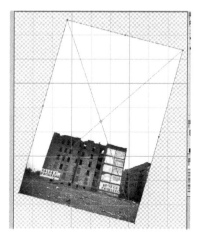

FIGURE 5-6 Image with FREE TRANS-FORM handles.

Selections

Selections allow you to isolate parts of an image for deletion, masking, shape creation, or for the creation of a transparent alpha channel. (Alpha channels add transparency to a raster image so that backgrounds are eliminated for compositing.) When you use selection tools, you place "marching ants," called marquees, around a section of pixels, or grab pixels by color. Once you have made a selection, you can move it, manipulate it, or drag it into another document to create a composite image.

Technique Lesson 5.8: Cropping an Image

Cropping allows you to select the portion of an image that you want to keep and discard the rest. Cropping affects the entire image. You can crop an image to eliminate unwanted framing, giving the image a different look. Crop photos in their original or copied image files and not in the final composite document.

QUICK STEPS (PS & FW):

Cropping

1. Cropping can be performed most easily using the CROP tool in the TOOL palette. Drag the CROP tool over the area you want to keep; the area to be cropped is outside that area. You can also rotate the crop box, and it will

rotate back the opposite way in the final image. Meaning that if your image is not straight, you can match the negative angle and the program will fix the image to the same positive value and straighten the image.

2a. Press ENTER to complete the crop.

or:

2b. Make a selection and go to IMAGE > CROP.

FIGURE 5-7 Cropping an image allows you to change the image and eliminate unwanted visual space.

Technique Lesson 5.9: Manual Selection and Inverse

Image areas (pixels) can be manually selected using the marquee selection tools. The most useful marquee tools are the ELLIPTICAL, RECTANGULAR, and LASSO tools. These tools give you precise control while making selections.

QUICK STEPS (PS & FW):

Manual Selection Using the Primitive Marquee Tools

1. Choose the ELLIPTICAL MARQUEE tool and drag it over any part of an image (make sure you are on the proper layer). Hold the SHIFT key while dragging if you want to constrain the selection to a circle.

Manual Selection Using the Freeform Marquee Tools

1. Choose the LASSO MARQUEE tool and hold down the ALT key: doing so allows you to click to make straight lines and drag to make curved lines. Choose a part of an image or an image outline to cut out (a person or object will work well). Using straight lines and curves, move the cursor around the contour (outline) of the object until the marquee encompasses the entire area you want to select. Clicking also binds the marquee in place.

2. Release the ALT key and the mouse button when you come to where you started. There will be a marquee around the selected area.

FIGURE 5-8 Image area with a marquee around it.

Deleting a Selection

Press DELETE. Whatever is inside the marquee will be deleted, and there will be a hole in the image. The hole will show either a background color, the image on the layer below, or the transparent checkerboard, depending on the contents of the document. Drag the selection within the document to move the selected pixels; this, too, will leave a hole in the image, through which either a background color or the transparent checkerboard will show.

Inversing a Selection

You can also inverse the selection. This selects the masked area—the area of the image you have *not* selected. This command is useful for eliminating backgrounds around people and objects. Select what you want to keep, then go to SELECT > INVERSE. Hit DELETE, and the pixels will be removed and the background color or transparent checkerboard will be visible.

or:

Select what you don't want to keep (for example, the solid color background behind an object or person), then use INVERSE to select what you want.

Moving a Selection

Select the MARQUEE tool and place the cursor inside the selected area. You will now be able to move the marquee without moving the pixels inside it.

Scaling a Selection

Select the MARQUEE tool and place the cursor inside the selected area, then go to SELECT > TRANSFORM SELECTION. This will allow you to scale the "marching ants" and not the pixels inside them.

Adding to and Subtracting from a Selection

Holding the SHIFT key while using a selection tool allows you to add to a selection. Holding the ALT key allows you to subtract from a selection.

Once you make a selection, you can:

* Inverse the selection to select the pixels in the masked area (described above).

* Retouch the isolated image area.

* Drag and drop the selection into another document.

* Copy and paste the selection.

* Tighten up the selection in QUICK MASK mode.

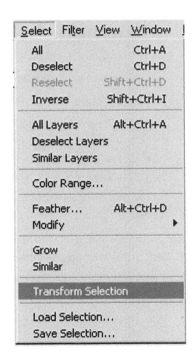

FIGURE 5-9 Scale and reposition the selection area without affecting the pixels inside by using the TRANSFORM SELECTION command.

- Feather the selection to soften its edges.
- Save the selection as an alpha channel and load the marquee into a saved Photoshop document.

Technique Lesson 5.10: Magic Wand Selections

The MAGIC WAND creates selections based on pixel color—the yellow in a banana, for example—without requiring you to trace an outline, as you would with a manual selection. You specify the color range, or tolerance, for the MAGIC WAND tool's selection, and all the pixels within that tolerance are selected. You cannot use the MAGIC WAND tool on an image in bitmap (one color) mode, or on 32-bits-per-channel images.

QUICK STEPS (PS & FW):

Magic Wand Selection

1. With the MAGIC WAND selected from the TOOL palette, choose NEW (the solid square in OPTIONS menu at the top of the document).

In the options bar, specify any of the following:

2a. The TOLERANCE will set the similarity or difference of the pixels selected. You can enter a value in pixels, ranging from 0 to 255. A low value selects the few colors very similar to the pixel you have selected with the MAGIC WAND. A higher value selects a broader range of colors. Be sure to select the ANTI-ALIAS check box to generate a smooth edge for the selections you create. Anti-alising blends pixels on screen to eliminate jagged lines in connected colors.

2b. Check CONTIGUOUS to select only those areas of the specified color adjacent to the pixel you selected originally; otherwise, all pixels in the entire image within the specified range will be selected.

2c. SAMPLE ALL LAYERS will select colors using data from all the visible layers; otherwise, the MAGIC WAND selects colors only from the active layer.

3. In the image, click the color you want to select. The marquee will appear around one or more areas of similar color.

FIGURE 5-10 Areas of solid color can be selected most easily using the MAGIC WAND. Holding the SHIFT key while using selection tools allows you to add range to the selected pixels. When you do this to add to a selection, you will see a small plus sign (+) next to the marquee. Holding the ALT key allows you to subtract range from the selected pixels. When you do this to subtract from a selection, you will see a small minus sign (−) next to the marquee.

TIP

Use the MAGIC WAND for selecting large areas of color quickly or small areas of color precisely.

Technique Lesson 5.11: Quick Mask Mode

QUICK MASK MODE allows you to precisely select pixels (or even a single pixel), using the PENCIL or PAINTBRUSH to "paint in" or "paint out" areas you want to select or deselect.

QUICK STEPS (PS & FW):

Cleaning a Selection Using Quick Mask Mode

1. Make a manual selection around the outline (contour) of an object using a marquee tool.

2. Go to the bottom of the TOOL palette and double-click on the QUICK MASK MODE icon directly under the COLOR PICKER. The icon next to the QUICK MASK MODE icon is the SELECTION MODE icon; clicking it will display the selection.

   Once you open the QUICK MASK MODE dialog box, you can set the color to represent the selected area or the masked area. The masked area is the

TIP

The best way to use QUICK MASK MODE is to create a manual selection first using a MAR-QUEE tool or the MAGIC WAND. Then use QUICK MASK MODE to fine-tune the selection to fit the desired selection area exactly.

area outside of the selected area (also known as the inverse). Keep the setting COLOR INDICATES > SELECTED AREA.

3. Upon clicking the QUICK MASK MODE icon, you will see a color overlay (red by default) covering the area that you selected with the MARQUEE tool. This does not add color to the image; it simply acts as a guide to show you the precise selected area. Notice that there are areas of the image that have been underselected and areas that have been overselected. Underselected means that you didn't select enough of the pixels you need; overselected means that you selected more pixels that you need. You will use the pencil tool to "paint in" or "paint out" the offending areas.

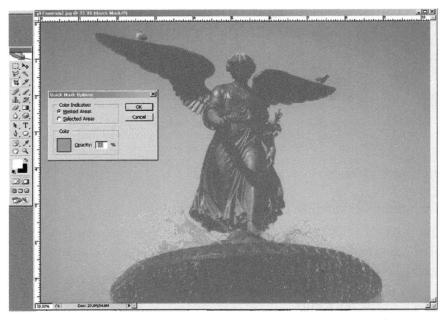

FIGURE 5-11 QUICK MASK MODE is used for cleaning up selections pixel by pixel. You can "paint in" or erase selected areas. Click back to SELECTION MODE to see the marquee. Color represents the selected or masked (unselected) areas.

4. Click on the PENCIL tool and set the BRUSH SIZE to 5 pixels in the options at the top of the application window.

5. Notice that the COLOR PICKER has turned to black and white. In quick mask mode, when the black square is the foreground (top) color you can use the paint and pencil tools to add to the selection area. When white is

the foreground color, you can use the paint and pencil tools to taking away selection area. This is known as painting in or painting out pixels.

6. Paint in areas that were missed in the manual selection and paint out areas that were added erroneously. Toggle back to SELECTION MODE to see the selection marquee on the image.

Technique Lesson 5.12: Drag-and-Drop Selections

You can make selections and then use the MOVE tool to drag and drop them into another open document.

QUICK STEPS (PS & FW):

Dragging and Dropping a Selection Area with the Move Tool

1. Use a marquee tool around the contour of an object to create a selection. Open a receptacle document to drag the selection into.

2. Go to the top of the TOOL palette and choose the MOVE tool.

3. Click on the selected area (make sure you are on the correct layer) and drag the selection into your final design document (receptacle).

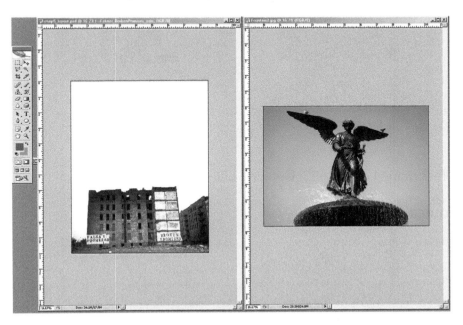

FIGURE 5-12A Drag and drop selected areas and layers from one document to another. In this sequence, a selected image was dragged into another document (Figure 512B, next page), then scaled using FREE TRANSFORM. Finally, the opacity of its layer was lowered.

TIP

Drag-and-drop
selections are
used quite often
when creating a
composite image
in a digital imaging
program such as
Adobe Photoshop
or Fireworks. You
can select an area
from one image
window and drag-
and-drop it into
another image
window. The
dragged selection
is added to a new
layer in the recep-
tacle document.

FIGURE 5-12B

Technique Lesson 5.13: Deleting Selections and Deselecting

QUICK STEPS

Deleting Image Areas

You can delete areas of an image by making a selection and hitting the DELETE
key. (This deletes pixels from the active layer, not the entire image.) You can also
delete pixels by using the ERASER tool on a selected layer.

Deselecting Image Areas

After you create a selection and delete pixels—or if you simply want to get rid of a selection—press CTRL + D (Windows) or CMD + D (Macintosh). You can also go to SELECT > DESELECT.

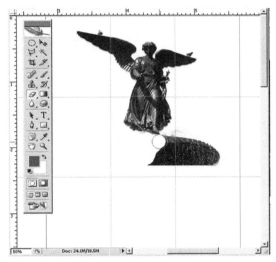

FIGURE 5-13 Use a marquee selection or the ERASER tool to eliminate image pixels from a layer.

Technique Lesson 5.14: Feathering Selections

By default, selections are hard-edged. Feathering a selection blurs its inner and outer areas, resulting in a softened effect.

QUICK STEPS (PS & FW):

Feathering a Selection in the Same Document

1. Use a marquee tool to make a selection around the outline of an object.

2. Choose SELECT > FEATHER.

3. Choose SELECT > INVERSE.

4. Press DELETE.

   The image background will be deleted, and the image will be feathered.

TIP

Feathering is used to eliminate the hard edge of a digital image or to create blended images within a digital montage. If you feather on a color background and press the delete key after the feather is set, you will create a color halo around the image. To avoid this, select the image and drag it onto a transparent background, then feather and drag it back into the receptacle document.

Feathering a Selection and Dragging It into a Final Design Document

1. Use a marquee tool to make a selection around the outline of an object.

2. Choose SELECT > FEATHER.

3. Using the MOVE tool, drag and drop the selected area into the final design document.

FIGURE 5-14 Softened pixels on the inside and outside of a selection create a feathered image.

Technique Lesson 5.15: Filling and Stroking Selections

You can fill a selection, or the entire layer if there is no selection, by using the FILL command. The STROKE command places a stroke along the selection marquee.

QUICK STEPS (PS):

Filling a Selection

1. Use a marquee tool to make a selection around the outline of an object, or create a shape (square, rectangle, circle, or ellipse).

2. Choose EDIT > FILL. (If there were no selection, the whole layer would be filled with the chosen color; this technique is useful for creating a solid color background layer.)

3. Go to CONTENT USE and choose COLOR; this will display the COLOR PICKER.

4. Pick a color. Make sure the opacity is 100%, the mode is NORMAL, and PRESERVE TRANSPARENCY is unchecked.

You can also add a fill to any object on a layer by using LAYER EFFECT > COLOR OVERLAY.

Stroking a Selection

1. Use a marquee tool to make a selection around the outline of an object, or create a shape (square, rectangle, circle, or ellipse).

2. Choose EDIT > STROKE. Set the WIDTH and click on the COLOR swatch; this will display the COLOR PICKER. Pick a color. Make sure the opacity is 100%, the mode is NORMAL, and PRESERVE TRANSPARENCY is unchecked.

You can also add a stroke to any object on a layer by using LAYER EFFECT > STROKE.

(A)

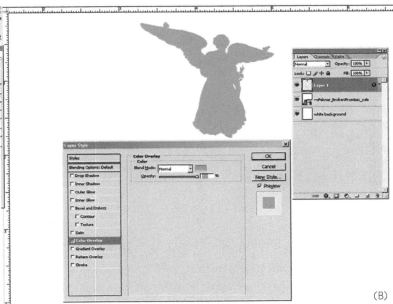

(B)

FIGURES 5-15, A–C You can add fill and stroke to any selected area, or to the pixels on an individual layer, using different techniques. The color overlay applied here creates a silhouetted image.

FIGURE 5-15C

Technique Lesson 5.16: Saving Selections as Alpha Channels

A selection is made up of a selected area and a masked area. Saving a selection as an alpha channel makes the masked area transparent when placed in a motion graphics program such as Adobe After Effects or Adobe Flash.

QUICK STEPS (PS & FW):

Saving a Selection

1. Use a marquee tool to make a selection around the outline of an object.

2. Choose SELECT > SAVE SELECTION. Name the new channel selection. Click OK.

3. Save the file as a .psd or .tif and make sure the ON check box under ALPHA CHANNEL is selected.

FIGURE 5-16 Saving complex selections saves time by allowing the selections to load immediately, thus eliminating the need to re-create them.

Load a Saved Selection

1. Open a .psd file with a saved selection.

2. Choose SELECT > LOAD SELECTION. In the Load Selection dialog box, select both the saved channel to be loaded and the layer the selection should be loaded on. Click OK.

Load a Selection from a Layer

1. Open a layered .psd file.

2. Choose a target layer and then choose SELECT > LOAD SELECTION. Click OK.

All the pixels (but not the transparent areas) on the highlighted layer will be selected automatically. If you go to SELECT > LOAD SELECTION on another layer, you can add to the selection area by selecting the pixels on it.

Masks

A mask is the inverse area of a selection. A mask covers something; in digital imaging applications, masks cover parts of an image and reveal selected parts—similar to looking through a keyhole or binoculars.

Technique Lesson 5.17: Layer Masks

You can create masks using gradients (pixels that move gradually from one color to another) on top of individual layers. These are known as layer masks. Layer masks are attached in the LAYERS palette and appear in a thumbnail box next to the layer thumbnail. A chain link shows that the mask and the image are linked. Click on the chain link to move either the object or the mask individually.

QUICK STEPS (PS & FW):

Creating a Layer Mask

1. Select a layer with an image on it from the LAYERS palette.

2. Go to the bottom of the LAYERS palette and click on the LAYER MASK icon.

3. Select the GRADIENT tool. Use the LINEAR GRADIENT from the TOOL palette (the specific colors don't matter).

4. Drag a gradient across the layer to reveal a layer mask based on the gradient direction. The gradient is determined by the direction in which you drag across the image and the gradient colors you select.

5. To APPLY or DELETE a layer mask to or from a layer, click on the LAYER MASK thumbnail in the layer and click the TRASH CAN in the LAYERS palette.

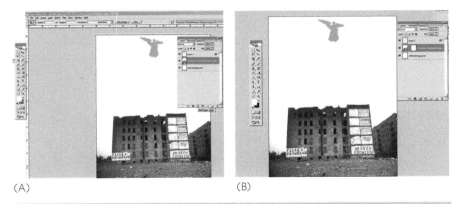

(A) (B)

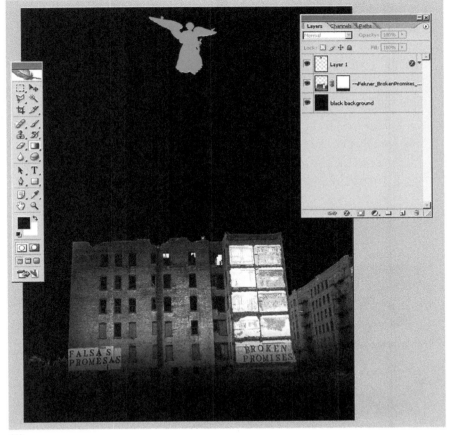

(C)

FIGURES 5-17, A–C Layer masks allow you to creatively crop and soften an image using a section as the mask. Here, the bottom layer is filled with black and the layer mask uses a gradient to soften the bottom edge of the image.

Technique Lesson 5.18: Type Masks

Type masks are selections in the shape of letterforms (fonts); they allow you to cut out an image in the shape of the letters. Type masks provide a creative visual effect—if used thoughtfully and sparingly.

QUICK STEPS (PS):

Creating a Type Mask

1. Select a layer with an image on it from the LAYERS palette.

2. Go to the TEXT tool on the TOOL palette; select and hold down the HORIZONTAL TYPE MASK tool.

3. Click on the document and type a word or a letter. Use a heavy font so that there is enough area inside the letterforms to allow the selection to show through. If you need to scale the text, go to SELECT > TRANSFORM SELECTION; resize handles will appear around the marquee. Scale the text marquee and press ENTER.

4. You will see the text in the form of a marquee. Go to LAYER > LAYER MASK > REVEAL SELECTION. The image will show through the selected area. You can click on the TYPE MASK icon in the layer and unlink it from the image. Then you can scale, move, or manipulate the mask or the image.

This technique also works with all selection marquees (elliptical, rectangular, and freeform).

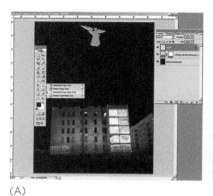

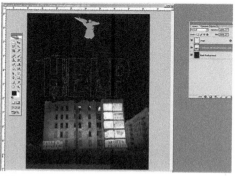

(A)   (B)

FIGURES 5-18, A–F Type masks use text as a selection mask. Here, the building is used to experiment with creating the type mask image.

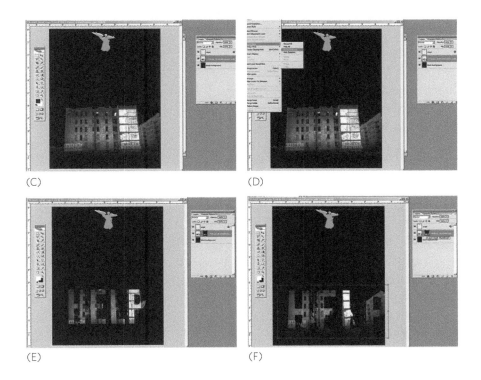

(C)

(D)

(E)

(F)

Color

Adobe Photoshop uses foreground and background swatches to represent color on the TOOL palette. Foreground color is the active color for brushes and fills, and background color, a quick cursor click away from foreground color, represents the document's background or base color.

Fireworks handles color in the TOOL palette differently. It provides color values for stroke and fill. Stroke is the color of the line around an object, and fill is the color(s) of the image or type. These fill and stroke properties are attached to a Web-safe palette or an index color palette. (For a review of color and color models, refer to chapter 3.)

Color Specifications to Remember

Print projects being output to a printing press need to be CMYK files. Work in RGB, and then convert to CMYK just before saving the final file.

Web projects being output to a screen need to be RGB or index (Web-safe) color. Work in RGB and optimize images for higher or lower quality and for final output in RGB or Web-safe color.

Technique Lesson 5.19: The Color Picker

There are several ways to access color in digital imaging programs. The Photoshop COLOR PICKER is a basic tool that will help you get started. Double-click on the TOOL palette swatches to display the COLOR PICKER, which is a swatch area that represents color using RGB and CMYK models. (HSL and LAB models are also represented, but you don't need to worry about them right now.) Always select the H (HUE) radio button; otherwise, you will not have access to the full range of RGB colors.

QUICK STEPS (PS):

Selecting a Color Using the Color Picker

TIP

Use the COLOR PICKER to quickly find colors and to view Pantone swatches. The Picker allows you to see the RGB and CMYK values of existing colors in order to match them to colors in other digital design program files.

1. Double-click the foreground color swatch in the TOOL palette.

2. Go to the color spectrum (rainbow) and select a HUE (base color) from the color ramp, and then move around the hue area to find the desired shade and value for your color.

Options:

For Web: Check off ONLY WEB COLORS for a Web-safe color palette. Use this option for solid-colored Web page backgrounds.

For spot color: Press COLOR LIBRARIES and look at the Pantone swatch palettes (both coated and uncoated are commonly used) and other swatch-based color systems.

3. After the color is selected, press OK.

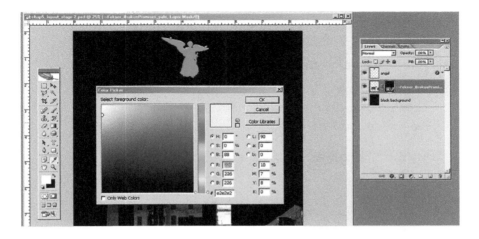

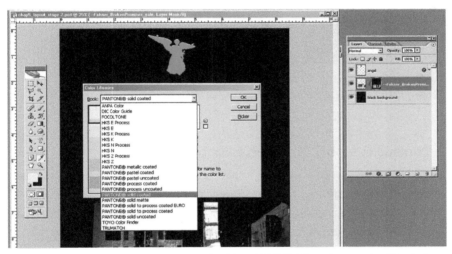

FIGURES 5-19, A, B The COLOR PICKER with RGB and CMYK (A), and spot-color (B) palettes.

Technique Lesson 5.20: The Web-Safe Palette

Although you can access the Web-safe color palette in either Photoshop or Fireworks, the process is a bit different in each program.

QUICK STEPS:

Selecting the Web-Safe Color Palette (PS)

1. In the TOOL palette, go to WINDOW > SWATCHES.

TIP

Use the Web-safe color palette for creating Web page backgrounds and solid-colored objects such as logos, text, and shapes.

2. Go to the drop-down arrow and scroll down to WEB SAFE COLORS to load the Web-safe color palette.

Using the Web-Safe Palette (FW)

1. Go to the color swatches at the bottom of the TOOL palette and click either FILL or STROKE. Use the drop-down arrow to see and select colors from the Web-safe color palette.

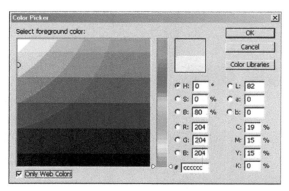

FIGURE 5-20 The Web-safe color palette should be used for solid colors.

Technique Lesson 5.21: The Eyedropper

The EYEDROPPER tool is used to sample color so you can set a new color in the foreground or background swatch in Photoshop and in the fill or stroke swatch for Fireworks. You can select a color sample from the active image or from anywhere else on the screen.

QUICK STEPS (PS & FW):

Sampling and Selecting Color with the Eyedropper

1. Select the EYEDROPPER tool.

2a. Click in the image.

or:

2b. Position the cursor over the image, press the mouse button, and drag anywhere on the screen to sample colors dynamically as you drag. Release the mouse button to pick the new color.

3. The new color appears in the foreground swatch on the TOOL palette in Photoshop, or the fill swatch in Fireworks.

Options:

To change the sample size of the EYEDROPPER, choose an option from the SAMPLE SIZE menu:

- POINT SAMPLE (PS) and 1 PIXEL (FW) read the precise value of the pixel you select.

- 3×3 AVERAGE or 5×5 AVERAGE read the average value of the specified number of pixels within the area you click.

FIGURE 5-21 The EYEDROPPER samples color and places it in the COLOR PICKER. Notice the eyedropper (top) in the red area of the image. It will add the selected color to the color picker swatch.

Technique Lesson 5.22: Gradients

Gradients, discussed earlier in this chapter, can be used to create layer masks. Gradients allow you to create mixes of graduated levels of color and transparency. Typical two-color gradients start at one color and stop at a different color. Gradients can also have transparency as an endpoint. You can use preset gradients, edit them, or create new ones.

QUICK STEPS (PS & FW):

Making or Editing a Gradient

1. Select or make a new layer to place the gradient on. (You can also place gradients inside of selections.)
2. Click on the GRADIENT tool on the TOOL palette. Options appear at the top (PS) and below (FW). Click the gradient sample to edit the gradients.
3. Double-click on the arrows below the gradient bar to display the color picker. Pick the gradient colors.
4. To add a STOP (new color bar) to the gradient, click underneath the gradient bar. To delete a STOP, click on it and drag down.
5. Press NEW to add the gradient to the presets.

Applying the Gradient to a Layer

1. Select or make a new layer to place the gradient on. You can also place gradients inside of selections.
2. Click on the GRADIENT tool on the TOOL palette. Choose or make a gradient.
3. Drag across the layer to create the gradient. There is a direct correlation between the area you drag over and the area in which the gradient appears. Change the options (LINEAR, RADIAL, ANGLE, REFLECTED, and DIAMOND) to change the gradient style.

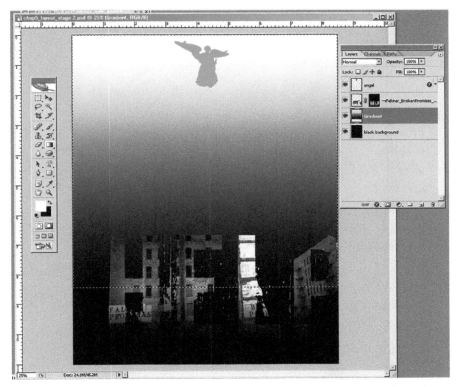

FIGURE 5-22 Gradients create smooth color transitions. Here, a selection was used to isolate the length of the gradient.

TIP

Gradients are useful for creating transitional backgrounds and graphics and for use in layer masks. Be thoughtful in your use of background gradients and graphics: the use of more than one gradient can become confusing and may distract from the overall message of the piece.

Shape Basics

Shapes can be created in all digital design programs. In digital imaging, shapes can either be raster (pixel) based or vector (line) based.

Technique Lesson 5.23: Making Shapes

You can create shapes in digital imaging applications by filling selections or using shape tools. The shape tools create shapes using fill pixels, a vector shape, or the PEN tool. This section focuses on shapes with fill pixels. Vector shapes and the PEN tool are covered in the next chapter, which is on vector graphics.

QUICK STEPS (PS & FW):

Making a Shape

1. Select or make a new layer to place the shape on.

2. Select a shape tool (ELLIPTICAL, RECTANGULAR, or POLYGON). Use the FILL PIXELS option (PS).

3. Choose a color and stroke value (FW). Use EDIT > FILL. PRESERVE TRANSPARENCY should be enabled.

4. Drag to draw the shape on the layer.
Resizing or Rotating a Shape

5. Go to EDIT > FREE TRANSFORM (CTRL + T for Windows or CMD + T for Macintosh; see Technique 5.7)

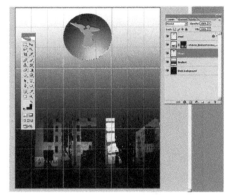

(A)

(B)

(C)

FIGURES 5-23, A–E Fill pixels can be used to create shapes. Here, a new layer was made, and the shape was created. The shape was then selected by holding the Control key and clicking the layer, and a gradient was applied. In addition, the color overlay was changed, and the shape was scaled down a bit and softened with a 5-point feather. You can toggle off the layer mask by right clicking and choosing Disable Layer mask to see what other variations can be built on.

(D)   (E)

Retouching Basics

Retouching images requires expertise and high-end computer equipment. However, some basic techniques in Photoshop and Fireworks can help make photographic images display better in print or on the Web. The trick to retouching is to
go slowly and use moderation; otherwise, you can do more damage than good.

Technique Lesson 5.24: Checking Image Sizes

An image's size also provides information about its resolution. Image
size is measured in pixels and can
be checked and changed by going to
IMAGE > IMAGE SIZE in Photoshop,
or MODIFY > CANVAS > IMAGE
SIZE in Fireworks. In this dialog box,
you will see the physical size of the
document in inches (print) or pixels
(Web). Avoid making the values in
the fields in this box larger; doing so

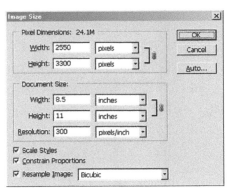

FIGURE 5-24 IMAGE SIZE dialog box.

will impair image quality. Always try to work at 100 percent of the final output size.

Technique Lesson 5.25: Adjusting Tonal Range Using Levels

Use the LEVELS command to correct images that are too light or too dark. Levels allow you to manipulate the tonal range of a photographic image by adjusting intensity levels of image shadows (dark areas), midtones (midvalue areas and grays), and highlights (light areas). These areas are also known as image key tones. The LEVELS histogram is a small graph, represented by a black mountain range, that acts as a visual guide for adjusting the image key tones. Use the PREVIEW feature to see what is happening to the image while you make adjustments.

QUICK STEPS (PS & FW):

Lightening or Darkening an Image Using Levels

1a. (PS) Choose IMAGE > ADJUSTMENTS > LEVELS.

   or:

1b. (PS) Choose LAYER > NEW ADJUSTMENT LAYER > LEVELS. Click OK in the NEW LAYER dialog box. The adjustment layer allows you to show or hide the image changes in order to compare them.

1c. (FW) Choose FILTERS > ADJUST COLOR > LEVELS.

2. Adjust the shadows and highlights manually by dragging the black-and-white INPUT LEVELS sliders to the edge of the first group of pixels on either end of the histogram. This is the basic technique for adjusting shadows and highlights.

3. To adjust midtones, use the middle INPUT slider. Move this slider in small increments; otherwise, you will damage the image's fidelity.

4. Click OK. View the adjusted histogram in WINDOW > HISTOGRAM.

TIP

Adjust levels on scanned and digital photographs to eliminate excessive shadows (dark areas) and highlights (light areas) by distributing the key tones.

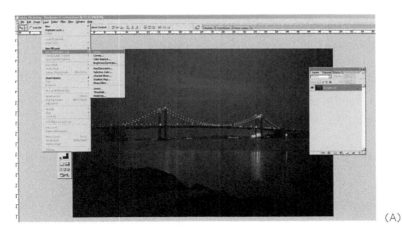

(A)

(B)

(C)

FIGURES 5-25, A–C
This image is too dark, and the histogram shows the pixels bunched at the shadow areas (A). Move the white (highlight) slider to the end of the data mountain to adjust the tonal range and correct the image's lights and darks (B, C). Next, the image's red color cast must be addressed.

Technique Lesson 5.26: Adjusting Color Balance

Color balancing lets you shift the colors of an image's pixels. The COLOR BALANCE command allows you to manipulate the color balance of the RGB and CMYK colors and the tonal balance of the highlights, shadows, and midtones. This technique is used to eliminate color casts, which are imbalances in color distribution in an image.

QUICK STEPS (PS):

Adjusting the Color Balance

1a. Choose IMAGE > ADJUSTMENTS > COLOR BALANCE.

or:

1b. Choose LAYER > NEW ADJUSTMENT LAYER > COLOR BALANCE. Click OK in the NEW LAYER dialog box. The adjustment layer allows you to show or hide the image changes in order to compare them.

2. Look at the image to determine what color is cast and what the colors should be. Then, move the color sliders accordingly. For example, if an image of a sunset is too red or too magenta, move the red or magenta slider to a negative number. If the image contains both water and sky, you might need to use the red slider to add cyan, rather than moving the magenta slider, which could make the sky and water green instead of blue. The important point here is that you perform subtle manipulations. Experiment with the tonal balances to see which will create the richest image detail.

TIP

Adjust color balance on scanned and digital photographs to eliminate excessive color casts caused by digital capture equipment, calibration faults, and light reflections.

FIGURES 5-26, A, B The red lights on the bridge are contributing to this image's red cast. This makes the sky and the water appear pink. Use color balance to subtract red and add cyan to correct this problem.

Technique Lesson 5.27: Replace Color

The REPLACE COLOR command lets you replace pixel colors in an image by creating a temporary mask to select specific colors and then setting the hue, saturation, and lightness of the selected areas. You can also use the COLOR PICKER to select a replacement color that will have the same shadows and highlights.

QUICK STEPS (PS):

Replacing the Color of Pixels

1. Choose IMAGE > ADJUSTMENTS > REPLACE COLOR.

2. Choose SELECTION as a display option. This will display the mask in the preview box. Masked areas appear black, and unmasked areas appear white. Partially masked areas (areas covered with a semitransparent mask) appear as varying levels of gray, according to their opacity.

3. Select the areas exposed by the mask whose color you want to replace by using the EYEDROPPER tool. Click either in the image area in the preview box, or in the image document, and select the color you want to replace.

4. Replace the color of the selected areas by performing one of the following operations:

   a. Drag the HUE, SATURATION, and LIGHTNESS sliders (or enter values in the corresponding fields).

   or:

   b. Double-click the RESULT swatch and use the COLOR PICKER to select the replacement color.

5. Use the ADD TO SAMPLE EYEDROPPER tool to add areas that you may have missed in the initial selection. As you select a color in the image area, the mask in the preview box is updated, and the color replacement is updated to show the newly selected areas as changed.

TIP

Use the REPLACE COLOR command for experimenting with new colors in order to change the look of an image—if, for example, you wanted to change the color of clothing.

FIGURES 5-27, A–C
Use the REPLACE
COLOR command to
change an image's col-
ors while maintaining
the shadows and high-
lights. Here the area to
be replaced (shirt color)
has been selected and
isolated. Use the eye-
droppers to select the
hue from the image,
then make adjustments
and preview the results.

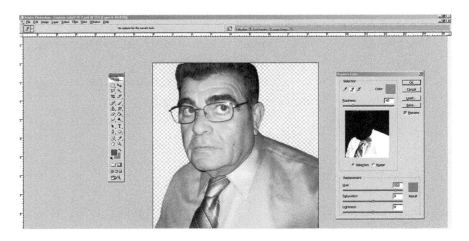

Technique Lesson 5.28: Saturate and Desaturate

The SATURATE and DESATURATE commands are used to add or subtract hue (color) from an image. Using the SPONGE tool, you can absorb color or add color.

QUICK STEPS (PS):

Saturating or Desaturating an Image Area

1. Select the SATURATION tool (SPONGE tool).
2. From the top of the options area, choose SATURATE or DESATURATE.
3. Choose a brush size from the options palette at the top.
4. Leave the FLOW at 50%.
5. Drag the sponge over the pixels whose hue you want to enhance or reduce. Excessive desaturation will lead to a gray color. Excessive saturation will create an undesirable, extremely vivid color.

TIP

Use the SATURATION and DESATURATION tools to enhance or reduce a color in an image. Manipulate the colors in small areas first to determine possible outcomes and avoid disturbing image clarity. Too much saturation will also create problems getting CMYK colors to print accurately.

FIGURES 5-28, A, B Desaturate layers to create grayscale images in an RGB document. Create selections to isolate portions of an image to be desaturated, or saturate colors to bring out additional hue using the SPONGE tool.

Technique Lesson 5.29: Dodge and Burn

When you use the DODGE tool, you lighten areas of the image. The BURN tool allows you to darken areas of an image. The tools are named for traditional photography's technique for regulating exposure on specific areas of a print.

TIP

Use the DODGE and BURN tools for pulling out or suppressing highlights (bright areas) or shadows (dark areas). This is useful when image areas may be "blown out" from an unexpected light reflection. The tools can also be used to create shadow areas—to enhance the abdomen muscles of a model to create a "six pack," for example—or for eliminating shadow areas, such as the dark circles under a model's eyes.

QUICK STEPS (PS):

Dodging (Lightening) and Burning (Darkening) an Image

1. Select the DODGE tool or the BURN tool.

2. Choose a brush size from the OPTIONS palette at the top.

3. Choose the key area and exposure (amount) from the option bar:

    Midtones will change the middle range of grays.

    Shadows will change the dark areas.

    Highlights will change the light areas.

    Specify the exposure for the DODGE tool or the BURN tool.

4. Drag over the part of the image you want to lighten or darken.

FIGURES 5-29, A, B
The DODGE and BURN tools are used to bring out or reduce highlights, shadows, and midtones. Here, the clock's highlights were dodged to brighten them.

Type in Digital Imaging Applications

Type is a critical element in communication design and can be generated in all types of applications. Digital imaging programs have specialized type tools that allow you to set type, distort type, and create type effects.

Technique Lesson 5.30: Using Type for Headlines and Body Text

The text tools in digital imaging applications work powerfully for small bits of text, such as headlines, buttons, graphical text headers for Web pages, text with effects, or even short paragraphs.

QUICK STEPS (PS & FW):

The TYPE palette in Photoshop uses the same character palette as the other Adobe CS applications. The type palette in Fireworks is on the PROPERTIES bar, which appears at the bottom of the screen by default.

Placing Type on a Document

1. Click on the TYPE tool in the TOOL palette.

2. Click on to the document; a cursor will appear.

3a. (PS) In the options palette at the top, set TYPEFACE, FONT SIZE, and COLOR.

3b. (FW) Go to the OPTIONS palette at the bottom and set the FILL and STROKE.

4. Start typing. Photoshop and Fireworks automatically create a new layer for the text. With the text tool selected, highlight the text to make necessary edits.

5. Go to WINDOW > CHARACTER to open the CHARACTER palette, which provides type, leading, kerning, tracking, and baseline shift controls.

6. Go to WINDOW > PARAGRAPH to open the PARAGRAPH palette, which provides alignment and indentation controls.

7. You can also drag using the text tool to create a text container in either Photoshop or Fireworks. The width of the container can be adjusted with manipulation handles so that you do not have to manually insert line breaks.

TIP

Digital imaging tools are great for applying special effects to text, and for adding headlines and short paragraphs to a layout. They are also good for creating buttons and graphical text headers for Web projects. When you have a meatier body of text that needs typesetting, however, the digital imaging applications won't do. To typeset larger bodies of text, or to create multiple-page documents, you will want to use a page layout program. You can also use a digital illustration program for setting type. Setting type is covered in the section on page layout (see page 245), and digital illustration programs are covered in chapter 6.

FIGURES 5-30, A–C Headline text and secondary text were set using Downcome (a type-face created by Eduardo Recife) at 249 and 24 point, respectively. The body text was set in medium-weight News Gothic Standard at 10 point. Eight-point Modern 880 type was added to the angel icon at the bottom to create a pseudo-logo for this experimental design. The final variation adds color and rotated text, created using the FREE TRANSFORM command.

Technique Lesson 5.31: Warped and Free Transforming Type

Photoshop's warp text tools give text visual variety and, when used correctly, can translate text into a graphical element that adds to the quality of a design. You can also use the FREE TRANSFORM command to scale, rotate, or manipulate the perspective of type.

QUICK STEPS (PS):

Warping Text

1. Create text and then select it using the TEXT tool.

2a. Go to LAYER > TYPE > WARP TEXT.

or:

2b. Click on the WARP TEXT icon in the OPTIONS palette.

3. The WARP TEXT dialog box will appear. Choose a warp effect.

4. Manipulate the BEND and DISTORTIONS.

5. To edit the warp, click on the text layer, highlight the text, and go to LAYER > TYPE > WARP TEXT (or click on the WARP TEXT icon in the OPTIONS palette).

Transforming Type (PS & FW):

Scaling and Rotating

1. Create type using the TYPE tool.

2. Select the type and press CTRL + T (Windows) or CMD + T (Macintosh); FREE TRANSFORM handles will appear around the text.

Scaling

1. Click on the corner handle; hold the SHIFT key and drag to scale.

Rotating

1. Place the cursor alongside any handle; when you see a curved line with an arrow, drag up or down to rotate.

Perspective (PS)

2. Click on a handle holding the CTRL key (Windows) or the CMD key (Macintosh); move the handles to manipulate perspective.

The FREE TRANSFORM command is useful for creating perspective after warping text, because you can move the entire FREE TRANSFORM box, rather than just a single handle.

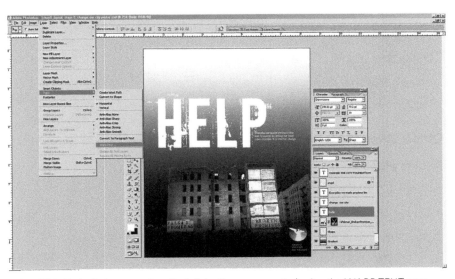

FIGURES 5-31, A–C An arc and vertical distortion were created using the WARP TEXT command. The final manipulation was done with the FREE TRANSFORM command and perspective manipulation.

FIGURES 5-31, B–C

Bitmap Filters

Digital imaging programs make dozens of bitmap filters available; they are, however, a secondary tool, and in many cases their use can actually hurt a design. This lesson covers the one filter I consider a staple in the digital designer's technique toolkit. Feel free to explore the other available filters, but be sure you can justify their results' value to the composition and the overall message.

 ### Technique Lesson 5.32: Motion Blur

Adding a motion blur (or any other blurring technique) to an image creates a feeling of motion and adds an element of abstraction.

QUICK STEPS (PS & FW):

TIP

Combining blurred and sharp images gives a composition an interesting visual overlap.

Adding a Motion Blur Filter to an Image or Text

1. Create text or place an image on its own layer.

2. Go to FILTER > BLUR > MOTION BLUR.

3. Set the ANGLE and DISTANCE.

4. Click OK.

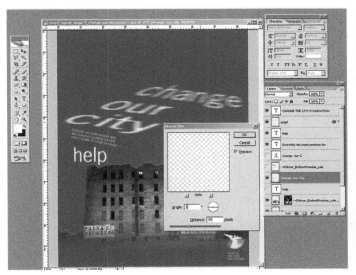

FIGURES 5-32, A, B MOTION BLUR applied to a layer's text object, creating a new variation.

Layer Effects

Technique Lesson 5.33: Drop Shadows

Adding drop shadows is easy in digital imaging applications. The same technique applies to both text and images.

QUICK STEPS (PS & FW):

Adding a Drop Shadow to Text or Image

1. Create text or place an image on its own layer with a transparent background. (Some portion of the transparent background must be visible in order to see the shadow.)

2. Select the text layer or the image layer.

3a. (PS) Go to LAYER > LAYER STYLE > DROP SHADOW.

    or:

3b. (PS) Click on the "f," which is the ADD TO LAYER STYLE icon at the bottom of the LAYERS palette.

    or:

3c. (FW) Go to the PROPERTIES bar at the bottom and select FILTERS. Choose SHADOW AND GLOW > DROP SHADOW.

TIP

Drop shadows add depth to an image and help eliminate flatness. Be aware of your angles and positions: they must be consistent so that they appear to come from the same light source. As a general rule, don't use drop shadows on text below 36 point: drop shadows work best with larger text.

4a. (PS & FW) Manipulate the shadow's POSITION, OPACITY, SOFTNESS, and ANGLE by entering numeric values into these fields.

or:

4b. (PS) Move the shadow directly on the document.

5. Click OK.

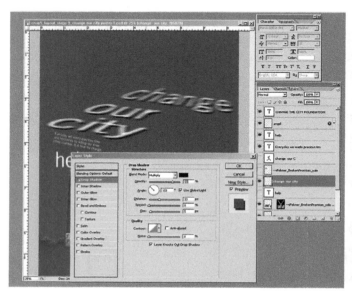 

FIGURES 5-33, A, B Drop shadows on type and on an image.

 Technique Lesson 5.34: Color Overlay

The color overlay layer effect is a handy tool that allows you to create colorized images and silhouettes.

QUICK STEPS (PS):

Placing a Color Overlay on Text or Image

1. Create text or place an image on its own layer.

2. Select the text layer or the image layer.

3a. Go to LAYER > LAYER STYLE > COLOR OVERLAY.

or:

3b. Click on the "f", which is the ADD TO LAYER STYLE icon at the bottom of the LAYERS palette.

4. Choose a color and manipulate the OPACITY. Leave BLENDING on NORMAL.

5. Click OK.

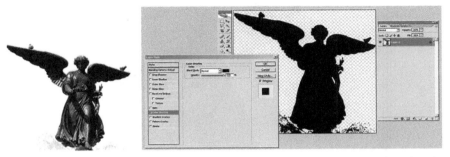

FIGURE 5-34, A, B Create silhouettes using color overlays. Here, the image was selected, and the background was eliminated. Then the overlay was applied to create the solid form.

Technique Lesson 5.35: Stroke

Strokes are outlines around objects. They call attention to an element and provide a way of highlighting something using the visual contour of a solid line.

QUICK STEPS (PS):

Adding a Stroke to Text or Image

1. Create text or place an image on its own layer.

2. Select the text layer or the image layer.

3a. Go to LAYER > LAYER STYLE > STROKE.

or:

3b. Click on the "f," ADD TO LAYER STYLE icon at the bottom of the LAYERS palette.

4. Choose a fill color and manipulate the SIZE, POSITION, OPACITY, and FILL TYPE. Leave BLENDING on NORMAL.

5. Click OK.

TIP

Stroke works well when you want to give an object a commercial appearance, rather than leave it in its natural form. Strokes create order with line and also lend variety to a composition when combined with photographic images.

FIGURE 5-35 Stroke can be added to text and objects.

Final Output for Print

Always save a layered Photoshop file (.psd) in RGB at 300 dpi as a source document backup.

When printing on a printing press, proofing machine, ink-jet, or laser printer, the final file should be in CMYK and should be saved as either an .eps or a .tif. These file formats create uncompressed files whose color data is saved internally.

The final resolution for print files is 300 to 350 dpi, at the final print size. Consult the commercial printer who is printing the job for exact file resolution specifications.

If you are using a laser or ink-jet printer, 300 dpi is acceptable. If the file formats and the color models are wrong, the images will not print correctly or as expected. Final images for a print project created in Photoshop may be placed into a page layout program such as Adobe InDesign or into a digital illustration program such as Adobe Illustrator.

Technique Lesson 5.36: CMYK Conversion

QUICK STEPS:

Converting a File to CMYK

1. Go to IMAGE > MODE > CMYK COLOR.

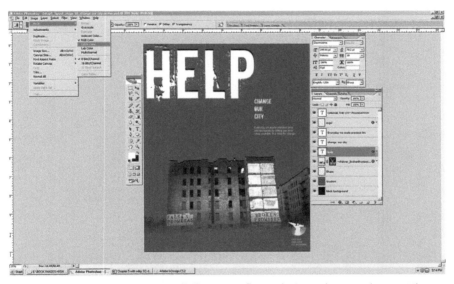

FIGURE 5-36 A CMYK conversion will allow you to flatten the image layers and convert the document to CMYK color for final print output.

Technique Lesson 5.37: Creating a Clipping Path

Transparency is not built in to raster images: you must create an alpha channel (discussed on page 156) for screen transparency (Web or broadcast); otherwise, if the image does not fill the page area, it will appear with a white bounding box.

The same is true with raster images placed in page layout and digital illustration applications. To insert a raster image in a page layout or vector application, you must first create a clipping path, which "clips" away the external background. The clipped area is defined in the image by a path, rather than a marquee selection.

QUICK STEPS:

Creating a Clipping Path Using a Selection Tool

1. Make a detailed selection of the image area needing **transparency**.

2. Go to WINDOW > PATHS to open the PATHS palette.

3. Click on the third icon, MAKE WORK PATH FROM SELECTION.

4. Double-click the italicized name *work path* and rename it.

5. Go to the drop-down arrow in the PATHS palette, then select CLIPPING PATH name; leave FLATNESS blank.

6. Click OK.

   You can also use the PEN tool to create a path around an image area, and then convert the path to a clipping path.

(A)

(B)

(C)

FIGURES 5-37, A–C Create clipping paths using the LASSO or PEN tool. Notice first (A) the selection around the guitar's headstock and tuners, then the converted path (B). A clipping path permits you to have a transparent background surrounding a printed image in a page layout or illustration program such as Adobe InDesign or Adobe Illustrator.

Technique Lesson 5.38: Saving as an .eps for Print

Whenever you create a clipping path, save your file in .eps format. Even though there is a vector path embedded in the file, the image is still a raster image and should not be scaled in the final layout program.

QUICK STEPS:

Saving a File in .eps Format

1. Go to FILE > SAVE AS > .EPS.

EPS stands for Encapsulated PostScript. All proofing machines and laser printers use the PostScript printing language to process files. The .eps file format is used for both raster and vector files. It is the primary format for saving final output vector graphics and is very reliable for the PostScript printer output of raster images.

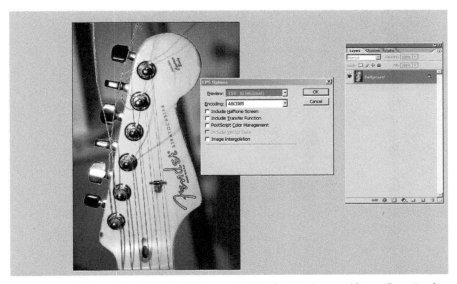

FIGURE 5-38 When setting EPS OPTIONS, use ASCII85 for Windows and Binary Encoding for Macintosh. Always use TIFF 8 bit preview. Make sure other boxes are unchecked.

Technique Lesson 5.39: Saving as a .tif for Print

QUICK STEPS (PS & FW):

Saving a File in .tif Format

1. Go to FILE > SAVE AS > .TIF.

TIF stands for Tagged Image File Format. Use this format for desktop ink-jet printers, as many use non-PostScript drivers to process files. However, .tif files also work well on PostScript devices such as laser printers, proofers, and large-format printers.

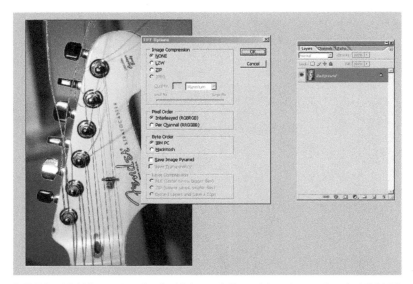

FIGURE 5-39 When outputting for high-resolution print, make sure to select IMAGE COMPRESSION > NONE.

Final Output for Web

Always save a layered Photoshop file (.psd) or a layered Fireworks file (.png) in RGB as a source document backup.

All screen graphics, including Web page graphics, are 72 ppi. When creating Web pages or graphics, or any content for the screen, the final file should be in RGB or Web-safe index color. Full-color image files should be saved as .jpgs with RGB color. In fact, you can use .jpg files for all artwork, including logos and line art. Flat artwork, such as logos or line art, can also be saved as .gifs with

Web-safe index color; however, the Web-safe index color palette cannot be used for photographic images.

If the file formats and the color models are wrong, the images will not show up correctly on the Web pages. Final images for a Web project created in Photoshop may also be placed into a Web page layout program such as Adobe Dreamweaver or Microsoft FrontPage.

Technique Lesson 5.40: Saving as a .jpg for Web

QUICK STEPS (PS):

Saving a File in .jpg Format (Photoshop Only)

1a. Go to FILE > SAVE AS > .JPG.

or:

1b. Go to FILE > SAVE > SAVE FOR WEB > JPEG.

2. Select QUALITY > HIGH 8 and BASELINE ("Standard").

JPG stands for Joint Photographic Experts Group. Use this format for all Web graphics. A Web .jpg file should be in RGB color.

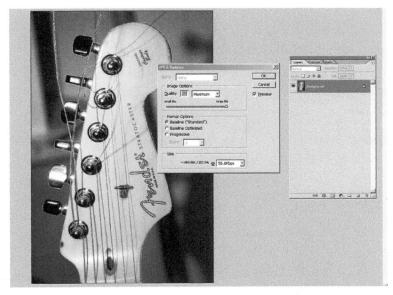

FIGURE 5-40 Used for Web graphics, .jpgs should be avoided for high-end print work because their file compression algorithm generates a quality loss on high-resolution devices.

Technique Lesson 5.41: Saving as a .gif for Web

QUICK STEPS (PS):

Saving a File in .gif Format (Photoshop Only)

1a. Go to FILE > SAVE AS > Compuserv.GIF.

or:

1b. Go to FILE > SAVE > SAVE FOR WEB > GIF.

2. Flatten the layers and use the Web-safe color index palette.

3. Select ROW ORDER > NORMAL.

The resulting .gif file will be in Web-safe index color.

GIF stands for Graphics Information Format.

Design Assignment

Assignment: Create a digital collage for a magazine article.

Tools: Digital imaging software and six digital images.

Specs: Imagine you are the graphic artist hired to create a digital montage for an article in *Rolling Stone* magazine. The image must fit on an 11 × 17" landscape page. You must direct the art and find up to eight related images (use four to six in the final piece) to composite in a digital collage that expresses unity.

Theme: Global warming and government. You can use specifically environmental images, or images of any subject—politicians, buildings, monuments, trees, animals, landscape images, natural textures, and so on.

Research the theme first, and then gather newspaper or magazine clippings, photos, and textures. Scan or photograph materials if needed. Next, practice using selections to isolate the desired visual elements from their backgrounds. Drag them into the final document and arrange them thoughtfully to create a digital montage.

Explore effects to create drop shadows and color overlays as well as filters for blurring images. Be sure to use filters or effects sparingly, as their overuse will diminish the quality of the design.

Follow the design principles and techniques presented in chapter 2 to create an appealing visual whole, or a gestalt. Make careful decisions about unity and variety, scale, repetition, texture, and visual rhythm.

Save the work file as a .psd and output the final file as a .tif or .eps, with a clipping path if needed. Advanced design assignments are available at the book's Web site: www.wiley.com/go/digitaldesign.

Online Movie Lessons

Tutorial movies for technique lessons are provided online. Each section contains step-by-step walk-throughs. They are available at the book's Web site: www.wiley.com/go/digitaldesign.

Bibliography

Muir, Peter. 2000. *Preflight: Avoiding costly printout problems through proper file preparation.* San Diego, CA: Windsor Professional Information.

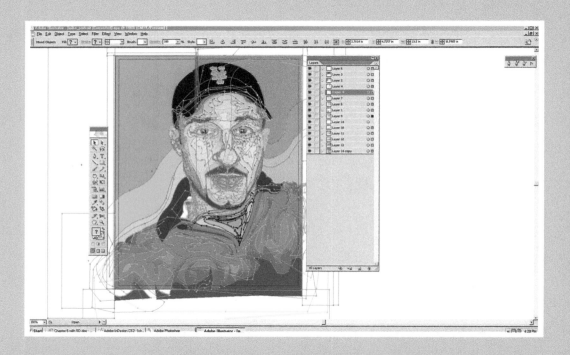

CHAPTER 6
Vector Graphics

Chapter Objectives

Identify and define vector graphics.

Identify and define the differences between vector graphics for print and for the Web.

Introduce basic vector graphics techniques.

Digital Illustration and Vector Graphics

Digital illustration is the creation of artwork using vector graphics applications. Vector graphics are also known as vector objects. Vector images are made with points and paths, which are described in the vector software and PostScript programming language as mathematical formulas. Vector graphics are complex because they use many points (or anchor points) and typically combine various vector objects inside of one graphic—a logo with a shape and text, for example. Points connect line segments, which can be open or closed objects that have a color fill or color stroke. Curved line segments have direction handles that allow you to manipulate the curve.

Vector Graphics for Print and Web

Vector graphics have built-in transparency. Instead of importing into a page layout program like InDesign or a digital imaging program like Photoshop, with a white bounding box, vector images (CMYK .eps files) have a transparent background.

The file format used for printing vector files is .eps. Vector graphics can be rasterized to convert them from points and paths to pixels. You must rasterize vector images before you can use them in a Web page. Exporting an image as a .jpg or .gif in a vector program, or opening the vector image in a digital imaging application such as Adobe Photoshop or Adobe Fireworks, will automatically rasterize the image and turn it into a bitmap graphic. However, vector formats are native to Adobe Flash, a vector-based motion graphics program; therefore, the same paths and points that exist in Illustrator are also utilized in Flash.

The most common graphical objects that are created in vector-based programs such as Adobe Illustrator are logos, line art graphics (buttons and icons), and illustrations. Text-based designs are also created using vector programs.

Vector graphics are high resolution and 300 ppi at any size. That is why they are the format used for logos, which usually have to be printed at many different sizes—on banners (big) *and* business cards (small), for example. Vector graphics also provide smooth, clean, sharp lines when printed on a PostScript printing device such as a laser printer or a wide-format poster printer.

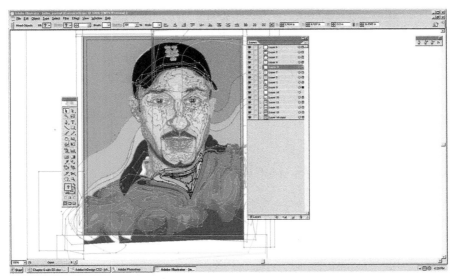

FIGURE 6-1 Vector graphics are made up of anchor points and line segments. Graphics created in vector programs can be scaled without losing quality.

Here are some concepts critical to outputting print and Web vector images:

- Vector images are resolution independent.

- Vector images for print projects are automatically created at 300 ppi to scale in vector applications such as Adobe Illustrator and Corel Draw.

- Always export vector images for Web projects at 72 dpi to scale.

- It is OK to scale vector images above 100 percent after they are placed in a page layout program; the image will not degrade (i.e., get jagged and lose detail). Create images at the size needed—or larger, if they may need to be enlarged in the future.

- Print projects are created in CMYK mode or using spot color (Pantone swatches).

- RGB color can be used for Web and broadcast graphics made in digital illustration (vector) programs. Never use CMYK for Web or broadcast graphics.

- The correct final output file format for vector graphics is .eps. These files can be placed in page layout programs such as InDesign and QuarkXPress.

- Digital illustration applications also allow output of raster images if needed. This is for convenience, not necessity. If you do this, export raster images for the Web as either .jpgs or .gifs. The .eps file format will not work in a Web page.

- The native, layered file format for Illustrator images is .ai; .eps also works as a native, layered file format for Illustrator.

- Integrating artwork between raster and vector programs is easy. You can drag and drop or import and place Illustrator files into digital imaging programs such as Photoshop or Fireworks. The images are rasterized automatically and will lose their vector attributes: resolution and scalability.

Vector Graphics Techniques

As discussed in the previous chapter on raster graphics, digital production projects are the culmination of a series of techniques that require familiarity with the various tools, palettes, and menus in the software application you use. There are thousands of techniques and a variety of digital imaging applications: all of them cannot be covered in a multisubject text such as this one. This chapter covers some of the most important techniques in order to help you get started creating layered illustrations, icons and logos, and page designs in digital illustration programs.

All of the techniques below are shown in Adobe Illustrator, but apply to other vector-based applications. Some lessons apply to programs that have vector tools. The names of menu commands, tools, panels, and palettes are written in ALL CAPS. Dialog boxes refer to boxes that appear after selecting tools, palettes, or menu items. They provide fine-tuning controls for executing techniques. Most menu items have dialog boxes associated with them.

You will eventually find your own comfort zone with digital illustration tools and use them accordingly when developing projects. In print workflows, Illustrator can be used for preparing vector-based images for other applications or act as a standalone tool for final design projects. In Web workflows, you can use Illustrator for Web page design and then open or drag your .ai files into Fireworks to perform optimization, slicing, and exporting.

The techniques below are presented in steps with corresponding sample project images that exemplify the techniques. You should explore various combinations of techniques in your work to discover divergent approaches to drawing and two-dimensional design in Adobe Illustrator. It is important to become comfortable using layers and familiar with this set of foundation techniques used in design projects.

As with most applications, there is usually more than one way to perform a technique in Illustrator, so don't be surprised if you discover other methods or shortcuts beyond those presented in this book. You can test yourself and explore these techniques by creating additional projects guided by the corresponding online movie lessons listed at the end of each technique lesson in this chapter. View these online tutorials by going to www.wiley.com/go/digitaldesign.

Document Setup

Adobe Illustrator allows you to create vector image documents for digital design projects. Setting up a new document requires the designer to make some choices about size and color.

Technique Lesson 6.1: Creating a New Document

This is the first step in creating a digital design project. Adobe Illustrator provides a simple setup box for new documents. The two main preset sizes are print (paper) and Web page. These setups provide the size settings automatically. Remember, Illustrator creates high-resolution (300 ppi) files by default.

Creating a New Document

1. Go to FILE > NEW.

2. Choose tabloid 11 × 17″, one of the preset setups in the drop-down menu. Use CMYK color for a print project; use RGB color for a Web project.

3. Choose ORIENTATION > LANDSCAPE.

4. Click OK.

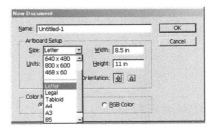

FIGURE 6-2 Illustrator's NEW DOCUMENT dialog box allows you to select print or Web page size presets.

> **TIP**
>
> Create a new final document or an image for placement in another application.

Technique Lesson 6.2: Guides and grids

The guides and grid are critical tools for helping you arrange items on a page. All digital design programs have guides and grid functions. In Illustrator, setting up a 3 × 3 grid for layouts will help you adhere to the rule of thirds and the law of thirds in your compositions.

TIP

Creating a grid before starting the design project helps with composition decisions. Arrange objects in your composition based on grid placements and the rule of thirds and law of thirds.

QUICK STEPS:

A 3 × 3 Grid Using Guides

To create a 3 × 3 grid in Illustrator using the grid lines function:

1. Go to EDIT > PREFERENCES.

2. Choose GUIDES and GRIDS.

    Now set the grid:

3. For a 3 × 3 grid, set the grid for 3.66 with 1 subdivision (11 divided by 3 = 3.66).

4. Click OK.

    The grid will appear on the document page.

Layers and Templates

Technique Lesson 6.3: Using Layers

Because compositing an image requires flexibility and control, most digital design programs, including Illustrator, employ a layers function within their interface. While you can work in Illustrator and other digital illustration programs without using layers much more easily than you could in a digital imaging program such as Photoshop, it is still recommended that you put each individual object on its own layer.

Illustrator layers work differently than layers in Photoshop. In Illustrator, line segments and anchor points are each color-coded to the corresponding layer. When you use the SELECTION tool (black arrow) and click on an object (either the path, point, or shape), it will appear with a color and a dot of the same color as the layer it is on.

QUICK STEPS:

The Layers Palette's Show Layers Only Option

In Illustrator, every object created gets placed on an individual sub-layer, which exists under the top layer. This can become daunting as many, many layers and sub-layers begin to pile up. It is, however, possible to work without sub-layers.

1. Go to WINDOW > LAYERS to open the LAYERS palette.

2. Go to the drop-down menu in the LAYERS palette.

3. Choose PALETTE OPTIONS.

4. Enable the SHOW LAYERS ONLY check box (this will hide the sub-layers).

5. In thumbnails, enable the LAYERS check box only.

Making a New Layer for Artwork

1. Go to WINDOW > LAYERS to open the LAYERS palette.

2a. Click on the NEW LAYER icon at the bottom of the LAYERS palette.

or:

2b. Go to the drop-down menu in the LAYERS palette.

3. Choose NEW LAYER.

Moving Objects from Layer to Layer

1. Click on a layer.

2. Grab the color dot and drag it to the layer on which you want the artwork to appear. The selection on that layer will be moved to the targeted layer.

> **TIP**
>
> Layers help you organize, view, and manage artwork. They are also needed for certain production techniques, so try to remember to use them, especially for complex projects with many objects.

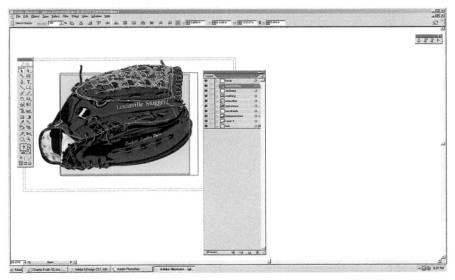

FIGURE 6-3 A layered illustration in Illustrator. Artwork by Michael Calandra.

Technique Lesson 6.4: Placing Artwork (Raster or Vector)

Illustrator is typically used as a tool for drawing individual images or creating a layered page design. Always create a final document (receptacle) and place or drag images into it (composite), rather than working from within an original image file. This preserves the original image in case it is needed in its original form.

You can use FILE > OPEN to open raster or vector images in Illustrator. You can work on them first—creating an illustration from a bitmapped image or making a logo, for example—and then drag and drop or copy and paste them into your receptacle document. Or you can save the images and, using the PLACE command, import them (in a variety of popular graphical file formats) into a new Illustrator document. Placed images all appear on the same layer, unless you create a new one before importing.

QUICK STEPS:

Placing an External Raster File

TIP

Place external images into documents to use for drawing templates or for layouts.

1. Go to FILE > PLACE.

2. Choose the image file you want to place (.tif, .jpg, .psd, .png, .eps, .bmp, or .gif) and open it.

3. The image can be resized using the FREE TRANSFORM tool in the TOOL palette. Grab a corner and hold down the SHIFT key to maintain the object's proportions when scaling it.

 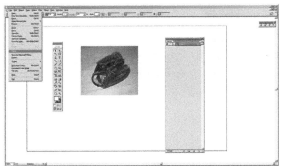

FIGURES 6-4, A, B Placed images in Illustrator can be used for layouts or as bitmap templates for creating custom illustrations.

Technique Lesson 6.5: Tear-Off Panels

Tear-off panels can be pulled from tools in the TOOL panel. Tools that have multiple tool sets have tear-offs. The PENCIL tool, for example, has a tear-off with the SMOOTH tool and the ERASER tool.

QUICK STEPS:

Using Tear-Off Panels

1. Go to the PENCIL tool.

2. Click and hold the mouse button.

3. Go to the end of the panel and drag it off.

TIP

You can use the tear-offs for the SHAPE, LINE, PEN, and PENCIL tools for quick access to entire tool sets.

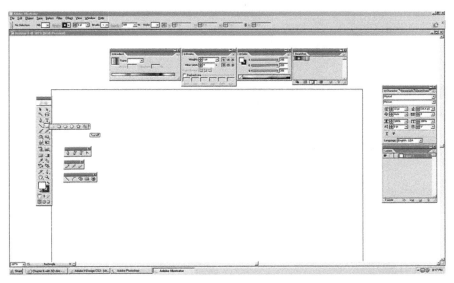

FIGURE 6-5 Tear-off panels.

Color

Technique Lesson 6.6: Fill and Stroke

You can add color to vector-based objects such as shapes and paths in two areas: fill and stroke. Fill refers to the inside of the shape or the inner portion of a path; stroke is the line that makes up shapes and open paths.

QUICK STEPS:

Adding a Fill to a Shape or Path with the Color Picker

1. Use the SELECTION tool (black arrow) to choose the shape or path you want to fill. (An object must be selected in order to fill it.)

2. Go to the TOOL palette and double-click on the FILL swatch (a square color chip) at the bottom.

   The COLOR PICKER will appear.

3. Choose a color.

4. Click OK. Click on any white space to deselect the object.

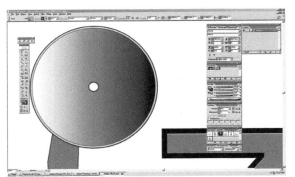 

FIGURES 6-6, A–C Strokes and fills can be applied to shapes and paths. Gradients, patterns, and solid swatches can all be applied to fills. This poster shows a variety of strokes and fills used on type, custom illustration, and a premade Illustrator symbol.

Adding a Stroke to a Shape or Path with the Color Picker

1. Use the SELECTION tool to choose the shape or path you want to fill. (An object must be selected in order to fill it.)

2. Go to the TOOL palette and double-click on the STROKE swatch (a framed box) at the bottom.

   The COLOR PICKER will appear.

3. Choose a color.

4. Click OK. Click on any white space to deselect the object.

Adding a Fill to a Shape or Path with the Swatches Palette

1. Use the SELECTION tool to choose the shape or path you want to fill. (An object must be selected in order to fill it.)

2. Go to the TOOL palette and click on a FILL swatch (a square color chip) at the bottom.

   The object will be filled with the color, gradient, or pattern. Gradients and patterns cannot be applied to strokes.

Setting the Stroke Width

1. Go to WINDOW > STROKE.

2. Enter a number in the WEIGHT field.

TIP

Fill and stroke are basic techniques used in every Illustrator project.

Technique Lesson 6.7: The Color Picker

There are a variety of ways to set color in Illustrator. The easiest way is to use the COLOR PICKER—the same one that appears in Photoshop—which is activated if you double-click on the FILL or STROKE icons in the TOOL palette. However, using the SWATCHES palette and COLOR palette is more useful.

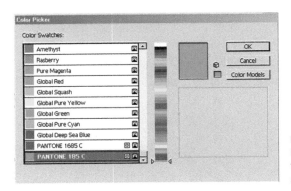

FIGURE 6-7 The COLOR PICKER is identical in Photoshop and Illustrator. You can also access color swatches from here.

Technique Lesson 6.8: Swatches

Swatches are grouped color chips that reside on palettes. You can both add color to and remove colors from the SWATCHES palette.

QUICK STEPS:

Opening the Default Swatches Palette

1. Go to WINDOW > SWATCHES.

   You'll see swatches for process (CMYK) colors, solid spot colors, gradients, and patterns.

Opening the Other Swatches Palette

1. Go to WINDOW > SWATCH LIBRARIES.
2. Choose either DEFAULT CMYK (for full-color print), WEB-SAFE (for Web), DEFAULT RGB (for broadcast or CD), or PANTONE UNCOATED (for spot-color printing) to get started.

Adding and Saving a Color to the Swatches Palette

1. Go to WINDOW > SWATCH LIBRARIES.
2. Pick the color or gradient you want to add from the COLOR PICKER, the document, or the GRADIENT palette.
3. Click the ADD SWATCH icon in the SWATCHES palette.

TIP

There are dozens of swatch sets in Illustrator, including important ones used over and over for print and Web design. Saving swatches is a very helpful production technique.

Deleting a Swatch from the Swatches Palette

1. Select the swatch.
2. Click the TRASH CAN icon in the SWATCHES palette.

Add a Fill to a Shape or Path with the Swatches Palette

1. Click on an object.
2. Click on a swatch.

   The object will be filled or stroked with the color, gradient, or pattern you selected. Gradients and patterns cannot be applied to strokes.

FIGURES 6-8, A, B The SWATCHES palette holds the swatches for solid colors, Pantone colors, gradients, and patterns.

Technique Lesson 6.9: Gradients

Gradients are graduated spans of color. Illustrator's default gradients are stored and available in the SWATCHES palette. You can also create custom gradients using the GRADIENT palette and drag them into the SWATCHES palette for future use.

TIP

Gradients are heavily utilized for creating seamless and subtle backgrounds. They are also used for digital illustration to add highlights and shadow areas to a two-dimensional surface.

QUICK STEPS:

Making or Editing a Gradient

1. Go to WINDOW > GRADIENT. The GRADIENT palette will open.

2. Place the cursor under the GRADIENT bar. Click on the triangle box sliders and pick a swatch, or use the COLOR PICKER to change the color.

3. Place the cursor under the GRADIENT bar and click to add to the triangle box sliders, which add colors to the gradient. Click and drag the sliders down to delete them.

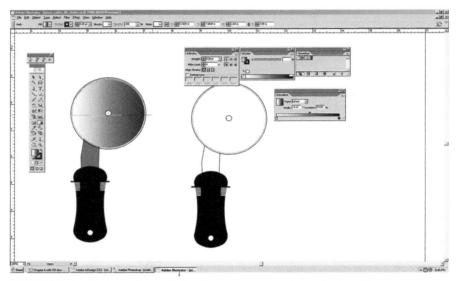

FIGURE 6-9 Gradients can be applied to fills to create a seamless color transition.

Technique Lesson 6.10: Patterns

Patterns are repetitive elements. There are several default patterns available in the SWATCHES Palette. You can also quickly create your own original patterns.

QUICK STEPS:

Creating a Custom Pattern

1. Make the object or set of objects that will form the pattern.

2. Select the objects with the SELECTION tool (black arrow).

3. Go to EDIT > DEFINE PATTERN.

4. Name the pattern.

5. Click OK.

The pattern now appears in the SWATCHES palette.

6. Use it to fill an object.

TIP

Patterns work well as background elements and create repetition in compositions.

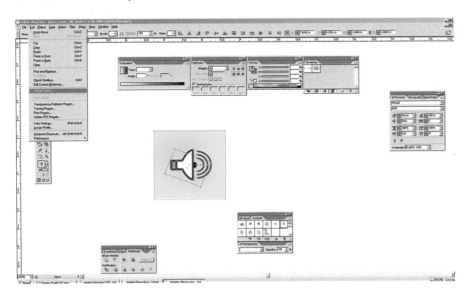

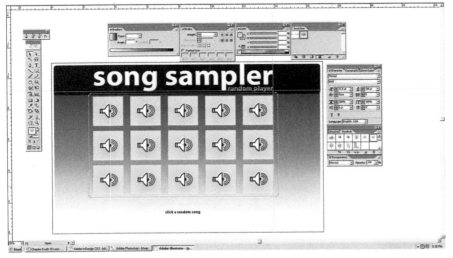

FIGURES 6-10, A, B Add a box filled with white (or any color) around an object in a pattern to create a cushion of space in the pattern.

Shapes and Paths

Technique Lesson 6.11: Making Shapes (Primitives)

Illustrator provides shape tools for creating closed-path shapes, including circles, ellipses, rectangles, squares, polygons, and stars. Shapes can be filled and stroked as well as overlapped and used in arrangement or layers.

QUICK STEPS:

Making a Primitive Shape

TIP

Shapes are the basis for illustration and are a main element in design across media. Shapes are a primary tool for creating all types of forms.

1. Select a SHAPE tool from the TOOL palette.

2. Drag the shape across the document. (Hold the SHIFT key to create a shape whose height and width are equal.)

3. Fill and/or stroke the shape with colors from the COLOR PICKER or the SWATCHES palette.

4. Click on white space to deselect the shape.

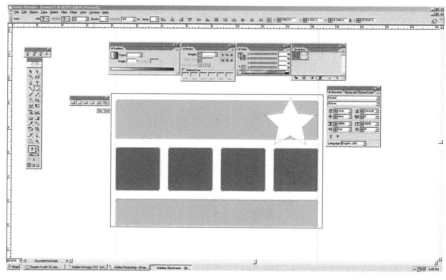

FIGURE 6-11 Use the primitive tools to draw shapes.

Technique Lesson 6.12: Selecting and Arranging Objects

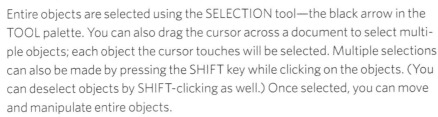

Entire objects are selected using the SELECTION tool—the black arrow in the TOOL palette. You can also drag the cursor across a document to select multiple objects; each object the cursor touches will be selected. Multiple selections can also be made by pressing the SHIFT key while clicking on the objects. (You can deselect objects by SHIFT-clicking as well.) Once selected, you can move and manipulate entire objects.

The DIRECT SELECTION tool—the white arrow in the TOOL palette—is used for selecting individual anchor points and line segments (paths). You can SHIFT-click to select multiple points or paths.

Objects are arranged in a stacking order on each layer. When you place multiple objects on one layer, they stack on top of each other.

QUICK STEPS:

Moving an Arrangement

1. Select the objects you want to move forward or back in the stacking order.

2. Go to OBJECT > ARRANGE.

3. Choose BRING FORWARD or SEND TO BACK.

TIP

Artwork on the same layer must be arranged to position it correctly and ensure it does not cover up other elements.

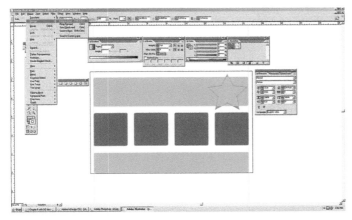

FIGURES 6-12, A, B Move objects from front to back using the ARRANGE command in the OBJECT menu.

Technique Lesson 6.13: Grouping

Once an object is selected, it can be grouped with other selected objects; this allows them to be moved and manipulated together.

QUICK STEPS:

Grouping Objects

1. Select the objects you want to group by dragging the cursor to touch each of them or by SHIFT-clicking them.

2. Go to OBJECT > GROUP.

Ungrouping Objects

1. Select the objects.

2. Go to OBJECT > UNGROUP.

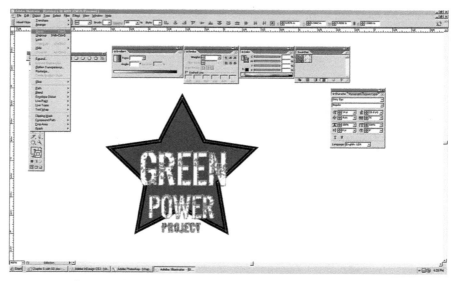

FIGURE 6-13 Grouping objects keeps them together, making it easier to move and manipulate them.

Technique Lesson 6.14: Align and Distribute Objects

Multiple objects can be aligned to the same horizontal, vertical, or center edge or distributed evenly in the same manner.

QUICK STEPS:

Aligning or Distributing Objects

1. Select the objects you want to group by dragging to touch them or SHIFT-clicking them.

2. Go to WINDOW > ALIGN to open the ALIGN panel.

3. Choose an alignment or distribution. The choices are vertically or horizontally aligned, or distribute each item along an edge or the center of the objects.

TIP

Use the ALIGN AND DISTRIBUTE panel to position multiple elements without moving each one manually or setting up an excessive number of guides.

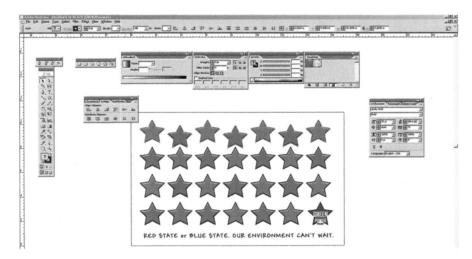

FIGURES 6-14, A, B
The ALIGN AND DISTRIBUTE panel allows objects to be aligned and spaced precisely—without manual positioning—thus saving time and ensuring consistency.

Technique Lesson 6.15: Scaling, Rotating, and Duplicating

Use the FREE TRANSFORM tool or the OBJECT menu to scale and rotate objects.

QUICK STEPS:

Scaling and Rotating Objects

1. Select the objects or groups you want to scale or rotate by dragging to touch them or SHIFT-clicking them.

2. Choose the FREE TRANSFORM tool from the TOOL palette.

3. To scale, grab a corner. Hold the SHIFT key to maintain the object's height and width proportion, or drag freely to change the object's aspect ratio.

4. To rotate, move the cursor just outside of a handle, and drag clockwise or counterclockwise.

Copying an Object by Dragging

1. Select the objects or groups.

2. Start dragging and then hold the ALT key (Windows) or the OPTION key (Macintosh). A copy will automatically be made.

   Be sure to drag the objects to the desired position.

Duplicating an Object

> **TIP**
>
> Scaling, rotating, and repeating are techniques frequently used to create visual variety as well as to size and position artwork properly.

1. Select the objects or groups.

2. Start dragging and then hold the ALT key (Windows) or the OPTION key (Macintosh). A copy will automatically be made. Be sure to drag the objects to the desired position.

3. Press CTRL + D (Windows) or CMD + D (Macintosh) to create another duplicate the same distance from the original as the previous one.

   The DUPLICATE command works for many functions.

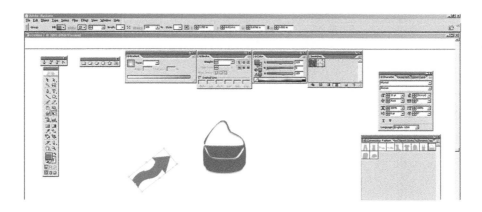

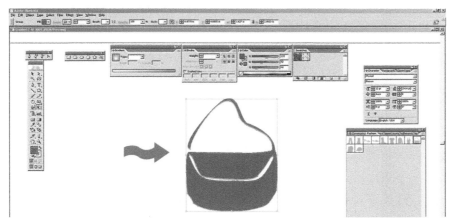

FIGURES 6-15, A, B Scale and rotate objects easily using the FREE TRANSFORM tool. Hold down the SHIFT key to maintain the objects' original proportions.

Technique Lesson 6.16: Creating Paths with the Pencil, Smooth, and Eraser Tools

The PENCIL tool allows you to draw paths freehand, just as you would with a lead pencil. There are two other tools in its set: the ERASER tool and the SMOOTH tool. The ERASER allows you to drag across an existing open or closed path to erase its line segments and anchor points. The SMOOTH tool allows you to smooth out curves and corners to eliminate any stray kinks in line segments. There are two attributes to this tool. Access them by double clicking the tool. Fidelity controls how far to move the mouse before Illustrator adds a new anchor point. Smoothness controls the amount of smoothing. Higher values yield smoother paths.

QUICK STEPS:

Drawing a Path or Shape with the Pencil Tool

1. Select the PENCIL tool from the TOOLBOX. You will see the PEN tool with the NEW PATH option (x) enabled. This means you can begin to draw a new path.

   2. Drag the PENCIL tool to create a line. Continue the line to the origin, and then hold the OPTION key to change to the PENCIL tool's CLOSE PATH option (o). Release the mouse button and the path will be closed, creating a shape.

Smoothing Lines with the Smooth Tool

1. Select the path or shape you want to smooth out using the SELECTION tool (black arrow) or the DIRECT SELECTION tool (white arrow).

2. Select the SMOOTH tool from the TOOLBOX.

3. Drag the SMOOTH tool across a line to smooth it.

4. Double-click on the SMOOTH tool to adjust its tolerance for the amount of pixels to smooth and their degree of smoothness.

Erasing Paths with the Eraser Tool

1. Select the path or shape you want to erase using the SELECTION tool or the DIRECT SELECTION tool.

2. Select the ERASER tool from the TOOLBOX.

3. Drag the ERASER across a section of a line segment (path) on an open path, or over a closed shape, to delete it. A shape becomes an open path when a section of it is erased.

TIP

Use the PENCIL, ERASER, and SMOOTH tools for freehand drawing, removing paths, and manipulating existing paths.

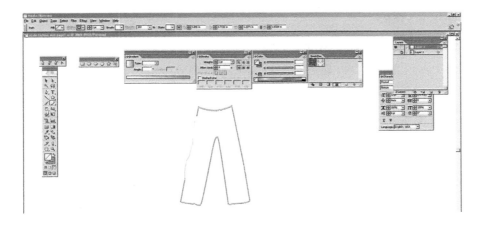

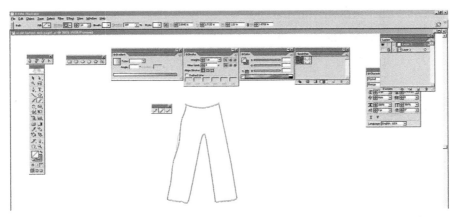

FIGURES 6-16, A, B The PENCIL tool is used for freehand drawing. Use the SMOOTH and ERASER tools to clean up pencil illustrations. (Use the PEN tool, below, for more precise drawing.)

Technique Lesson 6.17: Creating Paths with the Pen Tool

The BEZIER PEN tool allows you to create controlled paths. The way the PEN tool works can be challenging for beginning digital designers to understand because creating a path with the PEN tool is not like drawing freehand with the PENCIL tool. A key part of Illustrator's toolset, it is also available in many other applications, including Photoshop, InDesign, and Flash.

TIP

Use the PEN tool for controlled drawing—and accurate tracing. For example, create a template layer and then use a layer on top of it to trace over a photographic image. This common technique involves drawing in and coloring the different forms, shapes, and shadows in the photograph. It requires experience to become comfortable with this tool, so be patient and practice.

QUICK STEPS:

Drawing Straight Lines with the Pen Tool

1. Select the PEN tool from the TOOLBOX. The PEN tool's NEW PATH option (x) will display. This means you can begin to draw a new path.

   2. Click once where you want the line to start.

3. Move the PEN tool to where you want the line to end, then click once again. A line will appear.

   If you keep clicking, the PEN tool will continue to draw lines. When you cursor over the origin of the first line, the PEN tool will display the CLOSE PATH option (o). Click again to close the path.

Drawing Curved Lines with the Pen Tool

1. Select the PEN tool from the TOOLBOX. The PEN tool's NEW PATH option (x) will display. This means you can begin to draw a new path.

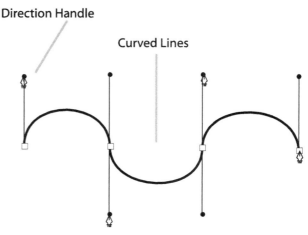

FIGURE 6-17 These PEN tool icons appear when you draw with the PEN tool.

2. Click and drag in the direction you want the curve to go (drag up approximately one-third of the line length you want). Stop and release the mouse button.

3. Move the cursor to where you want the curve to end. Click and drag in the opposite direction (drag down, approximately one-third of the line length you want). Stop and release the mouse button.

   A curved line will appear.

4. To close the path, move the cursor to the origin of the curve, hold the OPTION key, and drag in the opposite direction (upward). The path will be closed in the shape of an ellipse or a circle.

Technique Lesson 6.18: Tracing Raster Images

Tracing photographs is a professional technique that requires patience, skill, and a keen eye. This digital technique is like using tracing paper. Imagine you have a photograph and you place a piece of tracing paper on top of it. You use a pencil or black pen to trace around the contour (outer form) of the subject, and then add color to the shapes.

A template layer is a layer that can be used for tracing a bitmap. You can place a (photographic) raster image on a layer and make it a template layer, which will dim it and lock it. Then, just as you would with a piece of tracing paper, you can trace the photograph on a layer above the template layer.

QUICK STEPS:

Making a Template Layer for Tracing

1. Create a layer.

2. Place a raster image on it (FILE > PLACE).

3. Resize the image using the FREE TRANSFORM tool. Be sure to grab the corner and hold the SHIFT key to maintain the aspect ratio.

4. Double-click on the layer with the bitmapped image. In the dialog box that appears, enable the TEMPLATE check box. (The DIM IMAGES check box will be checked automatically.) You can adjust the IMAGE DIM percentage.

5. Create a new layer on top of the template layer for tracing lines and adding color.

> **TIP**
>
> Use the PEN or PENCIL tool to trace image contour and lines. Then add fills and strokes to create a digital illustration. Illustrator also has an AUTO TRACE tool that provides automated tracing; the freehand method is, however, more precise.

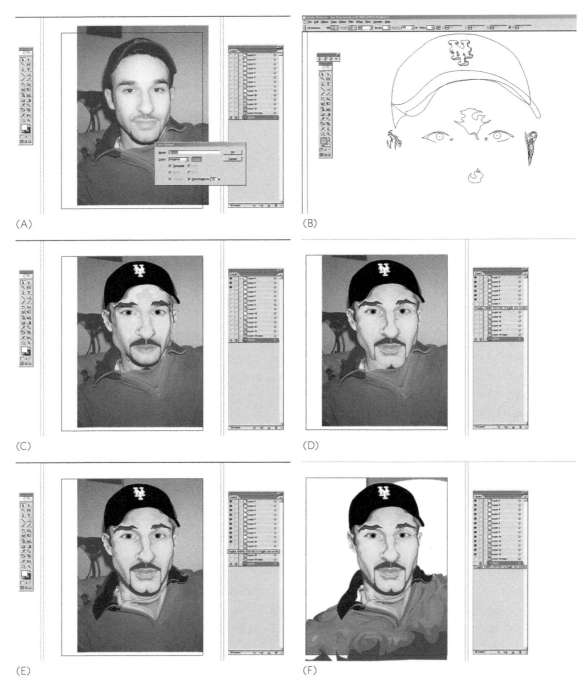

(A)

(B)

(C)

(D)

(E)

(F)

FIGURES 6-18, A–G Creating vector artwork from a photograph can be done with Illustrator's AUTO TRACE tool; use the PEN and PENCIL tools to trace artwork with more precision and flexibility. Layer by layer, this image was hand traced using the PEN tool. Overlapping the traced shapes created the form.

(G)

QUICK STEPS:

Tracing a Photographic Image to Create Line Art

1. Create a NEW LAYER.

2. Go to FILE > PLACE and place the bitmapped photo you want to trace on the layer.

3. Double-click the layer and make it a template layer (see page 217).

4. Select the PEN tool from the TOOLBOX. The PEN tool's NEW PATH option (x) will display. This means you can begin to draw a new path.

5. Use the PEN tool to draw around the contour of the image and to draw the individual shapes that comprise the image. Each new part of the drawing should be placed on its own layer and named descriptively. Begin with a contour line of the object. Create a rough outline and then add points and manipulate lines and points into the desired form.

TIP

This technique for creating line art from photographs enables you to create original artwork by utilizing reference photographs. When used for silhouettes, this technique creates uniquely stylized images.

6. Use fill and stroke to color the image and manipulate the line widths. You can also use solid fills to create a silhouetted graphic. Apply different brushes to stylize the tracing and create accurate marks.

7. Add shadow and highlight areas over the drawing to create visual depth. Use the TRANSPARENCY palette to lower the opacity of overlaid shapes.

Technique Lesson 6.19: Brushes and Symbols

Brushes are simply different types of lines that can be applied to object strokes or, put another way, different types of marks that can be applied to existing paths. Symbols are premade illustrations you can drag and drop into your Illustrator documents. You can also break the link to the symbol and edit the artwork's anchor points, line segments, and color.

TIP

Using a variety of brushes in different shapes and sizes creates different textures and values in line work. Experiment with different brushes when you create illustrations and logos to explore various styles and contrasts.

QUICK STEPS:

Adding Brushes to Paths

1. Select the path or shape to which you want to apply the brush using the SELECTION tool or the DIRECT SELECTION tool.

2. Go to WINDOW > BRUSHES to display the BRUSHES palette.

3. Select a scatter brush or art brush. A scatter brush scatters the brush along the path. The art brush you select will be represented as the stroke type. (You can also load other brushes by going to the drop-down menu in the BRUSHES palette: OPEN > BRUSH LIBRARY.)

QUICK STEPS:

Adding Symbols to a Composition

TIP

Use symbols as a starting point for designs and even for inspiration. You should break their links and edit the symbols you use; because they are in the public domain, others will use them, too.

1. Go to WINDOW > SYMBOLS to display the SYMBOLS palette.

2. Select a symbol and drag it onto the document. (You can also load other symbols by going to WINDOW > SYMBOL LIBRARIES.)

3. To break the link to the symbol and make it editable, click the right mouse button and select BREAK LINK TO SYMBOL. You can then edit the symbol's attributes. Or for a Mac with a single button mouse, hold CTRL and click the mouse. Use the DIRECT SELECTION tool to manipulate individual paths.

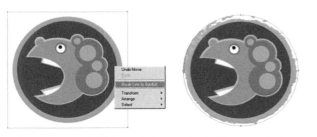

FIGURES 6-19, A, B This symbol was edited with a new stroke.

Typography

You can use Illustrator and other vector graphics applications to set type in layout projects such as brochures and manuals. Although the typesetting capabilities in Illustrator rival those in page layout programs such as InDesign, creating multiple pages of text is awkward. Vector-based programs are therefore best used for small chunks of text and text with special manipulations and effects. Type layout projects that are ideal for vector applications include one-page designs such as posters, packaging, mastheads, and logos.

Technique Lesson 6.20: Creating Type

Create type by using Illustrator's TYPE tool, which allows you to set text using the same typographic and paragraph controls found in Photoshop. You can set font, font size, leading, kerning, tracking, and baseline shift.

QUICK STEPS:

Putting Text on a Page

1. Select the TEXT tool from the TOOL palette.

2. Place the cursor and start typing.

3. Press CTRL + T (Windows) or CMD +T (Macintosh) to open the CHARACTER palette, which provides all the standard typographic controls.

TIP

Text in vector programs can remain editable; you can also convert it to outlines, which turns it into a graphic whose anchor points and line segments can then be manipulated.

FIGURE 6-20 Type can be set in vector programs using the same tools as those found in page layout applications. The CHARACTER panel and the PARAGRAPH panel are virtually the same in Illustrator, Photoshop, and InDesign.

Technique Lesson 6.21: Text Envelope Distortion (Warp and Mesh)

You can manipulate the text envelope, which is the skeleton of points and paths that make up an object. Altering the text's shape and appearance can be done using a warp or mesh approach.

QUICK STEPS:

Manipulating Text with Warp

1. Select the TEXT tool from the TOOL palette.
2. Place the cursor and start typing.
3. Select the text with the SELECTION tool.
4. Go to OBJECT > ENVELOPE DISTORT > MAKE WITH WARP.
5. Choose a WARP STYLE and adjust the horizontal and vertical bends and distortion.

Manipulating Text with Mesh

1. Select the TEXT tool from the TOOL palette.

2. Place the cursor and start typing.

3. Select the text with the SELECTION tool (black arrow).

4. Go to OBJECT > ENVELOP DISTORT > MAKE WITH MESH.

5. Choose the mesh dimensions by specifying rows and columns.

6. Use the DIRECT SELECTION tool to adjust the anchor points and line segments to create different effects.

TIP

This technique is good for creating special effects. It is especially useful for creating text that has perspective. Be judicious and use these effects with care, precision, and justification. Used indiscriminately, such text effects can detract from your design. These effects work well on larger, display text, and are not meant for body copy.

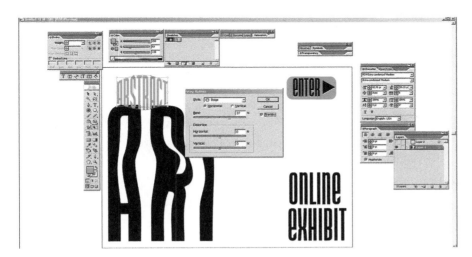

FIGURES 6-21, A, B This splash page mock-up shows both mesh and warp text distortion techniques.

Technique Lesson 6.22: Text on a Path

By placing text on a path or around a shape, you can create interesting text manipulations that follow the contour of an open path or of an entire shape.

QUICK STEPS:

Placing Text on a Path or Shape

1. Draw a path using the PENCIL or PEN tool (or create a shape).

2. Select the path or shape with the SELECTION tool (black arrow).

3. Select the TEXT ON A PATH tool form the TOOL palette.

4. Place the cursor on the line of the path or shape and begin typing.

   The text will conform to the path's boundaries. The text can be edited using the CHARACTER palette (CTRL + T for Windows, CMD + T for Macintosh): highlight the text and then manipulate its font, font size, color, tracking, and so on.

5. To move the text, click on the bottom of the text anywhere along the text string and drag. Don't click the mouse again: that will cause the text to flow wherever you have clicked.

TIP

This technique is used to create visually compelling textual graphics and to create logo type.

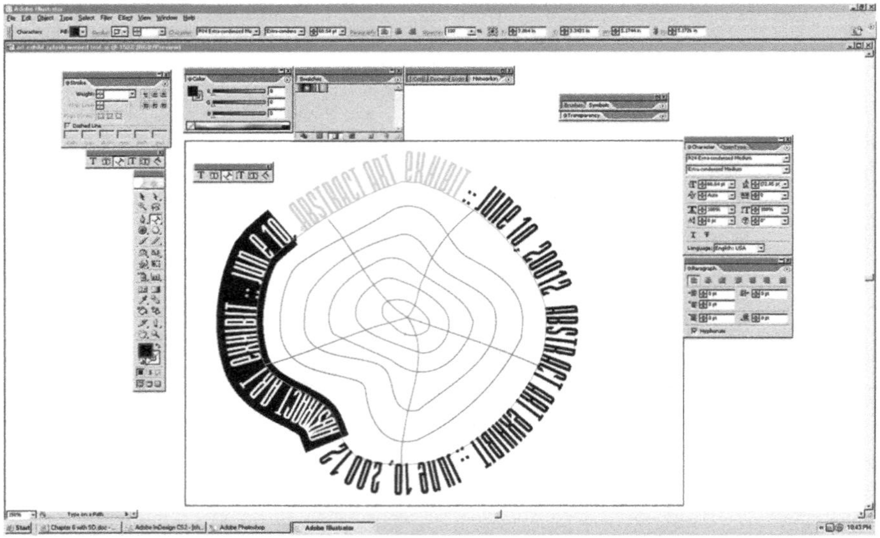

FIGURE 6-22 The TEXT ON A PATH tool allows you to place text on any open or closed path. When text is applied to a path, the path's stroke is set to none. Reselect it with the DIRECT SELECTION tool (white arrow) to add a stroke.

Technique Lesson 6.23: Converting Text to Outlines

Converting text to outlines creates a graphic out of type, providing the ability to manipulate the text's anchor points and line segments. It also eliminates the font data in the file, so when the graphic is placed in another application (such as InDesign) the font files do not have to be included: the font is now a graphic.

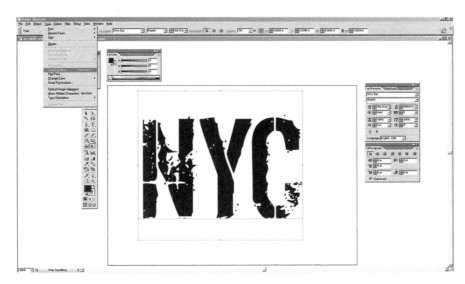

FIGURES 6-23, A, B The "NYC" text was converted to outlines so that the letterforms could be manipulated to complete the design. The outlined text has anchor points and line segments. The character and paragraph attributes cannot be edited after conversion, because the text is now a graphic. This is a critical production step in finalizing logo designs.

TIP

Text must be converted to outlines whenever a graphic includes text (such as a logo or masthead)— conversion eliminates the need to include the fonts with the .eps file. Always convert to outlines *after* saving a new .ai version of the file (SAVE AS) without outlines so an editable version of the file remains. This will give you the freedom to go back and edit the text.

QUICK STEPS:

Converting Text to Outlines

1. Select the TEXT tool from the TOOL palette.

2. Place the cursor and start typing.

3. After the type is set, go to TYPE > CREATE OUTLINES.

4. The text is no longer editable, but you can manipulate the letterforms using the DIRECT SELECTION tool. To manipulate individual letters, first select all the letters and go to OBJECT > UNGROUP.

Final Output for Print

When you create vector graphics to be printed, you must first create outlines of any text (see above). Then make sure that the color mode is set to CMYK or that the image is using spot colors (Pantone) or a spot color plus black (PMS + black). RGB colors are not used for print output.

Finally, the file to be printed should be saved as an .eps. These files can either be placed in InDesign or imported into Photoshop. For presentation purposes or for e-mailing a file to a client for proofing, save the file as a .pdf, and all color and text components will be embedded in the document so that it looks true; the client, however, will not be able to manipulate the file's content.

Final Output for Web

When you create vector graphics for placement on a Web page, you must first create outlines of any text. Then make sure that the color mode is set to RGB or index (Web-safe) colors. You can use the FILE > SAVE FOR WEB command to set your image color mode for the Web and decide on an output file format (use .jpg or .gif). You can also use FILE > EXPORT to export a vector file in raster formats such .tif, .jpg, and .gif. When an exported image is opened and rasterized in a digital imaging application, it takes on the resolution of the document.

Design Assignment

Create a magazine illustration for a feature article from a photograph.

Tools: Digital illustration software and one 8.5 × 11" digital image.

Specs: Imagine you are the graphic artist hired to create an illustration for a magazine article. Develop a concept and illustration based on a person. It can be a figurative or abstract illustration. Get a photo of the person, object, or setting, then place it in Illustrator and create a template layer (see 6.18, page 219). Then, use the PEN tool with overlapping fills and strokes to create a vector representation. The image can be traced true to life, as in a detailed illustration, or with less detail and high contrast, as in a pop art caricature. Experiment with representations to create a finished piece that satisfies your conceptual vision. Be a divergent problem solver in this assignment, and experiment. Add an appropriate headline to complete the layout composite. Advanced design assignments are available at the book's Web site: www.wiley.com/go/digitaldesign.

Online Movie Lessons

Tutorial walk-through movies for technique lessons are provided online. Each section contains step-by-step tutorial movies available at the book's Web site: www.wiley.com/go/digitaldesign.

Bibliography

Muir, Peter. 2000. *Preflight: Avoiding costly printout problems through proper file preparation*. San Diego, CA: Windsor Professional Information.

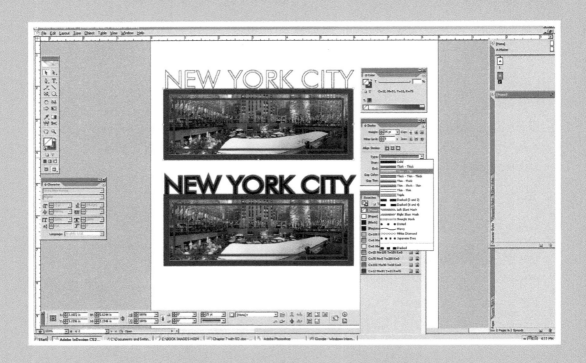

CHAPTER 7
Digital Page Layout for Print

Chapter Objectives

Define page layout for print.

Identify and define the differences between print- and Web-based page layout.

Introduce basic page layout techniques.

Digital page layout for print combines raster and vector graphics and elements of typography within the framework of print documents, including flyers and posters, brochures, magazines and newspapers, manuals, reports, corporate identity pieces, CD and DVD jackets, and books. Multipage publications typically require the use of page layout tools. InDesign is an application used for digital page layout; QuarkXPress is another page layout application. These programs' powerful typography and page setup tools facilitate graphic and publication design with type and images.

In digital page layout, images are combined with text on the page using image and text boxes—or frames—that act as containers for content. These text and image containers are arranged in a composition and then output.

Before page layout occurs, images and graphics are typically created, prepared, and output from raster and vector programs such as Photoshop and Illustrator. Photos are scanned and retouched, logos and line art are drawn, and text with special effects is created to develop content elements, which are the building blocks of a composition. Images in .eps, .tif, or .jpg format are placed in the page layout program in frames (InDesign) or picture boxes (XPress).

If you have a non-PostScript printer, such as an ink-jet, use .tif files, which output at the highest available quality. Files in .eps format can only be printed at high quality on PostScript printers, such as laser printers, high-end ink-jet poster printers, and commercial imagesetters. All raster files should be 300 ppi to scale, and you should avoid scaling or rotating raster graphics in the page layout program: doing so will cause a loss of resolution and adversely affect the image quality. Using .jpgs for print is not recommended because the format's poor compression algorithm causes quality loss when the file is decompressed and printed. Use .jpgs only for low-resolution output to desktop printers and, of course, for Web and screen design.

Files for print output generated in a raster or vector application and then placed in a page layout program must use the CMYK or spot color (Pantone) color models; RGB color is never used for print output and will cause printer output problems. CMYK or Pantone must also be used for text and other elements (boxes and rules) in the page layout application. Using these color models for print output helps ensure consistent color from the computer to the color proof to the final printed piece.

When you work in a page layout program, the graphics you work with are low-resolution representations used for placement only. When the file prints, the high-resolution originals must be available and in the same location as when they were placed in the page layout program. The files are then called on by the output device (the printer) and printed at a high resolution. Similarly, fonts used in a page layout program file must be available for printing. This means that you must submit the font files from your fonts folder to the print shop or service bureau that is preparing the files for final printing. Otherwise, the fonts you have chosen will not print as expected. InDesign and XPress have packaging features, which package the image and font files, and preflight features, which assess the files for technical accuracy. These help ensure that the needed files, color formats, and font files are available before sending a job to the printer.

Here are some concepts critical to the creation of page layouts:

- Page layout programs such as Adobe InDesign and QuarkXPress are container based; text and images are placed in text and picture frames (InDesign) or boxes (XPress) and are then arranged in a composition.

- It is OK to scale vector images above 100 percent after they are placed in a page layout program; the image will not degrade (i.e., become jagged and lose detail).

- Scaling raster images above 100 percent in page layout programs and digital illustration programs is inadvisable: it causes the images to degrade when output to the screen or to paper. Create images at the size needed for final output (or larger, in case the image needs to be scaled up in the future).

- Print projects are created in CMYK mode or using spot color (Pantone swatches).

- Make sure all image and font files are available and in place before printing. Use the page layout program's preflight and packaging features.

- Avoid rotating images in page layout programs. Instead, rotate them in a raster or vector application, then place them in the proper orientation in the page layout.

- Use .eps and .tif files in page layout programs. Avoid using .jpgs.

- Always create a paper dummy publication to establish physical page sizes, folds, and page sequences.

- Avoid using proprietary Photoshop (.psd) and Illustrator (.ai) files in InDesign. Instead, convert graphics to .eps or .tif format, and then place them in InDesign. Use only placed graphics in Quark Xpress.

- Both Adobe InDesign documents and QuarkXPress documents should be saved in their native formats (.idd and .qxd, respectively). These native files must be accompanied by any graphic and font files when the documents are sent for output.

Page Layout Techniques

This chapter will introduce you to some of the most important techniques for creating digital page layouts. There are hundreds of techniques and commands in page layout programs; this chapter focuses on the ones you need to get started. All of the techniques below are shown in Adobe InDesign, but also apply to other page layout applications, such as QuarkXPress and Adobe PageMaker. Some techniques are not executed identically in the other programs; however, with a bit of exploration, you'll be able to perform the technique in XPress or PageMaker as well. The names of menu commands, tools, panels, and palettes are written in ALL CAPS. Dialog boxes refer to boxes that appear after selecting tools, palettes, or menu items. They provide fine-tuning controls for executing techniques. Most menu items have dialog boxes associated with them.

In print workflows, page layout programs are used for composing and preparing pages and publications for final output. The techniques below are presented in steps with corresponding sample project images that exemplify the techniques.

Explore various combinations of techniques to discover divergent approaches to composition in Adobe InDesign and QuarkXPress. Become comfortable with using text and graphics frames, setting type, using color, and working with multisided and multipage documents. You can test yourself and explore these techniques by creating additional projects guided by the online movie lessons. The corresponding online tutorial video lessons are listed at the end of each technique lesson in this chapter. You can view the online tutorial lesson movies by going to www.wiley.com/go/digitaldesign.

Document Setup

To set up a document in a page layout program, you must create a new document, establish pages, and set guides. The setup of your document should reflect the size and setup of the final piece.

Technique Lesson 7.1: Creating a New Document

The size of a new document should be equivalent to final print size. (This means that you work at the final output size.) For example, for a book jacket that is 8×10″, you would set up a document at the same size.

InDesign has print document presets and also allows you to input a custom page size. You can also set up a book in InDesign. Book setup gives you custom control over page numbering and other long-document features. (The book feature is advanced and is not covered in this text.) As a novice, you need to learn about single- and multiple-page documents first; you can then move on to advanced layout projects for longer documents.

QUICK STEPS:

Creating a New Document with Three Column Guides

1. Go to FILE > NEW DOCUMENT.

2. Choose a preset page size, or input a custom size. Set the number of pages you want. You can add pages later also. Choose an orientation (portrait or landscape).

3. Set the number of columns. Using three columns will provide guides that split the page into thirds. Set the gutter, which is the space between columns (try .125″).

4. Set the margins, which provide a visual boundary to the edge of the page (try .25″).

    Enabling the FACING PAGES check box will create page spreads, which are useful for brochures and booklets. Enabling the MASTER TEXT FRAME check box creates a text frame on the first page that will also appear on subsequent pages you add, allowing you to flow text through the document. Do not enable this text box for documents that require more variation, such as pages with different numbers of frames or frames of different lengths.

    To begin, do not enable the MASTER TEXT FRAME or FACING PAGES check boxes. This will allow you to experiment with different text frames on each page.

5. Click OK.

> **TIP**
>
> Use column grids and margins each time you create a digital layout to establish a three-column page to use during the visual design process.

Your page should be divided into three equal columns.

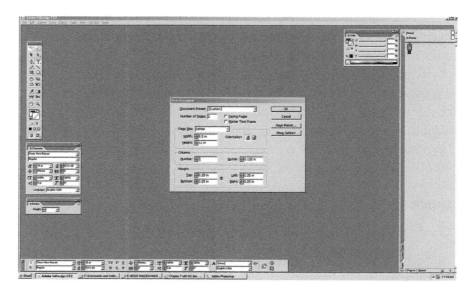

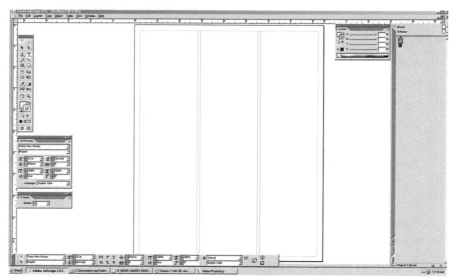

FIGURES 7-1, A, B InDesign's new document window.

Technique Lesson 7.2: Using Pull-Down Guides

In page layout applications, using guides enables the designer to place objects consistently along visual edges and to arrange text and graphics frames more easily.

QUICK STEPS:

Adding Horizontal and Vertical Guides

1. Create a new page.

2. Go to VIEW > SHOW RULERS.

3. Click on either the top (horizontal) ruler or the side (vertical) ruler and drag across the page to set the guide. Use 3.5" sections on an 8.5 x 11" page to make a 3 x 3 grid.

   Guides can be locked or hidden. You can also snap objects to the guides. Go to VIEW > GRIDS & GUIDES to access these options.

> **TIP**
>
> Using grids and guides makes it easier to place text and images on a page with precision. Use them to avoid sloppy compositions.

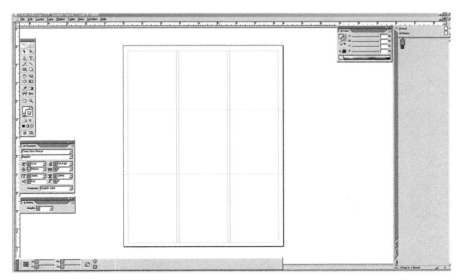

FIGURE 7-2 A three-column grid created by combining column guides with page guides.

Technique Lesson 7.3: Setting Up Document and Baseline Grids

Page layout programs typically have two types of grids: a document grid and a baseline grid. The document grid is like graph paper; it provides a set of horizontal and vertical grid lines that can be used for positioning and aligning objects. The baseline grid represents increments of space between lines of body text. It is usually measured using points, although it can be set up using inches. Using a baseline grid ensures that text in different columns and on different pages always sits on the same baseline.

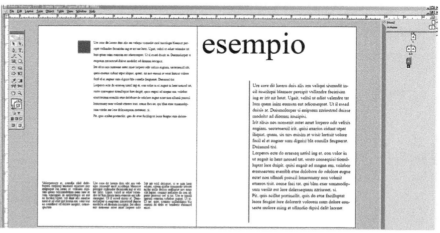

FIGURES 7-3, A, B The baseline grid keeps all text, regardless of its *specified* size and leading, at a consistent leading.

QUICK STEPS:

Changing Baseline Grid Settings

1. Go to EDIT > PREFERENCES > GRIDS (Windows) or APPLE menu > INDE-SIGN PREFERENCES (Macintosh). Set the baseline grid increments in points to create a consistent leading structure. Use the point size of your body text (try 11 point).

2. To view the baseline grid, go to VIEW > GRIDS & GUIDES > SHOW BASE-LINE GRID.

3. Select the text using the TOOL palette's TEXT tool.

4. In the PARAGRAPH panel or CONTROL panel, click the ALIGN TO BASE-LINE GRID icon. This will snap the text to the grid regardless of the leading that is set. You can also align only the first line of a paragraph to the baseline grid, allowing the rest of the lines to follow the specified leading value.

Technique Lesson 7.4: Adding Pages and Master Pages

One of the main strengths of digital page layout applications is their page-based tools. For example, you can add and delete entire pages, and create spreads out of two separate pages. Place an element on a master page, and it will appear on each page of a multipage document. Dragging a master page into the main document automatically creates a new page with the same setup as the master page.

QUICK STEPS:

Adding Single Pages or Facing Pages

1. Create a new document.

2. Go to WINDOW > PAGES. The PAGE palette will display.

You can now add pages in several ways.

3a. The easiest way is to click on the NEW PAGE ICON at the bottom of the palette.

or:

3b. Drag a single blank page (*None*) from the top of the palette into the document area above, below, or next to existing pages.

or:

3c. Use the drop-down menu in the palette and choose INSERT PAGES.

Adding Master Pages

1. Create a new document.

2. Go to WINDOW > PAGES. The PAGE palette opens.

3. Double-click on the *A-Master* master page at the top of the PAGES palette. The page will look the same as page one, but whatever you place on this page will appear on all the other master pages dragged into the document.

4. Using the LINE tool, draw a line on the master page and stroke it with the color red by double clicking the STROKE swatch at the bottom of the TOOL palette. Set the stroke value to 20 point (WINDOW > STROKE).

5. Drag master pages into your main document pages. Master items on a document page have a dotted border. If you cannot view master items on a document page, the master item may be hidden, so choose SHOW MASTER ITEMS from the PAGES palette. You will then see the red line on each master page.

   If you change items on the master page, all the document pages based on that master page will be automatically updated.

   If you want to move, manipulate, or delete a master page item on a document page, go to the drop-down menu in the PAGE palette and choose OVERRIDE ALL MASTER PAGE ITEMS. This will allow you to edit any master page item on that document page.

Adding Auto Page Numbers

1. Create a text frame on a master page and then insert text (the word *page*, for example).

2. Go to TYPE > INSERT SPECIAL CHARACTER > MARKERS > AUTO PAGE NUMBER. This inserts the automatic page number character.

   If your document has facing pages, add text and a page number to both the left and right master pages. Then apply the master pages to the document pages. The pages will now have numbers that update automatically if moved to another place in the document.

TIP

Master pages and page numbers are used in publication design and provide extended functionality for multipage documents. These functions save time and help ensure the consistent placement of standard page elements.

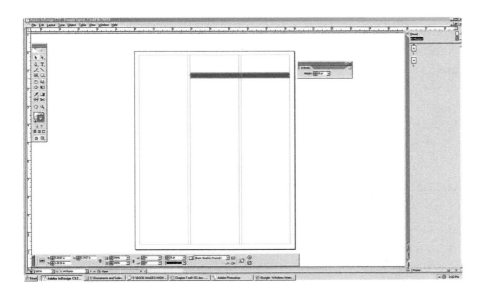

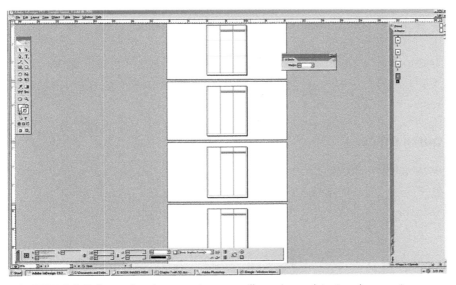

FIGURES 7-4, A, B Items placed on a master page will remain consistent on document pages based on those master pages. Here, the red line is the master page item: all document pages created by dragging that master page into the main document contain that line.

Using Color

In page layout programs, color can be added in three places: to type, to graphic and text frames (fill), and to text and graphic frame outlines (stroke). Always use CMYK or spot color (Pantone) when designing print documents in a page layout program. CMYK and spot (Pantone) colors that are embedded in imported graphics, such as .eps and .tif files, appear automatically in the page layout program's COLOR panel.

Color can be accessed in three ways:

1a. Use the COLOR PICKER at the bottom of the TOOL panel and go to WIN-DOW > COLOR to bring up the SWATCHES panel.

or:

1b. Go to WINDOW > SWATCHES.

or:

1c. Use the COLOR PANEL and go to WINDOW > COLOR.

These options provide RGB, CMYK, and spot color.

 ### Technique Lesson 7.5: Adding Fill and Stroke Color to Frames

Text and graphic frames can be filled and stroked with color and used as shapes, even when they contain text or graphic content.

QUICK STEPS:

Adding Fill or Stroke

1a. Create a text frame on the page by dragging the TEXT tool in the TOOL panel.

or:

1b. Use the RECTANGULAR FRAME tool to drag a box on the document page.

2. Select the frame using the SELECTION tool (black arrow).

3a. Go to COLOR PICKER and double-click the FILL swatch and choose a color. For stroke, double-click the STROKE swatch.

or:

3b. Go to WINDOW > COLOR to display the COLOR panel.

or:

3c. Go to WINDOW > SWATCHES to display the SWATCHES panel.

TIP

Using color for fill and stroke is a vital part of digital design and especially digital page layout, because it allows variance from simply using black text on a white page. Experiment with fill and stroke colors on text and graphic frames to explore visual options.

Under the FILL and STROKE swatches in each COLOR panel area is the FILL CONTAINER button, which applies color to the selected frame. Next to it is the TEXT COLOR tool, represented as a T.

4. Click on the one to which you want to apply the fill, stroke, container, or text.

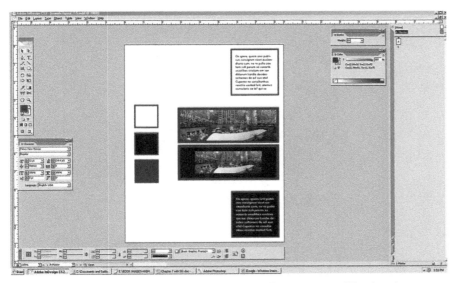

FIGURE 7-5 This document illustrates the various ways that you can use fill and stroke on text and graphic frames. Text with white or "none" background with a stroked frame. A graphic with a stroked frame. A graphic with a stroked frame and color background, and text with a stroked frame and color background.

Technique Lesson 7.6: Setting Stroke Values for Text and Frames

The stroke values for both text and frames can be customized.

QUICK STEPS:

1. Select the frame or text to which you want to add a stroke and choose a stroke color.

2. Go to WINDOW > STROKE. You can manipulate stroke weights, caps, and joins using the STROKE panel.

3. Adjust the weight value to thicken the stroke and manipulate the miter value to change the corner angles.

4. Set the caps of the strokes and the joins for rounded or angled ends.

5. Change the style of the stroke by choosing the type of stroke from the options in the STROKE panel. You can choose from thick, thin, dashed, dotted, wavy, and hashed strokes. You can also modify the color of the stroke and the gap colors in strokes.

FIGURE 7-6 The STROKE panel with its options displayed. The example shows text with strokes and fills as well as stroke types.

Technique Lesson 7.7: Creating and Saving a Process Color

Process color refers to CMYK color—colors made of a combination of cyan, magenta, yellow, and black. When the document is output, it will be printed on a CMYK device. Page layout programs such as InDesign facilitate the access and creation of process color.

QUICK STEPS:

Creating, Saving, and Naming a New Process Color

1. Go to WINDOW > COLOR to display the COLOR panel.

2. If the CMYK sliders are not visible, go to the drop-down menu in the COLOR panel and choose CMYK

3. Use the sliders or the rainbow spectrum to mix a color.

4. Go to WINDOW > SWATCHES to open the SWATCHES panel.

5. Drag the color swatch from the COLOR panel into the SWATCHES panel. (You can also drag a color from the COLOR PICKER.)

6. To name the color, double-click on it in the SWATCHES panel and uncheck the NAME WITH COLOR VALUE check box. Then type in a name for the color.

   You can also use the EYEDROPPER tool to sample a color from anywhere in the document. The sampled color resides in the COLOR PICKER and COLOR panel and can be dragged into the SWATCHES panel, saved, and named.

TIP

Process color is used in all full-color digital page layout projects. Creating new process colors is a way to fully utilize color as a design element.

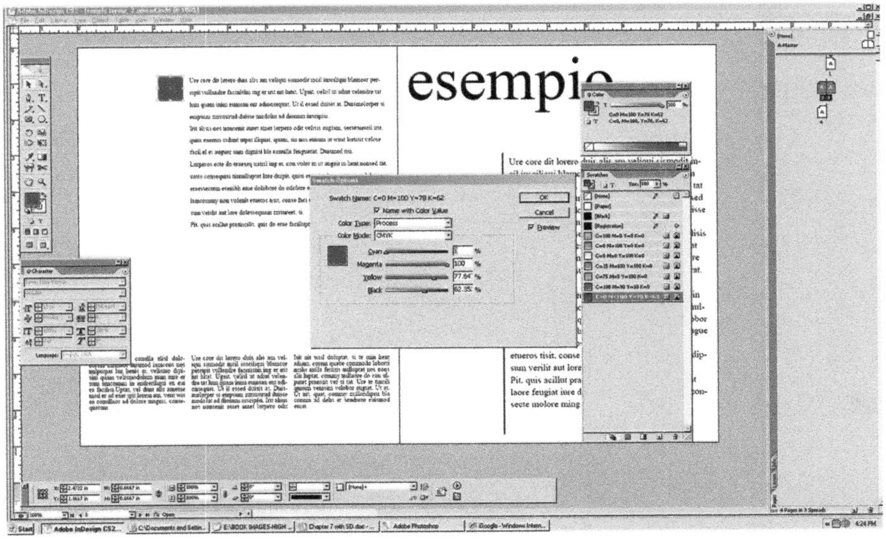

FIGURE 7-7 Create your own process colors by using the COLOR panel or the COLOR PICKER, and then add the color to the SWATCHES panel.

Technique Lesson 7.8: Creating and Saving a Pantone Color

Pantone or spot colors are off-the-shelf, premixed inks that are used instead of, or in addition to, CMYK process inks. Each spot color requires its own printing plate on a printing press.

QUICK STEPS:

Creating and Saving a Spot Color

1. Go to WINDOW > SWATCHES to display the SWATCHES panel.

2. Make a new swatch by clicking on the NEW SWATCH icon at the bottom of the SWATCHES panel.

3. Double-click on the new swatch. Go to COLOR TYPE > SPOT.

4. Then go to COLOR MODE > PANTONE SOLID COATED (for coated stock) or > PANTONE SOLID UNCOATED (for uncoated stock).

5. The swatch book will load. Pick a Pantone color.

   The swatch will appear in the swatches panel with the Pantone name and number.

TIP

Spot color is used when few colors are specified and color accuracy is critical—for logos and other corporate identity pieces such as letterhead and business cards, for example. Spot color is valued because, unlike CMYK color, it is invariable: because it relies on premixed inks, it produces consistent color across multiple projects.

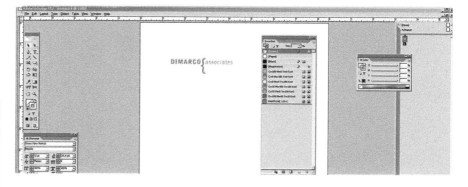

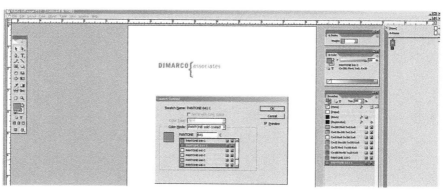

FIGURES 7-8, A, B When you place an .eps graphic from a digital illustration program, the spot colors it contains are added to the COLOR panel automatically. You can also create your own spot colors using the COLOR panel.

Text and Typography

Text and typography are cornerstones of digital page layout. Because page layout tools are built for moving chunks of type around on a page, they provide flexible features for the layout of text (and images) that go beyond those capabilities in illustration and imaging applications.

The three types of applications do, however, share many similar techniques and tools. The typographic panel tools in Adobe InDesign are exactly the same as those in Adobe Illustrator and Adobe Photoshop. The CHARACTER panel, which provides font, leading, kerning, tracking, and baseline shift settings, is identical. The PARAGRAPH panel is also the same, as are many of the other tools in the TOOL palette, such as the PENCIL and PEN.

The CHARACTER panel and the PARAGRAPH panel both have tabbed, floating attribute palettes that can be launched from the WINDOW menu. The features of both panels are also available in the CONTROL panel, which provides access to the attributes of each tool in one convenient, dynamic panel. To open the CONTROL panel, go to WINDOW > CONTROL.

Technique Lesson 7.9: Filling Text Frames with Text

InDesign's TEXT tool is represented on the TOOL palette by a T; select it and drag to create a text frame. Move the cursor inside the text frame, and it will change to a blinking cursor, allowing you to type. To edit the text, highlight it using the TEXT tool, then manipulate its font, size, and so on in the CHARACTER panel.

QUICK STEPS: (ID)

Creating a Text Frame and Filling It with Text

1. Select the TEXT tool from the TOOL palette.

2. Drag a text frame on the document page. Adjust its size with the SELECTION tool.

3. Click inside the text frame and the cursor will become a blinking cursor; begin to type.

4. Adjust the text frame by grabbing and dragging the frame's handles.

5. A red + at the edge of the text frame means there is more text inside the text frame than there is room to display. Widen or lengthen the frame to accommodate the additional text, if necessary.

Although designers prefer to have all of the text and graphics they need for a composition *before* creating a digital page layout, this is not always possible (and last-minute changes to text and graphics are common). In such situations, text frames can be filled with placeholder text (also known as Greek text): paragraphs of words in Latin (so it is never confused with live text). The placeholder text can then be styled, showing the designer what the live text will ultimately look like and allowing the composition to be developed even before the live text is available.

Filling a Text Frame with Placeholder Text

1. Select the TEXT tool from the TOOL palette.

2. Drag a text frame on the document page.

3. Click on the blinking cursor and go to TYPE > FILL WITH PLACEHOLDER TEXT.

   A red + at the edge of the text frame means there is more text inside the text frame than there is room to display.

Flowing Text into Another Frame

1. Click on the red + with the SELECTION tool.

2. Click and drag another text frame.

   The overflow text from the first frame will flow into the new frame. The link between the two frames is now interactive: adjusting the size of one frame (by grabbing and dragging the frame handles) will affect how the text sets in both frames.

TIP

Flowing text onto a page is one of the most common operations performed in a digital page layout application. Filling your page with placeholder text allows you to set up your text frames and master pages before the live copy is available.

FIGURE 7-9 Layout with placeholder text.

Technique Lesson 7.10: Adding Color to Text

QUICK STEPS:

Adding Color to Text

1. Create a text frame using the TOOL palette's TEXT tool.

2. Type in or copy and paste text from another program into the text frame. Or you can use FILE> PLACE to import text from a word processing application such as Microsoft Word.

3a. Go to WINDOW > COLOR to display the COLOR panel.

or:

3b. Go to WINDOW > SWATCHES to display the SWATCHES panel.

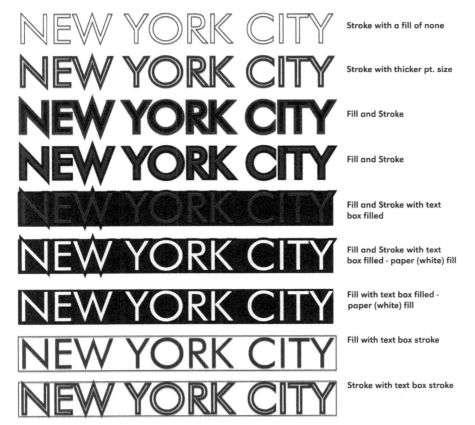

Stroke with a fill of none

Stroke with thicker pt. size

Fill and Stroke

Fill and Stroke

Fill and Stroke with text box filled

Fill and Stroke with text box filled - paper (white) fill

Fill with text box filled - paper (white) fill

Fill with text box stroke

Stroke with text box stroke

FIGURE 7-10 Variations of text with different stroke and fill values.

TIP

Adding color to
text and text stroke
adds variety to
typefaces and can
enhance or dimin-
ish the dominance
of a particular block
of text.

4. Highlight the text using the TEXT tool.

5. Next to the FILL CONTAINER button in each COLOR panel is the FILL TEXT COLOR button, which is represented as a T in the SWATCHES and COLOR panels. Click the FILL TEXT COLOR button.

The text will be changed to the selected color.

You can also add color to the stroke of text by selecting a range of text and clicking the STROKE COLOR button.

Technique Lesson 7.11: Adding Bleeds to a Layout

In print layout and digital page design, the term *bleed* refers to objects that extend (bleed) beyond the trimmed page. After the page is trimmed, these objects go right to the edge of the page, creating the "bleed."

Desktop printers and printing presses cannot print to the edge of a sheet of paper: there is typically a small area needed for a gripper, which the printer rollers use to grip and pull the paper through the device. Therefore, if the final output uses a bleed, the document size must be set smaller than the paper size so that there is room to extend the bleed and trim the paper.

You can set bleeds in a document by simply extending graphic and text frames off the page by at least 1/8". You can even set manual guidelines on the pasteboard, outside of the document's boundaries. In InDesign, you can also use the BLEED MARGIN feature in the NEW DOCUMENT window to set up margins outside of the page, which then give you a visual guide to which to extend frames.

QUICK STEPS:

Setting Up Bleed Marks in a New Document

1. Go to FILE > NEW DOCUMENT.

2. Create your document specifications at least 1/2" smaller than the paper size. For example, if the paper size is 8.5 x 11" (letter size), create the document at 8 × 10". This will allow for a bleed and trim area.

3. At the bottom of the NEW DOCUMENT window is an area titled BLEED AND SLUG.

4. Insert *.125* in the BLEED fields to create a 1/8" bleed margin around the document. Clicking on the CHAIN LINK icon at the end of the insertion fields sets

the numbers in all the fields to all the same value. The bleed margin is represented by red lines.

5. Extend frames with images beyond the page margin into the bleed margin.

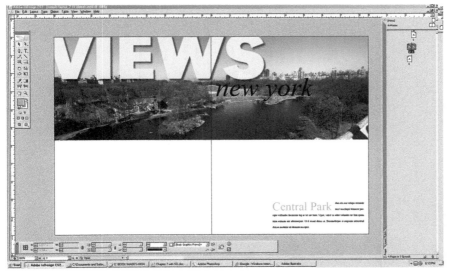

FIGURES 7-11, A, B Bleeds must be extended at least a ¹⁄₁₆″ beyond the live page area (more is better) to allow a commercial printing press to cut them accurately. This layout shows top and side bleeds for text and graphics.

TIP
Bleeds create the appearance that images and text are actually coming off the page, enhancing the level of visual intrigue and completely changing the gestalt and impact of a page layout. The effect becomes very obvious when used with tightly cropped photographs. Bleeds are used extensively in all kinds of design pieces, including magazine covers and spreads, book covers, print advertisements in newspapers and magazines, brochures, and postcards.

Technique Lesson 7.12: Setting Character Attributes

The CHARACTER palette and setting attributes are the same in InDesign, Photoshop, and Illustrator. The main functions include font, size, leading, kerning, tracking, and baseline shift (see page 76 for descriptions). Although horizontal and vertical scaling and skew functions also exist, avoid them unless their use is truly justifiable, because they distort the true letterforms of type.

QUICK STEPS:

Setting Character Attributes Using the Character Panel.

1. Create a text frame using the TOOL palette's TEXT tool.

2. Type or insert text.

3. Highlight the text you want to change and go to WINDOW > TYPE and TABLES > CHARACTER to open the CHARACTER palette At the top of the window, you can also toggle back and forth between character and paragraph attributes.

4. Change the settings for the attributes.

TIP

Digital designers spend a lot of time setting the character attributes of type. Become comfortable with manipulating text attributes by looking at typography all around you and by experimenting with attributes; your goal is to create unity and clear communication through letters and words.

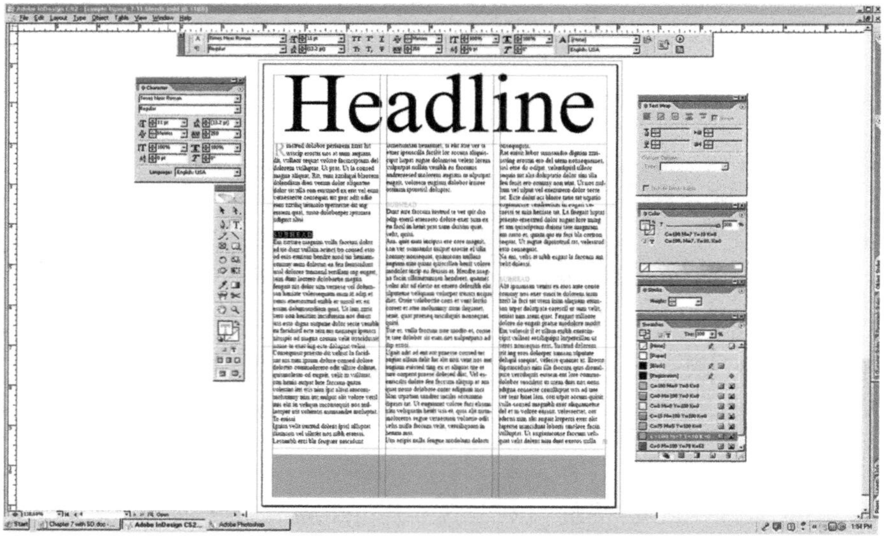

FIGURE 7-12 Use the CHARACTER palette or the character controls on the CONTROL panel to set typographic attributes such as typeface, point size, leading, kerning, and tracking.

Helpful Tips

- Use the CONTROL panel docked at the top (or bottom) of the document window to access all character and paragraph attributes.

- Keep body copy size between 7 and 11 point.

- Do not kern body copy; only kern type 24 point and larger.

- Avoid using horizontal and vertical scaling or skew, unless its use is justified by the design.

- Know the default values for each attribute (for example, 0 is the default value for kerning). Attributes do not reset themselves, so be wary when you create the next block of text: it will carry the previous block's attribute settings. If the type looks odd, reset its attributes to their default values.

Technique Lesson 7.13: Formatting Paragraph Attributes

Digital page layout programs such as InDesign and QuarkXPress have robust paragraph formatting tools that provide precise control over attributes such as spacing before and after paragraphs, indentation, alignment, drop caps, justification, bullets and numbering, columns, and baseline grid alignment.

In digital page layout, the end of a paragraph is represented by a paragraph marker, created by pressing the ENTER key. A paragraph, in typesetting terms, is physical space, and does not necessarily need to have any characters or words in it: when you press the ENTER key, you create vertical space in the document. You can also create vertical space by adding space before or space after a paragraph. Space is created on the right and left sides of the document by using indents and tabs.

Manipulating paragraphs is all about manipulating space on the page in relationship to the text. Paragraph formatting affects selected paragraphs only. Select the text frame, however, and the entire block of text within the frame is affected.

To see the paragraph markers in your text, go to TYPE > SHOW HIDDEN CHARACTERS. This will help you select the paragraphs that you want to format.

QUICK STEPS:

Alignment

Alignment can be horizontal or vertical. It is used to line up text within a text frame, so it is affected by the size and proportions of the frame itself.

Text can be aligned flush left or flush right, justified, or centered. Aligning left or right lines the paragraph flush to the left or right edge of the frame. (Flush left text is most common.) Center alignment centers the text within the frame. Use centering cautiously: it can detract from a design if it creates tension with other elements. Text can also be justified, with the last line aligned to the left or right, or centered. The last line can be force justified as well.

Horizontal Alignment

1. Highlight the text.
2. Go to WINDOW > TYPE and TABLES > PARAGRAPH.
3. Select HORIZONTAL ALIGNMENT.

Vertical Alignment

To affect the vertical alignment (or vertical justification):

1. Select the text frame with the SELECTION tool.
2. Right-click the mouse button, and go to TEXT FRAME OPTIONS (or type CTRL + B) > VERTICAL JUSTIFICATION.
3. Select TOP, CENTER, BOTTOM, or JUSTIFY.

   These selections will align the text vertically with the top of the frame, center it in the frame top to bottom, align the text with the bottom of the frame, or justify the text from top to bottom in the frame, respectively.

Columns

Text can be spread across multiple columns; shorter line lengths make it easier for the reader to absorb. You can set up two, three, four, or more columns per spread. When columns are set, they are spread across the text frame and separated by a gutter value, which you can control using the CONTROL panel.

1. Select the text or the text frame.
2. Open the CONTROL panel.
3. Set the number of columns using the COLUMNS icon at the right side of the CONTROL panel.

Indentation

Indents can be used to place space at the left or right edge of an entire paragraph; they can also be set to affect only the first line or last line of a paragraph.

1. Highlight the paragraph you want to format or select the frame to apply the formatting to the entire text block.

2. Go to WINDOW > TYPE and TABLES > PARAGRAPH.

3. Select an INDENTATION and place a value in the field. This will move the paragraph from the edge of the text frame.

Space Before and Space After

Placing space before and after paragraphs using the ENTER key to create extra paragraph markers is sloppy and often does not position the type precisely. A constant value for space before and after paragraphs can, however, be set using the SPACE BEFORE and SPACE AFTER commands.

1. Highlight the paragraph you want to format or select the frame to apply the formatting to the entire text block.

2. Go to WINDOW > TYPE and TABLES > PARAGRAPH.

3. Select SPACE BEFORE or SPACE AFTER paragraph options and place a value in the field. This will increase or decrease space.

Drop Caps

Drop caps are large capital letters that descend into (or sometimes rise several lines above) the body of the text. You must specify the number of lines of text the drop caps will displace, and the number of characters that will be set as drop caps (one is typical, but it is possible to set more).

1. Highlight the paragraph you want to format or select the frame to apply the formatting to the entire text block.

2. Go to WINDOW > TYPE and TABLES > PARAGRAPH.

3. Set the number of lines the drop cap(s) will descend into the text.

4. Set the number of characters (one or more) that will become drop caps.

Bullets and Numbering

You can use automatic settings to apply bullets and numbering to paragraphs.

1. Highlight the paragraph you want to format or select the frame to apply the formatting to the entire text block.

2. Go to WINDOW > TYPE and TABLES > PARAGRAPH.

3. Select the drop-down menu in the PARAGRAPH palette and choose BULLETS and NUMBERING.

4. Select either bullets or numbering and the bullet character or numbering style you want to use.

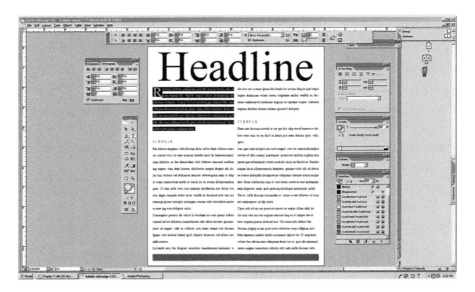

FIGURES 7-13, A, B Use the PARAGRAPH panel or the paragraph controls on the CONTROL panel to set paragraph attributes such as alignment, indents, space before and after, drop caps, columns, and align to baseline grid. Highlight an entire paragraph or text within a paragraph to apply these attributes to that paragraph. The SHOW HIDDEN CHARACTERS command will display hidden paragraph markers, making it easier to see where paragraphs begin and end.

Technique Lesson 7.14: Using Character and Paragraph Styles

Styles are preset formats that you create to help ensure consistency in the styling of characters and paragraphs. Character and paragraph styles allow you to set all the attributes for characters (font, size, leading, etc.) or paragraphs (indents, spacing, alignment, etc.) as a group. If you change one or more of the style attributes within that group, any text with that style attached to it will be automatically updated to reflect the change.

QUICK STEPS:

Adding a Character Style

1. Create a text frame and add text. Select the text and apply various character attributes using the CHARACTER panel.

2. Go to WINDOW > TYPE & TABLES > CHARACTER STYLE.

   The CHARACTER STYLE panel will appear.

3. Go to the drop-down menu in the CHARACTER STYLE panel and choose NEW CHARACTER STYLE.

4. The CHARACTER STYLE dialog box will appear. Name the new style and adjust the character formats and color, if necessary.

5. Click OK to close the dialog box.

   The style name will appear in the character style panel.

6. To apply the style, highlight a range of text and double-click on the style name in the CHARACTER STYLE panel.

Adding a Paragraph Style

1. Go to WINDOW > TYPE & TABLES > PARAGRAPH STYLE.

   This will display the PARAGRAPH STYLE panel.

2. Repeat the same steps for setting a character style, but create a new paragraph style and set paragraph formatting attributes instead. You can set character attributes in a paragraph style, too.

TIP

Styles are used to help ensure consistency and to save time when typesetting multi-page documents.

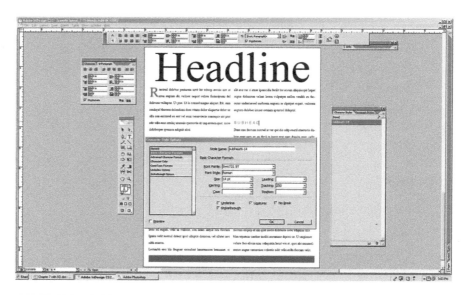

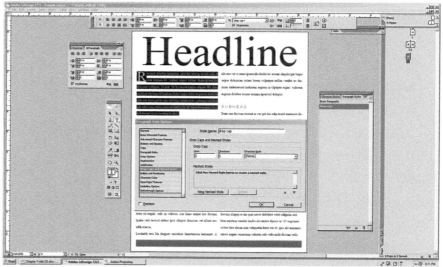

FIGURES 7-14, A, B Set text to the desired attributes and then create a new style based on those attributes. Character and paragraph styles then provide the ability to set text attributes with one highlight and one click. Character and paragraph styles are, therefore, time-saving ways to help ensure typographic consistency.

Working with Images

Images are placed inside rectangular, elliptical, or polygonal frames. The most frequently used frames for raster or vector graphics are rectangular. The graphic frame (blue box) is used to crop the image area by using the frame handles to resize the frame around the image, which can also hide a portion of the image. You can also crop the image by moving it around in the graphic frame by using the DIRECT SELECTION tool (white arrow) or the POSITION SELECTION tool (hand with a crop icon). You can also add color to the inside or to the stroke of a graphic frame. Once an image is inside a frame, you can move it around, center it, scale it, or fit it to the frame's boundaries.

Technique Lesson 7.15: Placing Graphics

Graphics are placed on a page in InDesign using graphic frames (and using picture boxes in QuarkXPress). A graphic is inserted into the frame; the frame acts only as a container that controls the position and size of the graphic. Only one graphic can occupy a frame.

There are three main image types that can be placed inside graphic frames (or boxes): .tif, .eps, and (for low-resolution output only) .jpg. All images get placed in the application as low-resolution placeholders, with the original image residing in a folder on the hard drive. This helps speed page scrolling, especially in large, multipage documents.

The designer must collect the images and make sure that they are available when the page layout file is printed. (The same is true for font files.) You can use InDesign's PACKAGE feature (FILE > PACKAGE) to collect all the needed files for final output, or you can collect the font and image files manually, like digital designers used to before preflighting functionality was integrated into page layout software.

You can scale raster graphics (.tif and .eps bitmaps)—which are typically photographs—in page layout programs, but only up to 5 percent over their original size (105 percent); scaling raster graphics any larger will distort the image when it is printed at high resolution. You can scale images downward to any size that is visibly legible when it is printed. There is no resolution loss for downward scaled images. Raster images should always be created at the size they will be used for final output. Vector files (.eps files) can be placed and scaled to any size without a loss of quality.

QUICK STEPS:

Placing and Fitting a Graphic into a Frame

1. Create a rectangular graphic frame using the RECTANGULAR FRAME tool in the TOOL panel on the document page. Make sure the frame is sized to accommodate the graphic you want to place.

2. Go to FILE > PLACE (CTRL + D for Win and CMD +D for Mac) and navigate to where your graphic file resides.

3. After the image is placed, fit the frame to the image size by going to OBJECT > FITTING > FIT FRAME TO CONTENT.

Moving and Scaling Images in a Frame

In InDesign, the image inside the frame has a brown boundary around it. You must move the image inside the frame to position it, or use a fitting command (see below). In QuarkXPress, you use the HAND tool to move the image around the picture box.

1. Move or resize a frame using the SELECTION tool (black arrow).

2. Move or resize an image inside of a frame using the DIRECT SELECTION tool (white arrow). You will see a brown boundary inside the blue graphic frame. The brown boundary can be moved and scaled to manipulate the image inside the graphic frame. Hold down the SHIFT key when scaling to maintain the image's proportions.

Fitting a Frame to an Image

1. After an image is placed, fit the frame to the image size by going to OBJECT > FITTING > FIT FRAME TO CONTENT.

Centering an Image within a Frame

1. After the image is placed, center the image in the frame by going to OBJECT > FITTING > CENTER CONTENT.

Fitting an Image within a Frame Proportionally

1. After an image is placed, fit the image in the frame at its proper aspect ratio by going to OBJECT > FITTING > FIT CONTENT PROPORTIONALLY.

Filling the Frame with the Image Proportionally

1. After the image is placed, fill the frame with the image at its proper aspect ratio by going to OBJECT > FITTING > FILL FRAME PROPORTIONALLY.

Tracking Images with the Links Panel

The LINKS panel provides a list of images that have been placed in a document. Images must be located where they are listed in the LINKS panel. If you move an image from one folder to another on your computer or a fileserver, the LINKS panel will display an exclamation point inside a triangle to alert you. You must relink the image to the document. You do this by double clicking on the image name in the LINKS panel and then click the RELINK button at the bottom of the window. Locate and select the graphic file on your computer and then click DONE.

TIP

Use these fitting options whenever you place an image. Never use FIT CONTENT TO FRAME because it disregards the image's original proportions.

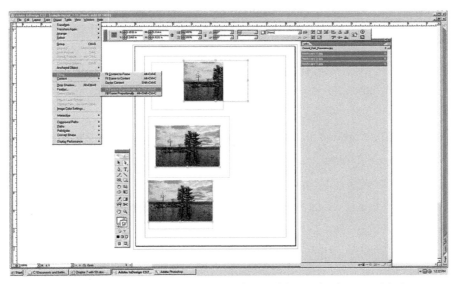

FIGURE 7-15 Placing graphics requires the manipulation of the graphic frame and the image inside of it using the fitting tools or the selection tools.

Technique Lesson 7.16: Text Wraps and Clipping Paths

Text can be wrapped around a frame or a graphic. To wrap text around a graphic, the image must be on a white background or it must contain a clipping path, as discussed in chapter 5 (page 185).

QUICK STEPS:

Wrapping Text around a Frame

1. Create a text frame and insert text—either placeholder text or your own.

2. Create a rectangular or elliptical frame and place it on top of the text frame.

3. Place an image inside the frame or add color.

4. Go to WINDOW > TEXT WRAP.

   The TEXT WRAP panel will appear.

5. Select the icon for WRAP AROUND BOUNDING BOX (second icon). The text will wrap around the frame. As the frame is resized, the text wrap will conform. You can add offset space by adding space (in inches) in the top, bottom, right, and left offset fields. Inputting space values in these fields will move the text closer or further from the image.

Wrapping Text around an Image with a White Background or a Clipping Path

TIP

Text wraps are an integral part of print design, and especially publication design. Use the technique when you have large blocks of text or text across columns. In most cases, text wraps are used when there is a fair amount of text.

1. Create a text frame and insert text—either placeholder text or your own.

2. Create a rectangular or elliptical frame and place it on top of the text frame.

3. Place an image with a white background or a clipping path.

4. Go to WINDOW > TEXT WRAP.

   The TEXT WRAP palette will appear.

5. Select the icon for WRAP AROUND OBJECT SHAPE (third icon from the right side of the palette).

6a. The text will wrap around the object if it has a clipping path; if so, choose CONTOUR OPTIONS > SAME AS CLIPPING.

6b. If the image is on a white background, InDesign can detect the edges of the image for the text wrap. Choose CONTOUR OPTIONS > DETECT EDGES.

7. Select the graphic frame with the image in it and go to OBJECT > ARRANGE > SEND TO BACK. The image frame needs to be in the back for text wraps with clipping paths or edge detection.

You can add offset space around the top, bottom, and sides of the frame by inputting numeric values into the top, bottom, left, and right offset fields.

(A)

(B)

FIGURES 7-16, A–F
Here text wraps are applied to a frame and to a clipping path. Then a final revision to the layout yields justified alignment and a better photograph.

(C)

(D)

(E)

(F)

FIGURES 7-16, D–F

Design Assignment

Create a full-page magazine advertisement using the Ayers No. 1 layout style (see below), placeholder text, one dominant visual element, and a bleed.

Tools: Page layout software and one digital image.

Specs: Imagine you are the graphic artist hired to create a full-page (8 × 10″) magazine ad for a local event. Before you create the ad, do the proper planning and conceptualization techniques (refer to chapter 3). Shoot or find a royalty-free electronic photo and use it in your design, or create an image using Photoshop or Illustrator. Experiment with bleeds. Utilize the Ayers No. 1 layout or the Inverted Ayers layout (see Figures 7-17, C–D) consisting of a picture, a headline (24 point or above), an 8-to-11-point block of copy (use placeholder text to represent the ad copy), and an advertiser's logo. (Either download one from www.brandsoftheworld.com for treatment purposes or create your own.)

(B)   (C)

FIGURES 7-17, A–D The classic Ayers No. 1 layout (A, B) uses a simple form to unify an image, headline, body copy, and logo in a composition. An inverted Ayers No. 1 (C, D) places the headline and text at the top of the composition.

FIGURE 7-17D

Advanced design assignments are available at the book's Web site: www.wiley.com/go/digitaldesign.

Online Movie Lessons

Tutorial walk-through movies for technique lessons are provided online. Each section contains step-by-step tutorial movies available at the book's Web site: www.wiley.com/go/digitaldesign.

Bibliography

Muir, Peter. 2000. *Preflight: Avoiding costly printout problems through proper file preparation.* San Diego, CA: Windsor Professional Information.

White, Alex W. 2007. *Advertising design and typography.* New York: Allworth.

CHAPTER 8
Web Site Design and Development

The Internet is a network of interconnected computers that serve up Web sites to people who have Internet access via dial-up (telephone-based) or broadband (DSL- and cable-based) connections. A Web site is a collection of Web pages that resides on a server connected to the Internet. To post a Web site you have created to the Internet, you need a Web address (a domain) and server space (a host). Regardless of the communication goals, specific tools, or technical specifications involved, there are two main stages to creating a Web site: design and development (authoring).

A Web page is a collection of media elements that resides in a programmable page framework such as .html or .php, which is recognized by http (hypertext transfer protocol) in Web browser software such as Internet Explorer, Firefox, or Safari. As a unit of design, a Web page consists of a Web screen, a term used because Web pages are presented on screen, not on paper. Web screens hold the graphical components of Web pages and must be designed and built using digital tools.

Acting as Web designers—not programmers—we create screen designs in Adobe Photoshop, Adobe Fireworks, or even Adobe Illustrator to establish the visual look and feel of the Web pages and Web site. Web page design must precede any Web development, or programming. Acting as Web developers, we use Web development software such as Adobe Dreamweaver to add structure and functionality to Web pages in the form of text items, links, rollovers, e-mail, and JavaScript (for added functionality).

Web page screens can be designed in any image editing program that optimizes and exports HTML Web pages. These screens can then be sliced, allowing entire pages to be cut up into individual graphics and sections. Sliced pages can then be exported into Web page layouts and individual graphical elements. Using image editing applications such as Photoshop and Fireworks to create Web screens provides to the option to design freely with type and graphics, as well as an accurate view of the Web page's ultimate size and color, instead of creating a page in a web page application and inserting the graphic content. Editing Web graphics is facilitated by creating Web screens composed of layers. After still graphics, motion graphics, and other multimedia components are created using various applications, Adobe Dreamweaver is used to create the receptacle pages—a Web site—that hold all those individual elements. A Web site is a dynamic digital design project that consists of multiple pages, connected through hyperlinks, that contain content in the form of images, text, motion graphics, animations, audio, and digital video.

Working through a project that has a definable product is the best way to learn about Web design. In this chapter, you will create a personal Web site that provides evidence of your skills and expertise in the form of artifacts (i.e., your photos, professional documents, artwork, audio, videos, and animations) from any discipline or field. Your Web portfolio will allow you to promote yourself, your skills, and your experience in a Web-based format—something all designers working today should be able to do.

Designing Web sites requires attention to technical as well as visual issues: technical and visual problems result in usability problems. Provide clear navigational aids for users through the consistent use of icons, typefaces, colors, and graphic styles in order to provide a transparent and intuitive site interface. Simplicity becomes a priority when designing for the Web. The interface shouldn't be a monster of complexity—for you or the user. Test your site to ensure that you have eliminated confusing, dead-end pages. Don't take navigation for granted: it needs to be well thought out. Otherwise, users will get lost—as will the message being communicated. Ensure that each page contains links to home, contact, and top-level pages, which are primary navigation elements that include the most critical links on the Web site. (Secondary navigation—links needed for pages that lie below the main level of the Web site—are referred to as subpages.) And always offer direct access to the information users want most. Provide a top-down structure that offers the most important items at the main level and branches down to lower, less important levels of content.

Creating a Web Site

You need to execute both design and development tasks to create a Web site:

Web Design Tasks

- Conceptualization
- Creation of a content list
- Creation of a content outline
- Creation of a three- to four-column script
- Creation of a flowchart
- Creation of rough storyboards
- Collection of content items

- Development of Web screens
- Slicing of Web screens
- Exporting sliced screens into HTML pages and .gif and .jpg graphics
- Exporting solo graphics to the images folder

Web Development Tasks

- Adding Web functionality to Web pages using hand coding or WYSIWIG software such as Dreamweaver

Specifically you will need to add or edit some or all of the following items:

- Navigation links
- Color
- Page titles
- Web text
- Pop-up windows
- Secondary navigation
- Functionality buttons (e.g., window close, sound off, etc.)
- E-mail links
- Content item updates (adding and removing graphics and multimedia components)

The Design and Development Process

Broadly speaking, the steps for creating a Web site are the same as those used to design any communication project. The seven-step design process presented below is a guide to solving the communication problem of developing your personal Web portfolio.

Step 1: Identify, Research, and Target

Complete the following sentence: "This Web portfolio promotes me as a _____." Fill in the blank in the way that best suits you. For now, let's assume you've filled it in with the words *digital designer and photographer*.

This is when you get a handle on what you need to accomplish and what you should focus on as the project evolves. First you need to identify, research, and target your prospective audience by brainstorming some of the important pieces you'll need for the Web products you plan to create. Prepare a written concept statement that defines the goals, audience, concept, message, images, style, and theme (or GACMIST) of the Web portfolio. Next, research Web portfolios in your discipline and others to determine possible categories of artifacts (i.e., your works) and visual themes.

Step 2: Conceptualize

This involves planning the site on paper.

Develop a content list: Write a loose list of projects you want to include in the Web site. Be specific and name each work descriptively (i.e., four-color brochure for the XYZ Co.).

Create a content outline: Write a detailed outline of all the pieces that will be included in the Web site, with categories (menu items) that group each item appropriately. Categories should be exclusive of each other.

Gather your work: Find the digital files for the projects in your content outline, or scan or photograph work that exists only as hard copies. Keep the presentation style of the individual projects consistent (don't mix digital graphic samples of brochures with photographs of brochures, for example).

Write descriptions of your work: These descriptions or captions for each project need not be long; they should simply provide a consistent set of information for each project. So if you decide to use the date and media type to describe your work, that information should appear in each caption.

Step 3: Information Design

The hierarchical presentation of information is the most important aspect of site structure. Just as a programmer uses pseudocode, a filmmaker writes a shot list, and a painter makes a paper sketch, Web developers must map out their projects. The flowchart is that map—or skeleton.

You are now ready to take the pieces in the content outline and place them into a three-column script, which segments the page name and number and lists the text, images, audio, video, and links by individual page. A flowchart can then be created to provide a visual skeleton of the Web pages and the various content pieces needed to fill those pages. The flowchart also serves as a visual pathway for identifying the navigation within the Web site and revealing the page and content count of the entire site.

Information design provides a data structure crucial to Web development. Navigation, usability, and organization are interconnected components that work together to create a successful site structure. When creating the flowchart, use boxes to depict pages and lines to depict connected links. List the content items needed for each page in the margins. When the flowchart is complete, you will be able to accurately assess the Web site's page count.

NAVIGATION

Navigation is steering for the user. Navigation systems are essential to the visual representation of information on a Web site and include buttons (also known as links); these allow the user access to the site's content. The user will navigate your Web site in search of content—and hopefully have a positive experience along the way. Navigation should be simplified to provide seamless usability and communicate a functional hierarchy—an understandable top-down structure. As the designer, it's your job to provide clear, direct navigation to your Web site's content.

Navigation consists of main and secondary (sub) categories. The main categories (topics) of the site hold the pathways to the secondary categories, or subtopics. Subcategories include your content (resume, project samples, etc.). Minimization is critical when developing navigation: design Web page navigation that minimizes user travel by creating the simplest and shortest path between any two points. Minimize depth by creating a hierarchy with the fewest possible levels: extra levels mean extra travel steps in the quest for information. Finally, minimize redundancy, eliminating multiple paths to the same place from the same screen, which can cause confusion about which path to use.

Step 4: Visual Design

This is when you begin to sketch out ideas for Web page layouts and the location of navigation and content items. These sketches can be very rough, using boxes and lines to represent items on the page. (Develop your Web portfolio site screens using a sketch pad before using Photoshop or Fireworks.) The goal is to recognize and fortify page layouts with regard to consistency, usability, and visual value.

Here are the basic components that you should include in your storyboards:

- **Image location** (relative to the page)

- **Text:** Where will it go?
- **Motion graphic or animation location:** How will media spots launch—within the page or from a pop-up window?
- **Navigation and subnavigation:** What guides the user to each page?
- **Pop-up windows with subnavigation:** If there is pop-up content, what will the windows look like?
- **Captions and close buttons:** Are your content items explained clearly and does the user have the functions needed to bypass them?
- **Controls for any audio track or sounds:** Will there be audio? If so, how is it accessed?

Step 5: Web Page Design

You now begin to work in either Photoshop or Fireworks to create Web page designs. Design at 72 ppi and create you home page and top-level pages—those accessed by the main navigation buttons. Print out the Web pages and use the paper prototypes to analyze (usability test) the design decisions that you made and to justify each component that fills the screen. Use FILE > SAVE AS to create copies that can be updated to reflect different elements but maintain items that require consistent positioning, such as navigation buttons and logos.

HTML AND GRAPHICAL TEXT

Two types of text can occupy a Web page: graphical and HTML (or browser-based) text. Web pages are typically designed with a combination of the two. HTML text, which is controlled through CSS (cascading style sheets), is plain text that can be typed into a Web page in Dreamweaver. It is easily edited, and consistent text and paragraph attributes can be structured using CSS. HTML text is used when there are large blocks of text and for navigation text, paragraph text, and scrollable text. Using HTML text limits you to the browser's font set on both Windows and Macintosh computers: Arial, Courier, Geneva, Georgia, Helvetica, Times, Times New Roman, and Verdana.

Graphical text is an image of type, but that text is not editable. It is used for page headings, navigation, and type used as an image. The best sites utilize both HTML text and graphical text.

TIP

I prefer to start off by designing in Photoshop because it gives me the most options and freedom to design. I then open the layered .psd file in Fireworks to slice and optimize the files and export them to HTML pages. Although Photoshop (and Illustrator) have slicing and optimizing tools, I prefer using Fireworks for these tasks.

When designing Web page screens, think about the basic components that you will need to place in the Web page (HTML text, videos, images, etc.), begin to design the graphics and layout of your Web pages, and leave space for page components that will be inserted later in Dreamweaver. For example, in the body of the page, you might leave room for a paragraph of HTML text or a spot for a Flash video. Later, in Adobe Dreamweaver, you could insert these components into the page using AP div tags (AP stands for "absolutely positioned," and divs, or divisions, are Dreamweaver's version of layers).

Only graphical text should be designed into the screens in the image editing application. Any text that needs to be edited or searched should be HTML based and inserted into the page *after* the screen design is created and optimized for the Web. (Use placeholder text to fill the areas where HTML text will ultimately be placed.)

Step 6: Slicing, Optimizing, and Exporting

The page must now be sliced into a table and individual graphics. Fireworks' SLICE tool is used to portion the Web page design residing in the digital imaging program into individual graphics, which are then set inside an HTML based table or an AP div layer. The table or AP div layer will contain cells with the sliced graphics. Optimization is setting the color mode (RGB or index) for the graphic and assigning the proper file format (.jpg or .gif) for the sliced image. Exporting refers to saving the sliced digital imaging document as an HTML page and also saving the individual slices as .jpgs or .gifs. This is the way designers create Web pages.

You can also create a Web page from scratch in Dreamweaver, using AP divs (layers) and tables to position elements freely in an environment not unlike that of a word processor. You can even create a Web page from scratch using HTML code. (This is the way programmers create Web pages.)

This book takes a hybrid approach to Web design. Using digital imaging programs such as Photoshop and Fireworks provides a graphical environment (as opposed to a Web application or programming environment) for the initial design stage. Once the pages and graphics are designed, Web development tools such as Dreamweaver are used to add functionality to the Web pages and to upload them to the Internet.

Step 7: Web Page Development

This phase, also known as authoring, is when you begin to work in Dream-weaver to add functionality to your Web pages. The screens you created in Fireworks become Web pages by being sliced, optimized, and exported into HTML tables or AP div layers using Adobe Fireworks. The resulting Web pages with tables or layers are opened in Dreamweaver. Tables can then be converted to layers, or kept as tables and vice versa. You can slice and export a page as AP divs directly from Fireworks if you want to avoid table conversions.

When you use tables, the cells hold all the graphics, which are named by default with the file name plus the suffix *r1_c1* in sequence, representing the row and column location of the graphic in the table (which was made by the slices). With AP div layers, the individual layer boxes contain the sliced graphics using the file name plus suffix convention also. More tables or layers are added for text elements. To add more content, use AP div layers, which float on top of the page; such layers can be positioned easily. Tables, on the other hand, which encompass the entire contents of a Web page, may need editing in HTML, which can be difficult for designers without coding experience.

Dreamweaver provides many different techniques for adding functionality to Web pages. Those discussed below are the most crucial for beginners—and the ones you'll need to get your Web site up and running. They include setting links, rollovers, adding HTML text, adding image and multimedia content to pages, editing CSS, creating AP divs, making tables, and creating pop-up windows.

Step 8: Uploading and Testing Site Pages

Your Web site pages must be uploaded to a server using either Dreamweaver (or another Web authoring program) or FTPed through a browser (or FTP application like Fetch). FTP, or file transfer protocol, is a fast method for transferring files to from one computer to another, such as a Web server.

When setting up your Web site locally, you create a folder that contains all the HTML pages and a subfolder that holds all the graphic and multimedia files that occupy those pages. After connecting to the Web server (the host) using FTP through a browser or Dreamweaver, you can drag your files from your computer on to the Web server. After you have a domain, or Web site address, you point the domain to the Web server and your site becomes live on the Internet.

Once the site is up, go through it to make sure all the pages look and load properly and that all the links work correctly. Ensure that any animations, videos, or motion graphics are loading efficiently and running smoothly on the Web server as well. There are formal checklists for usability, which measures the cognitive, visual, and navigational reliability of a Web site. Visit www.useit.com, the Web site of usability guru and pioneer Jakob Nielsen. His site provides extensive guidelines for Web site usability and also provides checklists you can use to test your own site.

Web Design and Development Techniques

This chapter will introduce you to some of the most important techniques for creating Web page layouts and performing basic Web development. The goal is to help you create your own Web site, in the form of a Web portfolio. There are hundreds of techniques and commands in Web development programs; this chapter focuses on the ones you need to get started, and shows you how to marry them to a fluid design process. The techniques below are shown in either Adobe Photoshop (PS), Adobe Fireworks (FW), or Adobe Dreamweaver (DW). The names of menu commands, tools, panels, and palettes are written in ALL CAPS. Dialog boxes refer to boxes that appear after selecting tools, palettes, or menu items. They provide fine-tuning controls for executing techniques. Most menu items have dialog boxes associated with them.

There are many ways to create Web pages; the techniques below exemplify the way *designers* take on the key tasks required to create a Web site—the Web design and development process. The corresponding online tutorial video lessons are listed at the end of each technique lesson in this chapter. You can view the online tutorial lesson movies by going to www.wiley.com/go/digitaldesign.

Web Design and Graphics Techniques

There are three main ways to create a Web page:

1. Hand code the page using HTML, a markup language that allows you to write coded instructions for how a Web page looks. Hand-coded methods are considered tedious by some and require the expertise of an experienced practitioner. In addition, unless the HTML coder is highly skilled, there is a strong chance the Web pages will turn out poorly constructed and visually weak.

2. Use WYSIWYG (what-you-see-is-what-you-get) software, such as Dreamweaver, to create Web pages. WYSIWYG software packages use intuitive interfaces and menus for user-initiated functions. This textbook uses methods that rely on WYSIWYG applications.

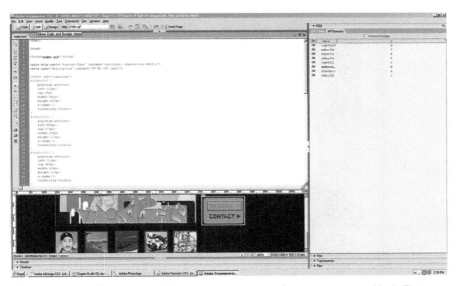

FIGURE 8-1 The HTML code of a Web page uses tags to define its structure and look. This image shows both code and design views in a split window.

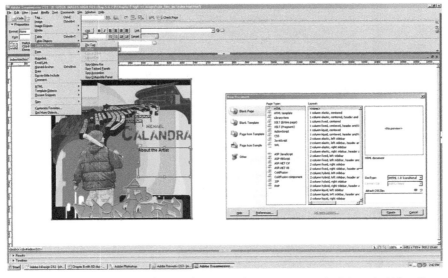

FIGURE 8-2 You can create Web pages from scratch, or you can manipulate and add functionality to sliced pages in WYSIWIG applications such as Dreamweaver.

3. Use a Web workflow that utilizes the design capabilities of Photoshop, Illustrator, and Fireworks and slicing tools. This method will be explained extensively in this chapter.

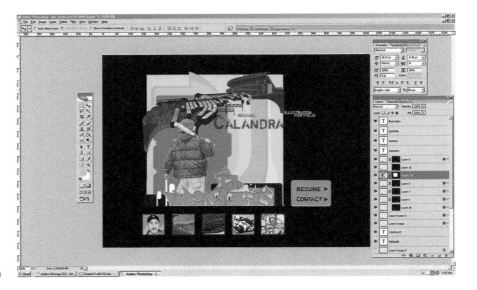

(A)

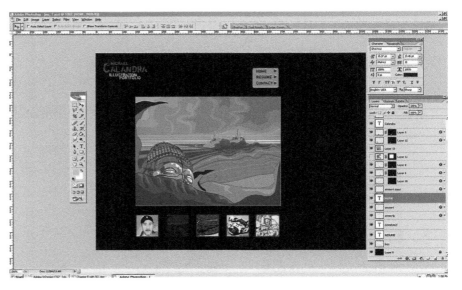

(B)

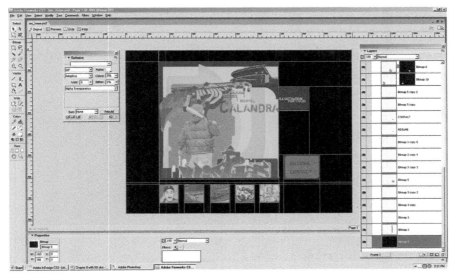

(C)

FIGURES 8-3, A–C You can create Web pages using the same applications and composition techniques used for print design. Web page designs can be created in Photoshop, Illustrator, or Fireworks. This Web page layout, for example, was created in Photoshop and then opened in Fireworks, where it was sliced and exported.

In Web workflows for designers, digital imaging or digital illustration programs such as Photoshop, Fireworks, and Illustrator are used for preparing and composing Web pages. Pages are sliced, optimized, and exported in a program such as Fireworks and then opened in a Web development application such as Dreamweaver.

Using Web development software, Web pages are given functionality and formatting using JavaScript and CSS. Web graphics and motion graphics programs such as After Effects and Flash are used for creating motion spots, multimedia, video, and animation content, which then gets embedded into Web pages using Web development software.

The techniques below will walk you through the Web design and development process using Fireworks. Keep in mind that Photoshop or Illustrator can also be used for Web screen design, but that the layered .psd or .ai files must then be opened in Fireworks to be sliced and exported to Dreamweaver.

Technique Lesson 8.1: Setting Up Files and Folders

You must set up your Web site file and folder structure before beginning to create your Web site. Begin by creating a dedicated folder that will hold all the content used for creating the Web site.

QUICK STEPS:

Setting Up the Folders

1. Create a folder on your computer that will hold the Web pages and additional folders for the final Web page graphic files, which include .jpgs and .gifs, as well as multimedia files such as Flash animations and videos (.swfs and .flvs). Call the folder *my_website.*

    This is your root directory—the top level of your file structure. This is the folder where you will place your HTML-based Web site pages. These files will ultimately get uploaded to the Web server.

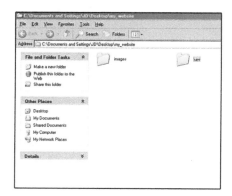

FIGURE 8-4 This is the typical initial folder setup for a Web site. An *images* folder inside the root holds the embedded graphics. A *raw* folder contains the files that are used to create pages and other content. The *raw* folder does not get uploaded to the Internet. The root directory (*my_website*) and images directory (*my_website/images*) are uploaded before your site goes live on the Web.

2. Inside the *my_website* **folder create two additional folders:**

    a. images

        This is the folder to which you will export (and place) all the graphics that occupy the Web pages. These images will be .jpgs, .gifs, and other final files that reside in the Web pages. These files will also get uploaded to the Web server.

    b. raw

        This is where you will keep all the native, layered files that you create during the design process, as well as native multimedia files. Hang on to these unedited versions in case you need to go back to them in the future. These files will be .psd files (layered Photoshop), .png files (layered Fireworks), and other source content files such as .fla (Flash) and .ai (Illustrator) files. These files will never get uploaded to the Web server.

Technique Lesson 8.2: Creating a Web Page Screen

After setting up the folders and going through the planning and conceptualizing phases, you can begin to create Web screens using Photoshop, Fireworks, or Illustrator. The examples in this section use Photoshop and Fireworks. Design your own pages in the application you are most comfortable using; if you work in Photoshop, the pages can later be opened in Fireworks, tweaked, and then optimized, sliced, and exported.

QUICK STEPS (PS & FW):

Creating a Home Page

Refer to your content outline, three-column script, and storyboards throughout the digital production process.

1. Go to FILE > NEW and create a document at the size you want your Web pages (try 800 × 600 or 1024 × 768 pixels).

2. Choose a Web-safe background color from the color picker. Fill a layer with the background color and make sure it remains on the bottom of the layer stack as you add layers.

3. Create a page header and navigation bar (this does not have to be an actual bar). Then fill in the body of the page, leaving space for elements that will be added in later, such as HTML text and multimedia content.

   You don't have to create a traditional-looking Web page, with a banner at the top and text-only buttons. Experiment with a functional and appealing design. Try a few variations and look at award-winning Web sites for inspiration.

4. In the page header, place an image or a logo. Then, using the TYPE tool, lay out the navigation buttons and main category level links.

   If you're not yet sure about your main navigation categories, use *home, resume, work,* and *contact*. These categories will work fine for a basic Web portfolio design. You can always redesign and expand your site as your skills increase and your experience grows.

5. Continue the design of the home page screen by adding content or background graphics. You can create and open individual images and graphics—such as a logo or buttons—in Photoshop or Illustrator, and then composite them into your Web page by dragging and dropping from one application

window to another, copying and pasting them, or importing them. (The easiest way is to drag and drop.) Each image will open (or be dragged into Fireworks) on its own layer.

6. Select the SCALE tool. A free transformation bounding box will appear around the graphic. Hold the corner node and the SHIFT key and scale the graphic; hit RETURN to complete the operation.

7. Go to FILE > SAVE AS and save a layered .psd file for Photoshop or a layered .png file for Fireworks. Save these files in the *raw* folder in the *my_website* folder.

8. Speed the production process and keep navigation elements consistent by using FILE > SAVE AS to save a copy of the page, rename it, and use it for a subpage. The entire navigation structure will already be in place: you will only have to change the page heading and the content.

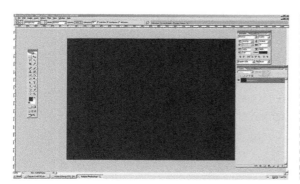

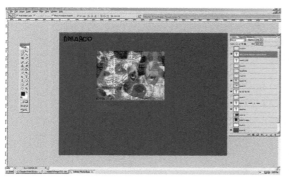
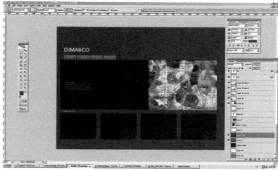

FIGURES 8-5, A–D Layered Web page designs can be created in Photoshop. Experiment with different navigation systems and layouts. Be sure to leave placeholder graphics and text for content that will be added later.

Creating a Pop-Up Window

Used in millions of Web sites, pop-up windows contain smaller Web pages that create a separate browser window space in which to display content. They function as micro-sites—modular sections of Web pages that load in a pop-up window outside of the main Web site's page framework. A pop-up window can be any size, provided it is smaller than the Web page it launches from. Pop-up windows are great for sectioning off portfolio works in concentrated Web pages.

For pop-up windows that contain your art and design work (or any project for that matter), you typically need a navigation system to present links through the works. Thumbnails or numbering schemes work well for this kind of subnavigation, as does a simple button that moves the viewer to the next image or movie. You also need a CLOSE WINDOW button so the user can get back to the main site.

1. Go to FILE > NEW and create a document at the size you want your Web pages (try 640 × 480 pixels or experiment with various sizes, but make sure all the pages in the micro-site and the pop-up windows are exactly the same)

2. Choose a Web-safe background color from the color palette.

3. Create a page header and concise navigation bar with a NEXT button and a CLOSE button. Leave space for elements that need to be added in later, such as a caption and an image or movie.

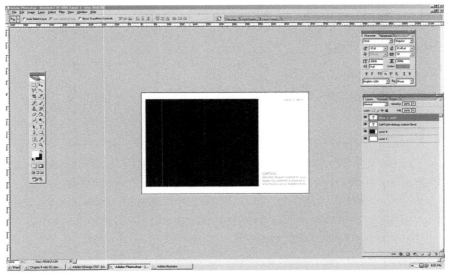

FIGURE 8-6 Pop-up windows can be simple but must be functional. Leave space for a caption, content, and interior navigation for viewing work and closing the pop-up window.

Technique Lesson 8.3: Slicing Graphics

Slicing allows you to turn a graphical Web page design into an HTML page. Using the SLICE tool, the page is sliced into rectangular boxes that have a green overlay. Sliced elements should include any item that needs to work as a link and any element that is a separate graphic on the page. When the slices are exported, all the graphics are optimized, converted to either a .gif or .jpg file, and assigned a sequential name.

Each slice is placed within an HTML table (or CSS layer—AP div —you can choose either option when exporting slices); the resulting output is an .html file and all the supporting graphics. The .html file is a Web page. Although Fireworks has some tools for adding functionality to a Web page, Dreamweaver is far better suited to perform any necessary Web authoring functions. (The .html file you generate from Fireworks can be opened in Dreamweaver.) Best of all, if you make updates to the Fireworks page and reexport the graphics, the Dreamweaver page is automatically updated.

Slice your Web screens using Fireworks. You can open a page saved as a Photoshop or Illustrator document and use the slicing and exporting tools and functions in Fireworks. Alternatively, you can create Web pages from scratch in Fireworks and then slice those pages directly. Feel free to explore the slicing and exporting tools in Photoshop and Illustrator, too. You may find that one of those applications fits into your workflow better than Fireworks does.

QUICK STEPS (FW):

Slicing a Web Page

1. Open a Web page created in Fireworks, Photoshop, or Illustrator in Fireworks.

2. Go to the TOOL panel and select the rectangular SLICE tool.

3. Strategically slice the entire page. Slices represent graphics and sections that link to content areas that will include other page components, such as video or animations. Do not overlap slices, and always slice the whole page; otherwise, Fireworks will fill in the remaining slices, which can result in slices that you didn't want to create.

4. Resize slices quickly and easily by pressing CTRL + T (Windows) or CMD + T (Macintosh) to display the FREE TRANSFORM handles around a slice.

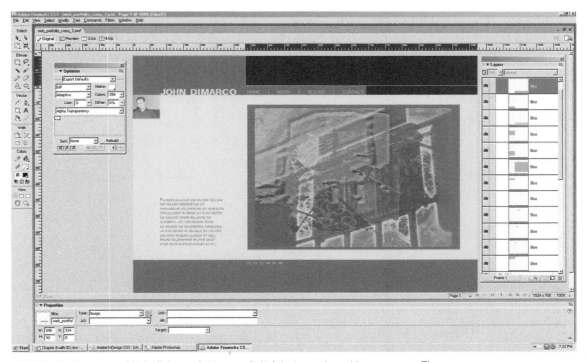

FIGURE 8-7 You can use Web slicing tools in many digital design and graphics programs. The slicing tools and export engine in Fireworks are reliable, easy to use, and integrate seamlessly with Dreamweaver. Slice Web pages to create tables or layers (AP divs) that act as containers for Web page content. Slice and optimize each piece of the Web page: unsliced areas will be automatically sliced when the page is exported.

Technique Lesson 8.4: Optimizing Web Graphics

Optimizing Web graphics assigns a color palette to a slice. Photographic images and full-color images must be optimized as RGB color .jpg files. Most flat, one- or two-color logos and icons can be optimized using Web-safe color and saved as .gif files. In Fireworks, you can click on each slice and use the OPTIMIZATION panel to determine if the graphic will be exported as a .gif or a .jpg. You can use the .jpg file format for all images. You cannot use the .gif file format for full-color photographs, however, because it will shift the colors and change the way the image looks.

QUICK STEPS (FW):

Optimizing a Sliced Graphic

1. Open a page with slices showing. With the SELECTION tool, select a slice (or SHIFT-click to select several slices).

2. Go to WINDOW > OPTIMIZE to open the OPTIMIZE panel.

3. From the EXPORT DEFAULTS menu choose either

   a. .GIF Web 216 (for flat color graphics)

   or:

   b. .JPG Better Quality File

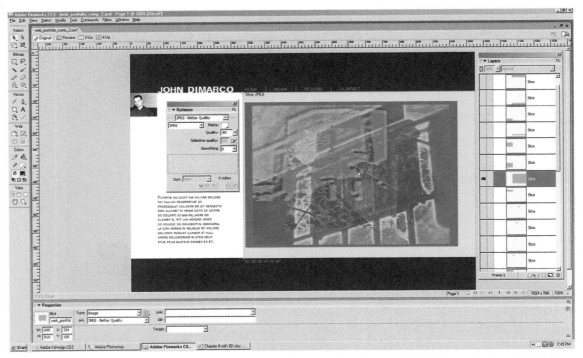

FIGURE 8-8 Optimization is used to set a slice to .jpg or .gif. Optimize each slice of the Web page that will represent content and navigation elements.

4. Increase the quality setting above 80 using the slider in the OPTIMIZE palette for higher-quality photographic images.

Remember, the .jpg format will work for all graphics, and it is sometimes easier to work with .jpgs because they use RGB color. The .gif format will only work well for flat, one- or two-color graphics.

Technique Lesson 8.5: Exporting Slices and the HTML Page

Fireworks and other applications allow you to slice graphics and export them with the HTML code that supports them, thus generating a Web page. This standard—and powerful—Web design technique allows you to take advantage of the design tools in programs built for visual design. Upon export, the HTML Web page can be opened in a Web authoring program such Dreamweaver or Microsoft FrontPage and supplied with full functionality.

QUICK STEPS (FW):

Exporting the HTML Web Page and All Graphics

1. Open, slice, and optimize a Web screen in Fireworks.

2. Go to FILE > EXPORT.

The EXPORT window will appear. Notice the different drop-down menu choices:

FILENAME: e.g., *index.htm* (*work.htm, contact.htm,* etc.)

Place the name of the Web page (with a .htm or .html file extension) in this field; both .htm and .html will work—just keep the naming convention consistent throughout the site. You *must* name the first page of the Website *index.htm*. The server will look for this index page when it loads the Web site. This page can be a splash page (with a graphic and an enter button) or the home page itself.

EXPORT: HTML and images

This tells Fireworks to export all images, and the HTML page that contains them, to a table with all the content. You can position the table in the browser window and set its margins.

You can also export to CSS LAYERS, which places the objects into layers (AP divs), rather than a table. You can always convert the table generated from Fireworks after you position the page elements in Dreamweaver.

HTML: Export HTML file

SLICES: Export slices

This tells Fireworks to export each optimized slice as an individual graphic.

3. Enable the following check boxes in the export window:

Current page only

Include areas without slices

Put images in the subfolder named images (the images folder is chosen by default). This is important so that your files are organized.

Upon export, Fireworks will ask you where to place the new graphic files and the HTML file that supports them. Refer back to the folder structure you previously created. It is very important to put the files in the correct folders.

4. For the site you are constructing, use the following structure:

   a. Export all .html pages to the root folder: *my_website* (don't export to the raw folder).

   b. Export all images to the images folder: *my_website/images*.

   c. Name the first page of the site (whether it is a splash page or a home page) *index.htm*.

   Always use all lowercase letters to name Web files, and never use spaces or nonalphanumeric characters (such as an asterisk, ampersand, bar, period, comma, or backslash) in their files names. Make sure you include the file extension for each file's name (.jpg or .gif for images, .htm or .html for Web pages).

5. After export, save a native Fireworks file (.png) complete with slices, layers, and text. Go to FILE > SAVE and navigate to the *raw* folder.

   The file may be used for editing and exporting later on. You should also save the initial design file if you used Photoshop or Illustrator for the Web screen layout. You now have a Web page with a table containing the sliced graphics that can be opened and manipulated in Dreamweaver.

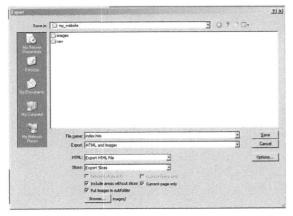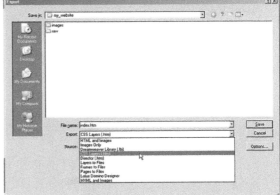

FIGURES 8-9, A, B Export your HTML page with either tables or layers. If you use the table method, each slice is a cell in one large table. If you use the layers method, each slice is an individual AP div.

Technique Lesson 8.6: Exporting Selected Slices

Web graphics need to be converted to .gif (Web-safe index color) or .jpg (RGB color) so they can be viewed on the World Wide Web. Individual graphics can be opened in any digital imaging program and exported or saved as a .gif or .jpg. In Fireworks, it is also possible to export a selected slice—or individual graphic—from any sliced Web screen page. This is extremely helpful in workflows involving a Web page image that must be updated frequently.

QUICK STEPS (FW):

Exporting a Selected Slice

1. Open the home page Web screen and hide the slice layers by clicking off the eye icon in the layers palette.

2. Import or drag and drop a new image onto the page to replace an existing image.

3. Resize the new image to fit the page space.

4. Show the existing slices by clicking on the eye icon in the layers palette and make sure the new image is in the slice area.

5. Right-click (Windows) or CTRL click (Macintosh) on the slice and go to EXPORT SELECTED SLICE.

   The EXPORT dialog box will appear.

6. Use the default settings and rename the graphic; otherwise, it will replace the existing graphic. (Keeping the name the same is helpful when you want to replace an existing graphic on a Web page without reexporting the HTML file and all the graphics again.) Make sure that the image is exported to and saved in the *images* folder in the root directory. Otherwise, it won't show up on the Web page and in its place, you will see a box with a red X.

7. Go to the HTML Web page in Dreamweaver to see if the image has been updated.

8. The exported graphics can be placed into layers and tables on your Web pages in Dreamweaver by clicking on the image you want to replace and going to INSERT > IMAGE, then navigating to the *images* folder to insert the image.

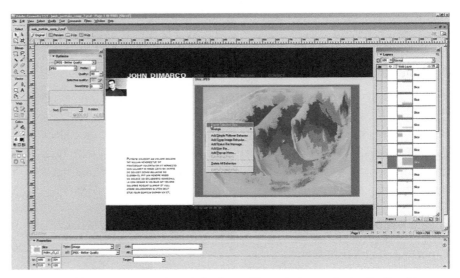

FIGURE 8-10 You can export a selected slice from a Fireworks layout. Saving the file with the same file name as the file to be replaced allows you to update images in your Web pages dynamically. Hide other layers to help make the process more manageable.

 ## Technique Lesson 8.7: Creating Buttons

Buttons can be text (graphical text), HTML text (text links), or graphics (icons and images). Whether they are represented by text or graphics, buttons should be intuitive, guiding users effortlessly where they need to go.

The advantage to using graphical text buttons is that it makes a wider range of typefaces and design elements available. With HTML text link buttons, you are limited to the browser's available fonts (Arial, Courier, Geneva, Georgia, Helvetica, Times, Times New Roman, and Verdana). Nonetheless, HTML text button links are both economical and communicate directly and simply. Many sites use both, but their application should be consistent. Graphical text works well for main navigation bars, while the clean line of HTML text is useful for secondary navigation such as CLOSE WINDOW buttons and NEXT links.

Buttons can be created in Web page layouts and then sliced and exported. Alternatively, they can be created individually, exported, and placed in an HTML page in Dreamweaver.

QUICK STEPS (FW):

Creating a Graphical Button Using a Shape and Text

1. For an individual button, create a new document at the size you want the button.

2. Select the ROUNDED RECTANGLE tool from the TOOL palette. Draw the button shape.

3. Apply a fill and stroke to the button shape.

4. Select the TEXT tool from the TOOL palette and type in the text for the button.

5. Lay the text on top of the button.

6a. Go to FILE > SAVE AS and save it as a .gif or .jpg in the *images* folder of your Web site.

   or:

6b. Keep the button document open and drag the button into your Web page layout window.

   Once saved, the button or the image will be available for import into other programs for Web design or Web development.

7. Save a layered .png file in the *raw* folder in case you want to make changes to the original file in the future.

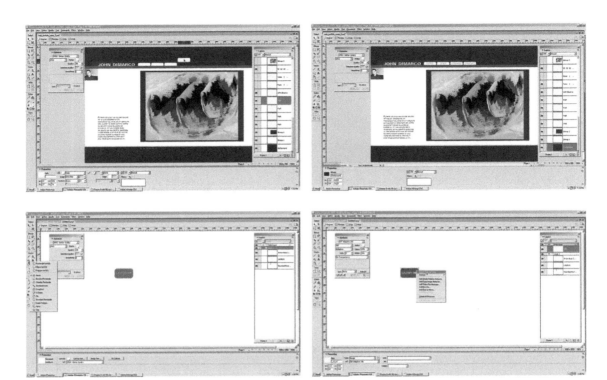

FIGURES 8-11, A–D Create buttons in your layouts during the page design phase. To edit a button—or to make use of a button that is part of an existing layout—create an individual document and then export or drag and drop the sliced button.

Technique Lesson 8.8: Creating Rollover Graphics

A rollover is a change in an image that provides visual feedback to the user. Rollovers can be used on text links and graphic text links, as well as with images. Creating HTML text rollovers is straightforward because they are automatically attached to links in Dreamweaver and set in the PAGE PROPERTIES dialog box. Image rollovers are a bit more complex; in addition to having the main graphic and the rollover graphic, you must then use JavaScript-based functions called behaviors in Dreamweaver to make them work.

First, making the graphics themselves will be discussed. After that, the Dreamweaver's SWAP IMAGE behavior will be used to create rollovers in a Web page. Corresponding rollover graphics should always be the same pixel size—especially when using them inside table cells.

QUICK STEPS (FW):

Creating an Image Rollover

1. Create a Web screen with graphical text navigation. Slice the Web screen and export it as an HTML page with all the supporting graphics.

2. Open the source .png page, which is a sliced Web screen.

3. Hide the slice layers and select one of the graphical text button layers.

4. Drag the layer to the NEW LAYER icon at the bottom of the LAYERS palette. This will create a copy of the layer.

5. Rename the layer *rollover text* and hide the original text layer.

6. Highlight the text and change the color or the button shape, or both.

7. Show all the slices and select the slice over the text button whose color you just changed.

8. Right-click (Windows) or CTRL click on Mac and go to EXPORT SELECTED SLICE.

9. Give the file the same name as the original graphic, but add the suffix *_rollover* to the end of the file name. (For example, the file name might look like this: *index_r1_c1_rollover.jpg*.) This will allow you to recognize the rollover graphic more quickly when you are using the BEHAVIORS PANEL dialog box.

10. Save the exported slice into the *images* folder of your Web site. You will use it once the Web page is opened in Dreamweaver and you apply the SWAP IMAGE behavior (see page 313).

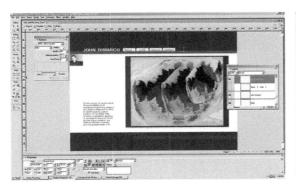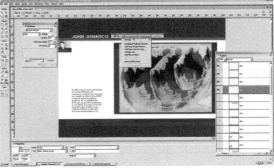

(A,B)

FIGURES 8-12, A–C Rollovers require the graphic to appear in at least two states: the original and the rollover image. Use existing layers and copy them, make a change, and then export the selected slice. The two graphics are used with behaviors in Dreamweaver to set the images to swap when the cursor rolls over them.

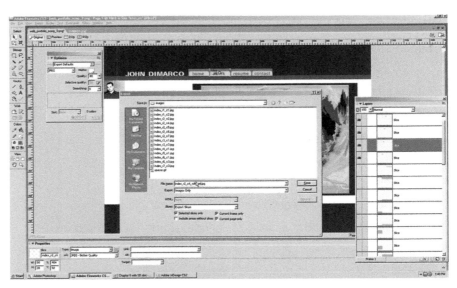

FIGURE 8-12C

Technique Lesson 8.9: Creating Thumbnail Images

Thumbnails are scaled-down versions of images used to represent media items. They typically function as buttons. Thumbnails are a natural approach to presenting small multiples of images: because they create repetitive order, they are easy for the eye to follow and the brain to understand.

Thumbnail images can be made a few different ways. The biggest problem with creating thumbnails is that the images they represent may not be the same size, so simply scaling an image won't necessarily work, because the images may not have the same proportions. And using layer masks becomes challenging to manage when there are many of them. So instead, create a new document at the size needed for each set of thumbnails. Creating the thumbnails then becomes a straightforward process of dragging, scaling, and cropping.

QUICK STEPS (FW OR PS):

Creating Thumbnails

1. Go to FILE > NEW and create a new document the size you want your thumbnails to be (try 100 x 100 pixels). Save the document as 100x100thumbnails.png in Fireworks or as a .psd in Photoshop.

2. Open the images you want to turn into thumbnails.

3. Click on one of the image documents and go to SELECT > SELECT ALL, which will make a selection of the entire image.

4. Drag the entire image into the thumbnail document. The image will be larger than the document size, so expand the application window and zoom out, so you can see the image's boundaries.

5. Press CTRL + T (Windows) or CMD + T (Macintosh) to display the FREE TRANSFORM resizing handles. Grab the corner of the image and hold the SHIFT key while dragging the image to make it smaller. Stop when the image is a little larger than the thumbnail document. Hit ENTER to execute the transformation. Now, position the part of the image you want in the document.

6. Select the CROP tool from the TOOL palette and drag it across the entire image to the edge. Hit ENTER to crop out the extra image area. The thumbnail is created.

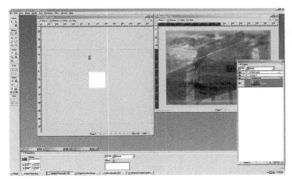
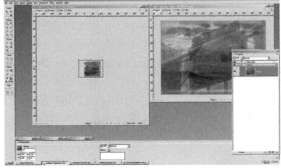
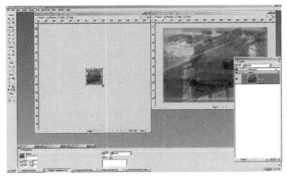
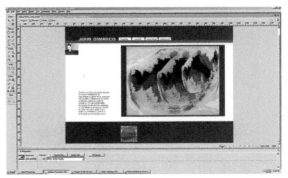

FIGURES 8-13, A–D   Create a separate thumbnail document if you need to produce many thumbnails. It will make managing and creating the images much easier than constructing them within the Web page layout itself. The thumbnails can then be dragged into the final Web page layout from the thumbnail document.

You can now drag it into another document, and it will be sized perfectly. Or you can use the SAVE AS command to save individual thumbnails as .jpgs.

Repeat these steps to make more thumbnail images. Each image will occupy its own layer. Save the layered thumbnail document as a .png file (Fireworks) or a .psd file (Photoshop). Saving the document keeps all the images available for editing and creates a template of the thumbnail document for future use.

Web Development Techniques

The Web pages you planned, conceptualized, and composed must now be turned into functional Web pages that work on the Internet. Web development is the process of adding functionality to these previously conceptualized Web pages. These pages can be created from scratch in Dreamweaver which can also be used to open an existing sliced page.

Go to WINDOW > PROPERTIES to launch Dreamweaver's PROPERTIES INSPECTOR, which is used for the precise manipulation of Web page elements. The INSPECTOR changes appearance depending on the page element that is selected. For example, if the page contains a table and you click inside a cell, the properties of the table cell become active. When an AP div is selected, the INSPECTOR enables you to enter new values for position, background color, and other attributes for that layer.

Creating a Web Page from Scratch in Dreamweaver

The process for creating, slicing, and exporting a Web page using Fireworks is only one way to make a Web page. You can also create Web pages by creating a new Dreamweaver document by going to FILE > NEW > HTML PAGE. This will create a blank white page that works like a word processing document, letting you type and add spaces.

Creating HTML pages in Dreamweaver is fairly straightforward. You can type and place graphics inline. You can change type color, link color, page title, and page color by going to MODIFY > PAGE PROPERTIES. And once you have created a new page and set its properties, you are ready to add content: just insert an AP div or a table to act as a container for that content by going to INSERT > LAYOUT OBJECTS > AP div. To control the content most effectively, create a layer and then insert a table inside of it (INSERT > TABLE). (Although a bit more complicated, you can also use CSS to position elements.)

From Fireworks to Dreamweaver

Fireworks and Dreamweaver are tightly integrated, allowing you to export HTML pages with their associated graphics files and save them in your Web site folder structure. You can then open the HTML pages (the files will be named .htm or .html) in Dreamweaver and add Web functionality such as HTML text, links, JavaScript, and simple motion using dynamic layers, which are AP divs that can be positioned along a timeline to create motion and other effects.

When you open HTML pages exported from Fireworks in Dreamweaver, the page you sliced in Fireworks will be represented by either a nested table or AP divs. The table will be constructed of rows and columns that hold the pieces of the Web page. Each of your slices become part of the table upon export. HTML tables allow you to arrange text, images, links, multimedia content such as Flash movies, other tables, and so on, into rows and columns of cells.

Complex tables can be created using the slice tools in a Web optimization application such as Fireworks. Slicing is easier than hand coding table rows and table data for large areas, such as entire Web pages. Slicing also allows the table to be edited using the table properties in Dreamweaver. Editing a complex sliced table is easier than creating a complex table from scratch in Dreamweaver.

Sliced images and buttons are nested in a table in the HTML page and consecutively named with an _r_c suffix. (The r stands for row, and the c stands for column.) The table can be edited and manipulated, but tables are sometimes challenging to work with. Floating design, which is design using layers (AP divs) is one alternative to building pages solely with tables. You can convert the complex table into free-floating AP divs that allow content to be added and edited easily. You can also use Fireworks to export a page directly to AP divs.

Technique Lesson 8.10: Setting Page Properties

Dreamweaver's PAGE PROPERTIES dialog box works like the page setup dialog boxes in other digital design programs. It allows you to set default global attributes for the Web page and to enter the page title information, which is the description of the page that loads at the top of the Web browser each time the page is visited.

QUICK STEPS (DW):

Setting the Page Properties for Margins, Links, and Page Title

1. Slice and export a Web page.

2. Open the HTML file in Dreamweaver (FILE > OPEN).

3. Go to MODIFY > PAGE PROPERTIES.

   The PAGE PROPERTIES dialog box will appear.

4. In the APPEARANCE settings, ignore the font information at the top; you will be using CSS for setting fonts later. Go to MARGINS at the bottom of the box and set the page margins. The margins will be applied to tables only: AP div tags are placed exactly and can be moved by selecting and dragging them. Tables, however, are relative to the browser and can be adjusted within the Web page using spaces and margins. For a flush left corner margin, enter *0, 0, 0, 0,* for all four margins: left, right, top, bottom.

5. In the LINKS settings, set the link colors for visited links and rollovers; set the underline style as well. You can set the link font in the document later, so you don't need to choose one now, but you can if you prefer.

6. In the TITLE/ENCODING settings, enter the page title. The title should provide some or all of the following information: site name, site page, site section, and your name. You can use any characters you like, including spaces, in page titles. When you launch the page in a browser, you will see the page title at the top of the browser window.

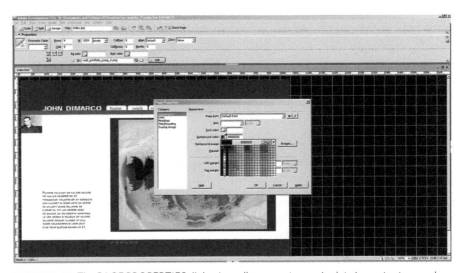

FIGURE 8-14 The PAGE PROPERTIES dialog box allows you to manipulate important page elements, such as background color, links, margins, and page titles.

Technique Lesson 8.11: Making and Manipulating Tables

Tables are containers for content. Dreamweaver gives you the ability to create simple tables and to nest tables inside of one another. Tables are made up of cells, which exist in rows and columns. You can add, delete, merge, and split rows and columns in tables, as well as align and pad content within them.

QUICK STEPS (DW):

Inserting a Table on a Blank Web Page (or inside an Existing Cell or AP Div)

1. Go to INSERT > TABLE.

2. To nest a table, click inside a table cell or AP div and go to INSERT > TABLE. Set the number of rows and columns of the table and set the cell spacing and padding, which add space outside and inside the table cells, respectively.

3. Resize the table by grabbing its edges.

4. Type F6.

   The table will appear in EXPANDED TABLE mode, which makes it easier to manipulate the table's cells.

5. Type F6 again to exit EXPANDED TABLE mode.

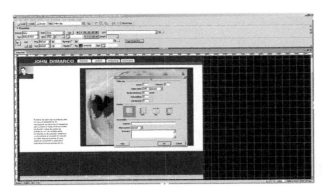 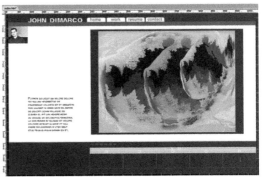

FIGURES 8-15, A, B Tables consist of rows and columns and work as containers for content. You can place tables inside of other tables or inside of AP divs.

Technique Lesson 8.12: Using AP Elements

Dreamweaver provides an environment for the layout of elements on Web pages. Called layers in previous versions of the software, they are now called AP elements (AP stands for "absolutely positioned"). AP elements are HTML page elements— div tags or any other tags (a tag is a page instruction)—that have been assigned an absolute position through the CSS panel fields or freely on the page. Most often absolutely positioned div tags, AP elements can be moved freely and placed anywhere on the Web page by using x (from the left edge) and y (from the top) coordinates. These are the kinds of AP elements Dreamweaver inserts by default. Put the AP together with a div and you get an AP div tag, which is, in simple terms, a layer on a Web page. AP divs essentially work as containers for content and are programmable objects. AP divs can hold text, images, or any other content that you can place in the body of an HTML document. They can also be controlled with JavaScript and CSS.

AP divs enable you to lay out Web pages without struggling with HTML coding or building pages with tables. You can place AP divs in front of and behind each other, hide some AP elements while showing others, and move AP elements across the screen. You can place a background image in one AP div, then place a second AP div containing text with a transparent background in front of it. You can insert tables inside AP divs to organize and control content within the AP div. And you control the attributes of the AP div from the CSS panel. This flexibility is why it is a good idea to convert tables to layers after slicing and exporting.

The AP ELEMENTS panel is where the AP divs reside. Each one can be named descriptively. Each AP div occupies a separate, layered position on the z-axis, which represents depth. (AP divs have a z-axis because they can be stacked on top of one another, thus creating depth.) The AP div will also have an assigned z-index number, which refers to the stacking order of the AP divs and to the load sequence on the page. The top-down stacking order is represented on the page in the same manner. The AP div at the top will have the highest number. The highest number loads last (on top), above the others indexes.

Here are some advantages to using AP divs:

- AP divs can be added and deleted easily from a Web page.

- AP divs can hold any Web asset or object.

- AP divs can be dynamically controlled using a timeline or CSS.

- AP divs can be resized, colored, and positioned to fit conveniently into your Web page design.

- Tables can be nested inside AP divs to provide extensive content control, and this provides an effective way to develop Web pages from scratch— without using Fireworks to create an entire page.

QUICK STEPS (DW):

Inserting an AP Div onto a Web Page

1. Go to WINDOW > AP ELEMENTS to display the AP ELEMENTS panel.

   This will show you a listing of and the stacking order for the AP divs that occupy that page.

2. Go to INSERT > LAYOUT OBJECTS > AP div.

   A new layer with a blue bounding box will appear on the page. *APdiv1,* representing the new layer, will appear in the AP ELEMENTS panel.

3. To move the layer (AP div), grab it and drag it. If you copy and paste it into another Web page, it will be positioned at the same (absolute) position. (This makes building multiple pages go more quickly.)

4. To position the layer precisely, type numeric values into the L (left) and T (top) fields on the PROPERTY INSPECTOR. For example, L = 100 and T = 100 would move the top corner of the layer down 100 pixels from the top and over 100 pixels from the left.

5. To further manage the positioning of layers, use the rulers, PROPERTIES INSPECTOR positioning fields, and the grid (VIEW > GRID). Using the grid is advantageous because you can position items on the Web page consistently and accurately.

6a. To scale a layer, click on it on the page or inside the LAYER INSPECTOR, grab an anchor handle, and drag. (Use a corner handle to resize two sides at once.) Resize layers to snuggly fit their content.

   or:

6b. Type size values into the WIDTH and HEIGHT fields on the PROPERTIES INSPECTOR to scale the layer to a precise numeric size.

Inserting an Image, Flash Object, or Text into an AP Div

1. To place an image, go to INSERT > IMAGES and navigate to the *images* folder in the root directory of your Web site.

2. To place a Flash object, go to INSERT > MEDIA > FLASH. (To insert a Flash video, go to INSERT > MEDIA > FLASH VIDEO.)

3. Navigate to the .swf (object) or .flv (video) file and insert it. (These files should reside either in the *images* folder or another folder in your Web site's root directory.)

4. To place text, click on the cursor and start typing. You can also insert a table to help you control the text.

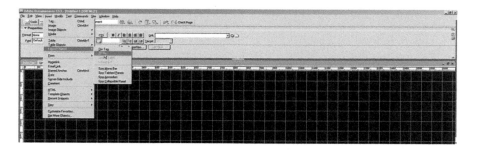

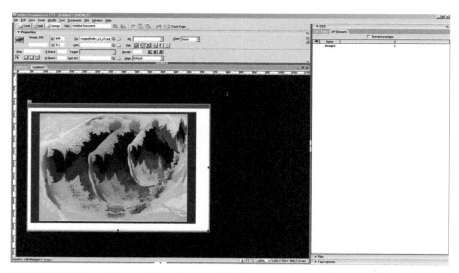

FIGURES 8-16, A, B Using AP divs is the most flexible way to create Web pages from scratch, because they allow the designer to work in a composite environment, rather than tinkering with the difficult code manipulations required for table-only Web pages . When AP divs are added to a page, they are listed in the AP div panel, which is similar to the layers palettes in graphics programs. The z-index number refers to the stacking and loading order of AP divs.

Technique Lesson 8.13: Putting AP Elements in Motion

You can make AP divs move across the page using timelines—an easy way to create simple motion pieces on your Web pages.

QUICK STEPS (DW):

Adding Motion or Timing to an AP Div

1. Go to FILE > NEW > HTML.

2. Open the timeline by going to WINDOW >TIMELINE.

3. Go to WINDOW > AP ELEMENTS to display the AP ELEMENTS panel.

4. Add an AP div to the Web page by going to INSERT > LAYOUT OBJECTS > AP div.

5. Name the AP div descriptively in the AP ELEMENTS panel.

6. Position the AP div where you want it to start using the L (left) and T (top) fields on the PROPERTY INSPECTOR.

7. Select the AP div and go to MODIFY > TIMELINE > ADD OBJECT TO TIMELINE.

   You will see the layer name on the timeline in a gray bar with a line and two dots (when selected, the gray bar becomes purple). The dots represent key frames. There is a start and an end to every animation; key frames represent the start, middle, and finish points of the motion—moments in time when change occurs. There are always at least two key frames (start and finish).

8. Drag the bar anywhere on the timeline. To make the AP div appear after some time, move the bar farther down the timeline.

9. Click on the last key frame dot and move the AP div across the Web page to where you want it to stop moving.

   You can also extend the time it takes the layer to move from start to finish by selecting the last key frame and dragging it down the timeline. If you want to change the object during that span of time, you can add a key frame in between the beginning and ending key frames by CTRL-clicking on the time-line of the AP div.

10. Enable the AUTOPLAY check box. To loop the animation, enable the LOOP check box. (A looped animation can become annoying—use it only when it fits your communication goals.)

11. Preview the Web page in a Web browser by pressing F12. You should see the AP div move across the page.

    If it does not move at all, go back to Dreamweaver and make sure the AUTO-PLAY check box, located on the timeline, is enabled. Then press F12 again to preview the animation.

Dreamweaver will now offer to add a behavior to your Web page code to allow the animation to start or replay automatically. Behaviors provide easy, intuitive JavaScript functionality without requiring extensive coding knowledge. (For more about behaviors and JavaScript, see page 317.)

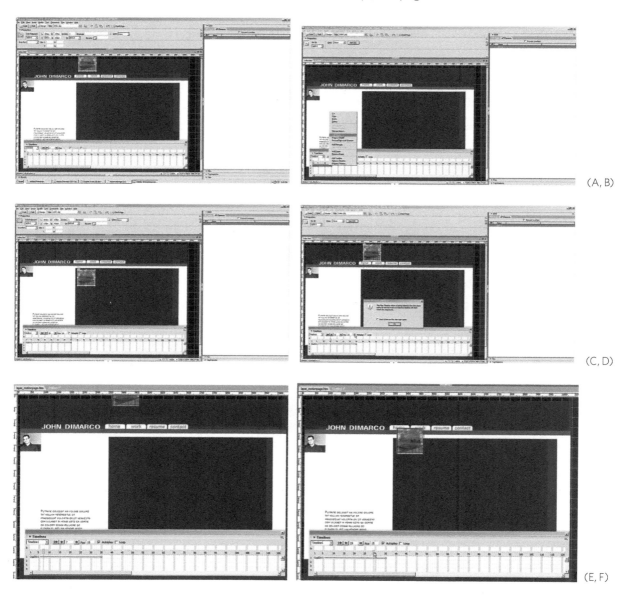

(A, B)

(C, D)

(E, F)

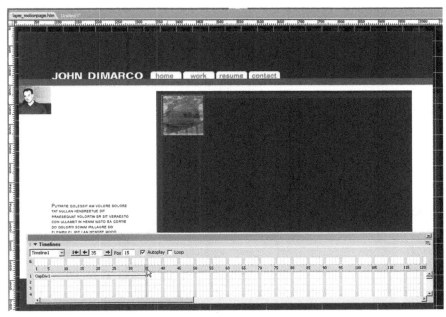

(G)

FIGURES 8-17, A–G You can add motion to AP divs with Dreamweaver to create simple movements and animations. Here, a thumbnail image exported from Fireworks was placed into an AP div. The thumbnail was set to move using the timeline by positioning the layer off the page at -110px (px stands for pixels) and then moving the object to its endpoint on the page. The key frames (dots) represent the start and end of the motion. AUTOPLAY is enabled so the motion will start automatically.

Technique Lesson 8.14: Converting Tables to Layers

Although CSS layers (AP divs) can be exported from Fireworks, it is a bit easier to maneuver and position a big table. You can therefore export HTML and images from Fireworks, generating a big table that holds the content. Tables are created when Web pages are sliced and the HTML files are exported from Fireworks with their images using the HTML AND IMAGES export setting. But tables, the main containers for Web pages, are difficult to manage and manipulate efficiently, especially for nonprogrammers. The better solution is to use AP divs. After slicing and exporting from Fireworks, you can convert the table to AP layers so that the page elements can be edited more easily.

QUICK STEPS (DW):

Converting Tables to Layers

1. Open a sliced page that was exported as HTML and images.

   The page should contain a table with all of the page's content.

2. Select the table and go to MODIFY > CONVERT > TABLES TO AP divS.

   The table cells are now broken into AP divs and listed in the AP ELEMENTS panel.

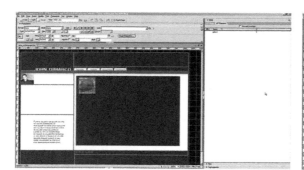 

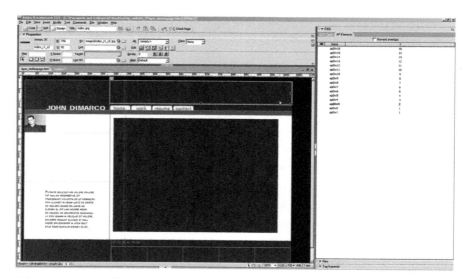

FIGURES 8-18, A–C This page was exported from Fireworks as HTML and images, producing a table that holds the page elements. It was then converted to AP divs to make it easier to edit. After conversion, the layers are listed sequentially in the AP div panel. Each slice (table cell) becomes a layer. The AP divs can be moved, edited, or deleted. Leave them in their positions after conversion to maintain the original design.

Technique Lesson 8.15: Adding Browser-Based Text to a Page and Using CSS for Text Formatting

HTML (browser-based) text is limited to the fonts available to the Web browser on the viewer's computer. You must therefore use only certain fonts for HTML-based text: Arial, Helvetica, Times, Times New Roman, Geneva, Courier, Georgia, and Verdana.

Add text to a Web page by clicking on the page itself, or on a Web page content container such as an AP div or table cell, and begin typing. To set font attributes, highlight the text and go to the PROPERTIES INSPECTOR, where you can edit the values for font, font size, and font style. Once you set the font the way you want, Dreamweaver will assign a generic name to the font and attach it to the document using CSS.

CSS, which stands for cascading style sheets, provides a collection of formatting rules that control the appearance of content items in a Web page. CSS styles creates a set of rules (settings and attributes) to control content. CSS rules separate content from formatting by creating two separate files. The HTML file holds the content of your page; the CSS rules defining the formatting of the code is in another file.

The CSS rules can get saved into a .css file, which is an external style sheet. If a separate, external .css file is not saved, the CSS is embedded in the head section of the HTML document. If they are embedded, you can apply the fonts and edit the CSS rules in Dreamweaver's CSS STYLE panel. You can rename the styles right from the PROPERTIES INSPECTOR.

Using CSS enables you to control the appearance of the Web page, including its text properties. The properties that can be manipulated include fonts and font sizes; font styles (bold, italic, underlining, and text shadows); text color and background color; and link color and underlining. Letting CSS control your fonts gives your Web page a consistent appearance across multiple browsers.

QUICK STEPS (DW):

Editing and Setting Type Using Embedded CSS

1. Open the PROPERTIES INSPECTOR (WINDOW > PROPERTIES) and CSS STYLES panel and (WINDOW > CSS STYLES).

2. Enter text inside a page, AP div, or table cell.

3. Highlight the text and set the attributes (rules) from the PROPERTIES INSPECTOR. Set the font, size, color, and font style.

   The CSS text style will appear; its default name in the PROPERTIES INSPECTOR's STYLE drop-down menu will be *style1*. You can apply the saved styles from the drop-down menu to that Web page only.

4. Rename the style descriptively by selecting RENAME from the STYLE drop-down menu; this will facilitate its later application.

5. Click on to the CSS STYLES panel to edit the style rules and add properties to the style.

   Not all properties will manipulate the text—some are used for other page elements. You can test each added property by setting it and seeing what happens on the page. Properties can be deleted by selecting them in the CSS STYLES panel and then clicking on the TRASH CAN icon at the bottom of the panel. You can also edit the styles by clicking on the CSS STYLES panel's EDIT STYLE button (pencil icon) at the bottom of the panel. This will bring up the CSS rule definition for that style. To save the styles embedded in one document into a new document, go to FILE > SAVE AS and give the HTML document a new name.

Saving a Style Sheet as a .CSS File

Saving an external style sheet creates a file that can be attached to each page and used throughout your Web site. You don't have to save external .css files: Dreamweaver automatically embeds the CSS styles you create in the Web page for which you create them; however, using an external file saves time and guarantees consistency across all Web pages in a site.

1. Create styles and rename them inside of an HTML document (Web page).

2. Go to WINDOW > CSS STYLES to display the CSS styles panel.

3. In the panel, click on the NEW CSS RULE icon (the document with a +) to open the NEW CSS RULE dialog box.

4. In the dialog box, use these settings:

   a. SELECTOR TYPE: Class

   b. NAME: Add a style name (use eight letters or less and no spaces). This will create a new style.

c. DEFINE IN: Select NEW STYLE SHEET FILE and click OK. The SAVE STYLE SHEET FILE AS dialog box will appear. There you will save the entire style sheet to the root directory (*my_website*). The file will be named with a .css file extension. The CSS file will need to be uploaded for the styles to appear when the Web site is live on the Internet.

5. To attach a saved style sheet in another location to other HTML pages, open the page and go to the PROPERTIES INSPECTOR, then click on the STYLE drop-down menu and select ATTACH STYLE SHEET. You will have the option to link or import. Choose IMPORT so that the CSS file is placed in the root directory, thereby making it available for upload.

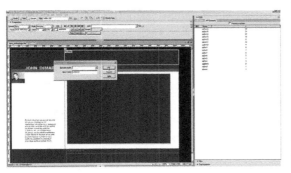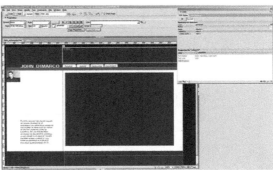

(A,B)

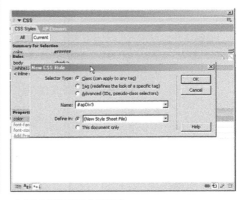

(C,D)

FIGURES 8-19, A–D You can save CSS styles directly in Dreamweaver's PROPERTIES INSPEC-TOR. To create a cascading style sheet, establish a font, size, and color and then rename the style descriptively. The styles will be embedded in the page—no external file is needed. You can also save an entire .css file (style sheet), which will allow you to import those styles into other Web pages and Web sites.

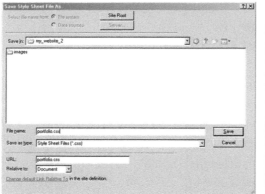

(E,F)

FIGURES 8-19, E-F For the styles to appear when the pages are live on the Internet, the .css file must be uploaded with the HTML and graphic files. Style properties and attributes can be edited using the CSS STYLES panel. To create a new cascading style sheet, click on the NEW CSS RULE icon in the CSS STYLES panel.

Technique Lesson 8.16: Setting Links to Text or Images

Links, short for hyperlinks, are navigational elements in a Web page that connect one page or piece of content to another. Links can be HTML text based or, using an image map, attached to images or virtually any other Web page content. Links load new pages, either in the same browser window, a new browser window, or a pop-up window.

Links can be absolute or relative to your Web site. Absolute links exist outside of a Web site's root directory—they are external to the site (e.g., http://www.portfoliovillage.com). Relative links exist inside the root directory and are shortened to the file name, such as *work.htm*. This means that the work.htm page location, which exists in the root directory of the site, can be called by any page inside the root directory simply by linking to that file name.

QUICK STEPS (DW):

Applying a Link to Text or an Image with the Properties Inspector

1. Select the text or image that will trigger the link.

2a. Go to the PROPERTIES INSPECTOR panel and click on the LINK field. Enter the page name (*contact.htm*).

or:

2b. Enter a Web site address (URL, or uniform resource locator) to link the page to a Web page external to the site.

3. Go to the PROPERTIES INSPECTOR and select the TARGET field. Select _SELF to load the linked page in the same browser window (the default setting) or _BLANK to open the Web page link in a new window.

Applying a Link to an Image Using an Image Map

An image map is a hot spot that you place over image content on a Web page. To apply an image map, select an image, and then drag a hot spot tool (the rectangular tool works best) over the part of the image that you want to trigger the link. The image map hot spot tools are in the PROPERTIES INSPECTOR and become active when an image is selected.

1. Select the image that will trigger the link.

2. Go to the PROPERTIES INSPECTOR panel and click on the MAP field. Enter the image map, which references the graphic map.

3. Drag one of the hot spot tools (square, oval, or polygon) onto the area of the graphic where you want the link.

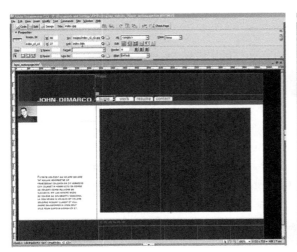 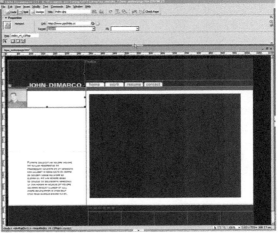

FIGURES 8-20, A, B   HTML links can be set using the PROPERTIES INSPECTOR's LINK field or by using image maps, which allow you to designate hot spots on a Web page's content.

4. Type the link destination (URL or Web page) into the link field.

5. Add an alt tag (text description) if desired. This is good to do because it provides additional usability for the graphics elements.

6. Test the map's link by going to FILE > PREVIEW IN BROWSER.

Technique Lesson 8.17: Setting an E-Mail Link

The most intuitive and straightforward method for getting feedback from your visitors is to provide an e-mail link for them. You can apply e-mail links to text or images. Many sites use the *contact* link to launch an e-mail client window.

QUICK STEPS (DW):

Applying an E-Mail Link to Text or an Image

1. Select the text or image that will trigger the e-mail link.

2. Go to the PROPERTIES INSPECTOR panel and click on the LINK field.

3. Type *mailto:* and then your e-mail address (for example: *mailto:bsomeone@ gmail.com*). Be sure to type your e-mail address behind the colon after *mailto* accurately.

   When users click the linked text on their computer, their e-mail client program will pop up, ready to send a message to the address in the link field.

Behaviors

Designers are sometimes at a disadvantage when performing Web development tasks due to a lack of experience with hand coding HTML or JavaScript. Dreamweaver provides WYSIWYG tools that make use of software functions—instead of coding functions—to accomplish certain tasks. Behaviors are one such feature.

Behaviors are client-side JavaScript code that run in browsers and are triggered by actions. A behavior is added to a page through the BEHAVIORS panel, in which an action and the event triggering that action are specified. After you attach a behavior to a page element, the behavior calls the action (i.e., JavaScript code) associated with an event whenever that event occurs for that element.

Actions are prewritten JavaScript code for executing Web functions such as opening a browser window, showing or hiding an AP element, playing a sound, or swapping images for rollovers. For example, if you attach the OPEN BROWSER WINDOW action (for pop-up windows) to a link and specify that it will be triggered by the onClick event linked to a button, then that pop-up window will appear whenever a visitor clicks on the link associated with that button. The actions available vary among browser versions.

Events are messages generated by browsers indicating that a visitor to a Web page has done something, such as moved the cursor over a link. When this happens, the browser generates an onMouseOver event for that link; the browser then checks whether it should call some JavaScript code in response to the event (a SWAP IMAGE action, for example). One event can even trigger several actions, such as a swap image and the appearance of a pop-up window triggered by an onMouseOver event and then an onClick event.

Technique Lesson 8.18: Using Behaviors for Graphical Rollovers

You can use behaviors for a host of actions that make your Web pages more interactive. Graphical rollovers, which are called SWAP IMAGE actions in the BEHAVIORS panel, are among the most common. Rollovers provide visual feed back to the user by swapping an image when the cursor rolls over it.

There are two ways to create rollovers in Dreamweaver. The first is to use the SWAP IMAGE behavior. The other is to go to INSERT > IMAGE OBJECTS > ROLLOVER IMAGE. Both ways are effective, and are described below; choose the one that you are most comfortable using. You can also set the rollover properties for HTML text links by going to MODIFY > PAGE PROPERTIES.

The simplest rollovers require you to create two graphics. One is the graphic that will be rolled over. This is usually a navigation button or a graphic that triggers the appearance of the other graphic. The second graphic is the replacement image that displays when the mouse-over occurs. When a navigation bar is involved, the second graphic usually contrasts visually with the first graphic, typically by graying out the graphic, changing colors, or adding a border.

Make sure that the rollover image is the same size as the image being swapped; if the container (table cell or AP div) is too small to accommodate it, the image will become distorted upon rollover.

QUICK STEPS (DW):

Using the Swap Image Behavior to Create Rollovers

You must have a rollover graphic ready before opening the BEHAVIORS panel (see Technique Lesson 8.8, page 292). Make sure you have the image that will be used in the rollover saved in the *images* folder of your Web site.

1. In the Web page, select the image that will be swapped or will trigger the event.

2. Click on the + in the BEHAVIORS panel and choose SWAP IMAGE.

   The SWAP IMAGE dialog box will appear, and you will be prompted to choose an IMAGE and SET SOURCE TO destination.

3. In the IMAGES field, navigate to the image you want to swap from.

   The image you have selected previously will be selected by default, so you do not have to reset it if you are doing a single-state (two-image) rollover.

4. The SET SOURCE TO field represents the image that is swapped in on roll-over. Navigate to the graphic that you exported from Fireworks or saved into your *images* folder. If you named it with an identifier, such as *_rollover*, you should be able to find it quickly. Be sure that the rollover image is the same size as the selected image.

5. After choosing the image, click OK.

6. In the BEHAVIORS panel, set the event to onClick or onMouseOver.

7. Press F12 to preview the rollover in the browser.

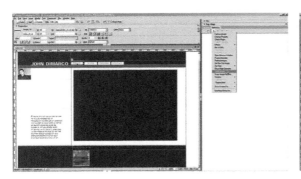

(A,B)

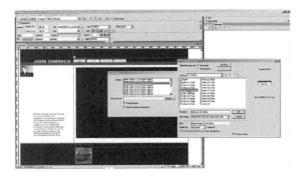
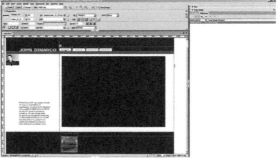

(C,D)

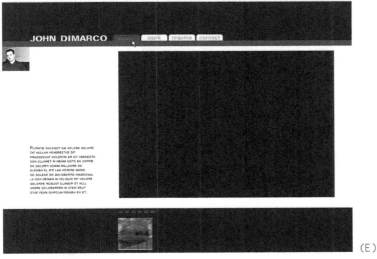

(E)

FIGURES 8-21, A-E   Constructing graphical rollovers requires you to first create a different image state, then generate the rollover JavaScript using a SWAP IMAGE behavior.

Creating Multistate Rollovers

You can also create multistate rollovers, which let you swap multiple images on a page with an event.

1. Perform the SWAP IMAGE behavior process described above for each item you want to have swapped to the same trigger graphic.

2. Select the graphic (button) that will trigger the event, then set the image that will be swapped out in the IMAGES section (at the top of the SWAP IMAGE dialog box).

3. Browse for the image that will be swapped in.

4. Set the BEHAVIORS panel event to onMouseDown and onMouseOver for each individual event.

    Naming the image descriptively in the PROPERTIES INSPECTOR will help you find it in the SWAP IMAGE dialog box more easily. This is not a file name, but merely a descriptor for coding purposes.

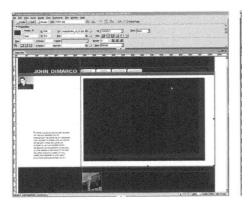
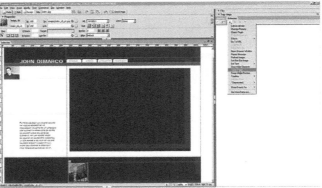
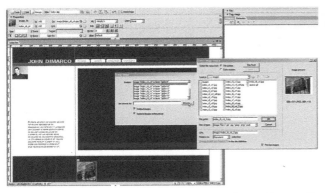

FIGURES 8-22, A–D   For multistate rollovers, start by naming the image you want to swap in the PROPERTIES INSPECTOR. Select the trigger graphic—the image that initiates the event when clicked. Next, select the SWAP IMAGE behavior and set the IMAGES area to the image that will be swapped. Then navigate to the SET SOURCE TO image.

Using the Insert Menu to Create Rollovers

Use this method if you are starting from scratch, and no images yet exist on the Web page. (If there are existing images on the page, use the SWAP IMAGE behavior.) Make sure you have the image that will be used in the rollover saved in the *images* folder of your Web site.

1. Go to Insert > Image Objects > Rollover Image.

   The INSERT ROLLOVER IMAGE dialog box will appear.

2. Choose the original image (this will be replaced by the swapped image).

3. Choose the rollover image. This image should be the same size as the original image.

4. Add a link destination.

5. Press F12 to preview the rollover in the browser.

There are also other methods for swapping images: using the SHOW-HIDE ELEMENTS behavior, for example, allows you to show and hide entire AP divs and images on the page.

Technique Lesson 8.19: Using Behaviors for Pop-Up Windows

Pop-up windows are browser windows that load on top of an existing window. Because their size can be controlled (unlike external windows, which open through _blank window_ links), pop-up windows are ideal for isolating content.

In the BEHAVIORS panel, the JavaScript function for pop-up windows is OPEN BROWSER WINDOW. Although their sizes can vary, a pop-up window should always be smaller than the Web page that launches it. Try 600 x 400 pixels for showing off graphics and image-related work. Use 400 x 300 pixels for smaller work that requires smaller windows, such as videos or animations. Try 600 x 800 pixels for long, text-based pages such as an interactive Web resume.

You are always safe using white as a background color. Work on one pop-up page until you are satisfied with its size and look. Then choose the SAVE AS command to use the page as a template again and again for each new piece of work.

Pop-up windows should be kept simple and contain a minimum of graphics and text. Basic navigation for the next pages and a CLOSE WINDOW button should always be included. The layout of the pop-up page should consist of a few strategically placed layers—a work layer and a navigation layer. No other content is needed. You do not want to distract the viewer from the main content.

QUICK STEPS (DW):

The Open Browser Window Behavior

Apply this JavaScript to text or a graphic button to trigger the event.

1. Highlight the text or graphic that will trigger the browser window to open (the event) and go to the BEHAVIORS panel. Do not to add a link to the text or graphic; doing so will cause multiple windows to open.

2. Click on the + in the BEHAVIORS panel and choose OPEN BROWSER WINDOW.

   The OPEN BROWSER WINDOW dialog box will appear.

3. In the dialog box, next to URL TO DISPLAY, click on BROWSE.

This will display the navigation window showing your files.

4. Navigate to where your Web site resides (*my_web folder*) and choose the HTML page you want to load in the pop-up window.

5. Set the width and height of the pop-up window in the corresponding fields. Experiment with sizes and text to make sure the content fits properly.

6. Enable the SCROLLBARS AS NEEDED and RESIZE HANDLES check boxes if the page will scroll or need resizing. Otherwise, leave all the attributes blank to generate a blank window.

7. Set the event in the BEHAVIORS panel to onClick.

8. Press F12 to preview the pop-up window in a browser.

Technique Lesson 8.20: Using JavaScript to Close a Window

QUICK STEPS (DW):

Making a Close Button

You can also "call" JavaScript without using behaviors. JavaScript can be typed directly into the PROPERTIES INSPECTOR's LINK field. This book is not about JavaScript, but the technique for creating close buttons is very straightforward— and one that's important to have in your arsenal of Web page design skills.

A close button provides an easy, intuitive method for a visitor to close a pop-up window and return to the home page. While a visitor will often close the window by clicking the *X* in its title bar, it is still prudent to provide a close button in your pop-up window's design. You can do so using some simple JavaScript. Add forward and back buttons to the pop-up window, and you've created a rudimentary user navigation system. (This system should be very discreet and in the same location on each page.)

1. In a pop-up window, make a new layer, type the words *close window,* and apply a CSS style (or make a new text style). (Don't put this on your home page or it will close its window.)

2. Highlight the text and in the PROPERTIES INSPECTOR, go to the LINK field, and type *javascript:self.close().*

3. Set the event to onClick.

4. Press F12 to preview the close button in a browser. Test the button to see if it closes the window.

Using the Call JavaScript Behavior

You can also use behaviors to call JavaScripts in Dreamweaver by using the BEHAVIORS panel and choosing CALL JAVASCRIPT.

1. In the CALL JAVASCRIPT dialog box, type *self.close()*.
2. Set the event to onClick.
3. Press F12 to preview the behavior in a browser.

This provides the same result as typing *javascript:self.close()*.into the PROPERTIES INSPECTOR's LINK field.

Uploading Files to the Internet

To place your Web pages on the Internet at a World Wide Web location, you need to have a Web address (domain name) and server space on a host computer. Hosts provide server space and registrars provide Web addresses, also known as URLs (for uniform resource locators).

There are many advertisements on the Web for companies from which you can purchase these components. Until you have them, you will only be able to run your Web site locally—on your own computer. Once you secure a domain name and a host, you can begin to upload your Web site files to the Internet. To upload files to a Web server (host), you use FTP (file transfer protocol), either within a Web development program such as Dreamweaver, through a dedicated FTP application such as Fetch, or directly from a Web browser to the Internet.

Technique Lesson 8.21: FTPing Files from Adobe Dreamweaver

To upload files to a host computer from Dreamweaver, you must first set up a site.

QUICK STEPS (DW):

Uploading Files via FTP

1. Go to SITE > NEW SITE.

   The SITE DEFINITION dialog box will appear. Click the ADVANCED tab.

2. Enter in the settings for your local Web site and your Web hosting server.

3. Select the LOCAL INFO category and complete the following fields:

   a. SITE NAME: Add a name for the Web site.

   b. LOCAL ROOT FOLDER: Navigate to where your Web site files reside on your computer (*my_website*).

   c. DEFAULT IMAGES FOLDER: Leave this field blank.

      LINKS RELATIVE TO: Document.

      HTTP ADDRESS: Type in your Web site's URL
      (e.g., *www.portfoliovillage.com*).

4. Select the category REMOTE INFO and complete the following field:
ACCESS: FTP.

5. Type in the FTP host, the log-in, and the password. (You get all of these from your Web hosting provider.)

6. Go to WINDOW > FILES.

This will display the FILES panel, which provides a file tree—the location of your files on your computer.

7. From the drop-down menu, choose REMOTE VIEW. Dreamweaver will log on to the host server.

6. Expand the window by clicking the EXPAND WINDOW button at the top of the FILES panel.

You will see the host folders and your folders in a split-pane window.

7. Go to your local Web site folder (*my_website*) and drag the index.htm Web page onto the host server (usually the *HTML* folder, although some hosts name this folder *public_html*).

Dreamweaver will ask you if you want to PUT DEPENDENT FILES.

8. Click YES.

The image files that are coded into the Web page will be moved into the *images* folder on the host server automatically. If you click NO, you will have to drag the image files over to the *images* folder manually.

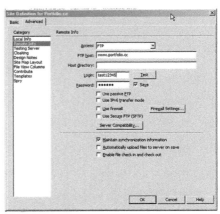

9. Type your Web site address into a Web browser to see if the pages and graphics have uploaded correctly.

(A)

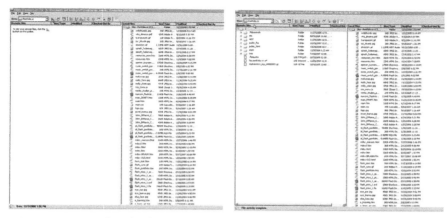

(B,C)

FIGURES 8-23, A–C   To upload to the Internet through Dreamweaver, you must have a host and a local site set up using the SITE menu. Once set up, you then connect to the host and transfer your files from your local computer to the host computer.

Technique Lesson 8.22: FTP Files from a Web Browser

You can upload files to a server directly from a Web browser such as Internet Explorer.

QUICK STEPS:

Uploading Files via FTP from a Browser

1. Type *ftp://* followed by the name of your Web site into your browser.

   A window asking for the FTP username and password will appear.

2. Enter that information.

   The browser will open the host server and your folders will appear.

3. Drag files from your Web site's root directory folder (*my_website*) directly into the host's HTML and images folder. If an *images* folder does not exist, either create one or drag your images folder over to the host server.

4. Open a new browser window and type in your Web site address to see if the pages and graphics uploaded correctly.

Design Assignment

Create a five-page Web site that presents a photo narrative. Choose a theme (e.g., food, trees, people) and shoot some digital photographs. Retouch, scale, and crop the images. Design a Web page with links to each of the photos. Use text, thumbnails, or buttons for links.

Tools: Digital imaging software, Web development software, and five digital images.

Specs: Imagine you are the digital designer hired to create a pitch site to get the account of a well-known photographer. Develop a five-page site that demonstrates design, composition, navigation, and ease of use.

Online Movie Lessons

Tutorial walk-through movies for technique lessons are provided online. Each section contains step-by-step tutorial movies available at book's Web site: www.wiley.com/go/digitaldesign.

Bibliography

Adobe Systems 2009. Adobe Fireworks and Adobe Dreamweaver HELP menus for CS4.

Curtis, Hillman. 2000. *Flash Web design: The art of motion graphics.* Berkeley, CA: New Riders.

———. 2002. *MTIV: Process, inspiration, and practice for the new media designer.* Berkeley, CA: New Riders.

DiMarco, John. 2006. *Web portfolio design and applications.* Hershey, PA: Idea Group.

Kristof, Ray, and Amy Satran. 1995. *Interactivity by design: Creating & communicating with new media.* Mountain View, CA: Adobe Press.

Figure Credits

3-1 "GWB II". Screenprint, State 3, Edition of 15. Courtesy of Richard Kirk Mills.

3-2 "P.A.S. - Park Avenue South". Screenprint, Edition of 35. Courtesy of Richard Kirk Mills.

3-3 "Garden Pot 3". Etching with Aquatint, Edition of 3. Courtesy of Richard Kirk Mills.

3-4 "Golden Arch 1". Monoprint. Courtesy of Richard Kirk Mills.

3-5 "Florida Sketchbook: Where Shopping is a Pleasure". Monoprint. Edition of 10. Courtesy of Richard Kirk Mills.

3-6 Courtesy of Kristen Krawford.

3-7 Courtesy of Kristen Krawford.

3-7 Courtesy of Kristen Krawford.

3-7 Courtesy of Kristen Krawford.

3-8 Photo by John DiMarco.

3-11 Image by John DiMarco.

3-12 Design by Kristen Krawford.

3-13 Design by Kristen Krawford.

3-14 Design by Kristen Krawford.

3-15 Design by Kristen Krawford.

3-16 Design by Kristen Krawford.

3-17 Image by John DiMarco.

3-18 Image by John DiMarco.

3-19 Image by John DiMarco.

3-20 Image by John DiMarco.

3-21 Image by John DiMarco.

3-22 Art direction, design, illustration: Stefan Sagmeister. Additional Illustration: Peggy Chuang, Kazumi Matsumoto, Raphael Rüdisser. Photography by Bela Borsodi. Paint Box by Dalton Portella. Courtesy of Sagmeister Inc.

3-23 Courtesy of Pentagram Design.

3-24 Courtesy of Milton Glaser.

3-25 Courtesy of Pentagram Design.

3-25 Courtesy of Pentagram Design.

3-26 Screen Actor magazine cover designed by Alvin Lustig, September 1942 / Alvin Lustig, 1 magazine cover; 30 x 23 cm. Courtesy of the Alvin Lustig papers, 1935-1955, Archives of American Art, Smithsonian Institution. Courtesy of Elaine Lustig Cohen.

3-27 Conference on Art Education, May 6-8, 1948 / Alvin Lustig. Leaflet: 1 folded sheet; 48 x 29 cm. folded to 13 x 10 cm. Courtesy of the Alvin Lustig papers, 1935-1955, Archives of American Art, Smithsonian Institution. Courtesy of Elaine Lustig Cohen.

3-28 Conference on Art Education, May 6-8, 1948 / Alvin Lustig. Leaflet: 1 folded sheet; 48 x 29 cm. folded to 13 x 10 cm. Courtesy of the Alvin Lustig papers, 1935-1955, Archives of American Art, Smithsonian Institution. Courtesy of Elaine Lustig Cohen.

3-29 Screen Actor magazine cover designed by Alvin Lustig, December 1942 / Alvin Lustig. 1 magazine ; 30 x 23 cm. Courtesy of the Alvin Lustig papers, 1935-1955, Archives of American Art, Smithsonian Institution. Courtesy of Elaine Lustig Cohen.

3-30 Cover of Interiors magazine designed by Alvin Lustig, July 1946 / Alvin Lustig, 1 magazine cover; 31 x 23 cm. Courtesy of the Alvin Lustig papers, 1935-1955, Archives of American Art, Smithsonian Institution. Courtesy of Elaine Lustig Cohen.

3-31 The Makers of Modern Literature poster design, ca. 1949 / Alvin Lustig, artist, print: 1 mock-up: ink; 36 x 28 cm. Courtesy of the Alvin Lustig papers, 1935-1955, Archives of American Art, Smithsonian Institution. Courtesy of Elaine Lustig Cohen.

3-32 New Directions Books poster design, ca. 1949 / Alvin Lustig, artist. Print : 1 mock-ups : ink ; 36 x 28 cm. Courtesy of the Alvin Lustig papers, 1935-1955, Archives of American Art, Smithsonian Institution. Courtesy of Elaine Lustig Cohen.

3-33 World Inventors Exposition catalogue cover designed by Alvin Lustig, ca. 1947 / Alvin Lustig, 1 exhibition catalog: ill.; 29 x 22 cm. Courtesy of the Alvin Lustig papers, 1935-1955, Archives of American Art, Smithsonian Institution. Courtesy of Elaine Lustig Cohen.

3-34 Metropolitan Los Angeles: One Community book cover design, ca. 1949 / Alvin Lustig. 1 book jacket ; 28 x 24 cm. Courtesy of the Alvin Lustig papers, 1935-1955, Archives of American Art, Smithsonian Institution.

3-35 Illustration by John DiMarco.

4-2 From Flash Web Design by Hillman Curtis.

4-3 Courtesy of Kristen Crawford.

4-4 Courtesy of John DiMarco.

4-5 Client: SKY Cinema Classics, Italy. Design agency: Flying Machine NYC. Courtesy of Micha Riss.

4-6 Courtesy of Turnstyle.

4-7 Courtesy of Kristen Crawford.

4-8 Courtesy of Turnstyle.

4-9 Courtesy of Pentagram Design.

4-10 Courtesy of Kristen Crawford.

4-11 Courtesy of Turnstyle.

4-12 Courtesy of Pentagram Design.

4-13 Courtesy of Turnstyle.

4-14 Courtesy of Turnstyle.

4-15 a. Courtesy of Kind Company.

4-15 b. Courtesy of Sony BMG records and Soul Associates Inc.

4-16 Courtesy of Turnstyle.

4-17 a. Courtesy of Milton Glaser.

4-17 b. Courtesy of Milton Glaser.

4-17 c. Courtesy of John DiMarco

4-17 d. Courtesy of Turnstyle.

4-17 e. Design director, Stefan Sagmeister. Designer, Matthias Ernstberger. Courtesy of Sagmeister inc.

4-17 f. Courtesy of Soul Associates Inc.

4-17 g. Courtesy of John DiMarco

4-17 h. Courtesy of Pentagram Design.

4-17 i. Courtesy of Pentagram Design.

4-17 j. Courtesy of Pentagram Design.

4-17 k. Courtesy of Pentagram Design.

4-17 l. Courtesy of Pentagram Design.

4-18 Courtesy of the Division of Mass Communication at St. John's University.

4-19 a Courtesy of Kristen Crawford.

4-19 b Courtesy of Sagmeister Inc.

4-20 Courtesy of Pentagram Design.

4-21 Art Direction by Stefan Sagmeister. Design by Stefan Sagmeister, Matthias Ernstberger. Photography by Tom Schierlitz. Courtesy of Sagmeister Inc.

4-22 Courtesy of Pentagram Design.

4-23 Randal Ford, photographer. Courtesy of Pentagram Design.

4-24 Courtesy of Pentagram Design.

5-1 Image courtesy of John Fekner and Don Leicht.

5-1 Image courtesy of John Fekner and Don Leicht.

5-4 Image courtesy of John Fekner.

5-5 Image courtesy of John Fekner.

5-6 Image courtesy of John Fekner.

5-7 Image courtesy of Kevin Fornito.

5-8 Image courtesy of John Fekner.

5-10 Image courtesy of Kevin Fornito.

5-11 Image courtesy of Kevin Fornito.

5-12 Images courtesy of John Fekner and Kevin Fornito.

5-13 Image courtesy of Kevin Fornito.

5-14 Image courtesy of Kevin Fornito.

5-15 Image courtesy of Kevin Fornito.

5-16 Image courtesy of Kevin Fornito.

5-17 Image courtesy of Kevin Fornito.

5-18 Image courtesy of Kevin Fornito.

5-18 Image courtesy of Kevin Fornito.

5-19 Image courtesy of Kevin Fornito..

5-25 Image courtesy of Brian Fendt, Refelctions Photography, LLC.

5-26 Image courtesy of Brian Fendt, Reflections Photography, LLC.

5-27 Image courtesy of John DiMarco.

5-28 Image courtesy of John Fekner.

5-29 Image courtesy of Kevin Fornito.

5-29 Image courtesy of Kevin Fornito.

5-30 Image courtesy of John Fekner.

5-31 Image courtesy of John Fekner.

5-32 Image courtesy of John Fekner.

5-33 Image courtesy of John Fekner.

5-36 Image courtesy of John Fekner.

5-37 Image courtesy of Brian Fendt, Reflections Photography, LLC.

5-38 Image courtesy of Brian Fendt, Reflections Photography, LLC.

5-39 Image courtesy of Brian Fendt, Reflections Photography, LLC.

5-40 Image courtesy of Brian Fendt, Reflections Photography, LLC.

6-1 Image courtesy of Michael Calandra.

6-3 Image courtesy of Michael Calandra.

6-4 Image courtesy of Michael Calandra.

6-6 Image courtesy of John DiMarco.

6-8 Image courtesy of John DiMarco.

6-9 Image courtesy of John DiMarco.

6-10 Image courtesy of John DiMarco.

6-11 Image courtesy of John DiMarco.

6-12 Image courtesy of John DiMarco.

6-13 Image courtesy of John DiMarco.

6-14 Image courtesy of John DiMarco.

6-15 Image courtesy of John DiMarco.

6-16 Image courtesy of John DiMarco.

6-17 Image courtesy of John DiMarco.

6-18 Image courtesy of Michael Calandra.

6-20 Image courtesy of John DiMarco.

6-21 Image courtesy of John DiMarco.

6-22 Image courtesy of John DiMarco.

6-23 Image courtesy of John DiMarco. Fonts by Eduardo Recife.

7-5 Photo courtesy of Kevin Fornito.

7-6 Photo courtesy of Kevin Fornito.

7-11 Photo courtesy of Kevin Fornito.

7-15 Image courtesy of Brian Fendt, Reflections Photography, LLC.

7-16 Images courtesy of Brian Fendt, Reflections Photography, LLC.

7-17 Image courtesy of Brian Fendt, Reflections Photography, LLC.

8-2 Image courtesy of Michael Calandra.

8-4 Windows XP professional window.

8-5 Images courtesy of John DiMarco.

8-7 Images courtesy of John DiMarco.

8-8 Images courtesy of John DiMarco.

8-10 Images courtesy of John DiMarco.

8-11 Images courtesy of John DiMarco.

8-12 Images courtesy of John DiMarco.

8-13 Images courtesy of John DiMarco.

8-14 Images courtesy of John DiMarco.

8-15 Images courtesy of John DiMarco.

8-17 Images courtesy of John DiMarco.

8-18 Images courtesy of John DiMarco.

8-19 Images courtesy of John DiMarco.

8-20 Images courtesy of John DiMarco.

8-21 Images courtesy of John DiMarco.

8-22 Images courtesy of John DiMarco.

8-23 Images courtesy of John DiMarco.,

Index

Page numbers in *italic* type refer to illustrations.

APPENDIX I
Using the Seven-Step Design Process

Kristen Krawford

1. Identify the audience, problem, and communication goals by creating a scope document, abbreviated **GACMIST, that specifies the following:**

   G: Goal—the goal is to produce a poster that will grab the attention of college students and educate them on the need for having an online portfolio.

   A: Audience—college students.

   C: Concept—the concept for this poster is based on the portfoliovillage.com Web site, which explains why a college student needs an online portfolio.

   M: Messages—the messages and copy will be provided, but I will be able to add or eliminate copy based on design purposes. The main message is that everyone needs a professional portfolio.

   I: Images—some suggestions of imagery for a college-based online portfolio include college students, a portfolio, a laptop or computer, and postmodern graphics.

   S: Style—the style of this poster should be hip, fresh, and very edgy and graphic, with bright or muted colors—something that will stand out to both average and more artistic college students.

   T: Theme—the theme of the poster is based on new and exciting tools available to a college student.

2. Research the audience and the medium to clarify themes and output specifications. Gather information to be used in the conceptualization and creation of the work.

In order to create a poster that will attract college students, I began by considering the colors, symbols, and fonts that are associated with young students. Once I started researching magazines and advertisements targeted to this audience, I noticed edgier graphics, the nontraditional placement of images and words, bright colors, line art, and so on.

3. Use concentric circles to identify keywords from which themes may emerge. These themes will lead to the emotional center of the product or idea. Ask your client, research subjects, and yourself, "What will make people respond?"

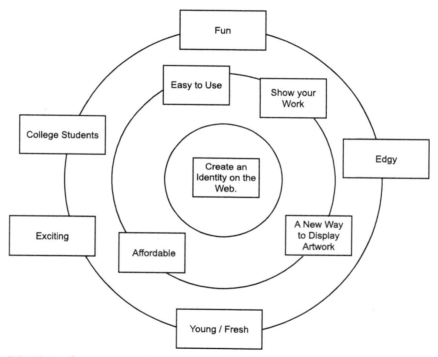

FIGURE A1-1 Concentric circles help identify themes.

4. Conceptualize on paper using outlines, flowcharts, sketches, storyboards, and integrated site maps to connect the concept and theme. Brainstorm using divergent (nonlinear) thinking to find creative solutions first; then use convergent (linear) thinking to solve process problems. Use thumbnails to rough out possible creative directions.

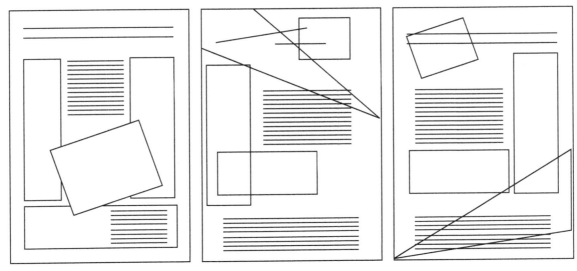

FIGURE A1-2 Sketches are a vehicle for creative design planning.

5. Create simple solutions in the form of visual comps, prototypes, and treatments using digital design tools.

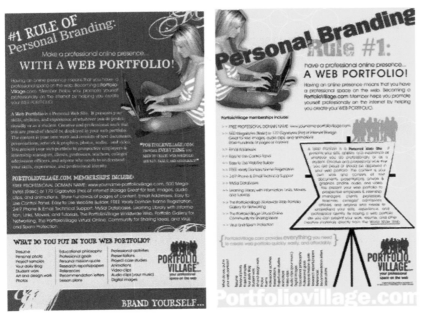

FIGURE A1-3 The initial designs provide direction.

6. Revise by filtering, simplifying, and justifying the work.

FIGURE A1-4   The final designs represent simpler solutions.

7. Evaluate the design against the communication goals and scope document to measure your success and make recommendations for future updates.

Have the visual communication goals been achieved in the final piece? Goals:

Use of Line Art

Use of Graphic Images

Use of Photo or Graphic of a Portfolio

Use of Edgy Fonts

Use of Color

Inclusion of Information to Attract the College and Designer Audience

APPENDIX II
Digital Photography

Rex Thomas, MFA

Of the myriad factors that have contributed to digital photography's ongoing integration into professional applications, the two most influential are the personal computer and the photojournalist. The computer has become the hub from which we communicate, create, and interact, And the peripherals we use to connect to one another have evolved in tandem with it. Historically, photojournalists have always been early adopters of new technologies. In the mid-1920s, they were among the first to embrace the 35 mm film camera because it offered the ability to capture high-quality images without all the travails that came with the sheet-film cameras of the time. Similarly, photojournalists have transitioned to digital photography because it provides the freedom to record and deliver an assignment without the restrictions that came with processing and distributing film.

Today, commercial, fashion, and portrait photographers are embracing digital systems. In part, this is because digital photography allows for faster turnarounds of finished work product, but it is also because digital photography offers photographers a greater creative freedom to experiment, provides their clients with immediate proofs, and easily integrates images into design applications.

Exposure = Aperture + Shutter Speed

Aperture

Aperture is the opening in the lens that permits light to pass through it. Aperture is measured in f-stops. A larger f-number (e.g., f/16) indicates a smaller aperture, meaning that less light will pass through the lens opening to the image sensor. A smaller f-number (e.g., f/2.8) indicates a larger aperture or lens opening, thus allowing more light to reach the image sensor. A "fast" lens is one that has a smaller f-number, thereby allowing more of the available light to pass through a lens and for use of a faster shutter speed. A faster shutter speed captures action in low-light situations without the need of a flash, and still achieves the correct exposure.

Shutter Speed

Shutter speed is the amount of time the shutter has to remain open, or the digital sensor has to remain activated, in order to achieve the correct exposure. Shutter speed is measured in fractions of a second (e.g., $1/8$, $1/125$, $1/250$); the higher the number, the faster the shutter speed.

Aperture and shutter speed always work in tandem. If you set your camera to aperture priority, you choose the aperture value and the camera selects the shutter speed accordingly; if you select *shutter priority*, you choose the shutter speed and the camera selects the aperture automatically. Full manual control means you select both the aperture and shutter speed.

Depth of Field

Depth of field (DOF) is the distance between the nearest and the farthest objects that are in focus. It is important in achieving a strong compositional narrative because it establishes a visual and emotional connection between the subject and the foreground and background elements.

FIGURE A2-1 A large DOF provides a global view of the subject's relationship to all the elements in the foreground and background.

Achieving a large DOF depends on the lens's focal length and f-number. A telephoto lens, or a zoom lens set to its narrowest viewing angle (largest focal length), compresses space. A wide-angle lens, or a zoom lens set to its widest viewing angle, increases what will be seen in a frame, providing the opportunity for a larger depth of field. The f-number you use also affects the DOF: as you decrease the f-stop (use a larger f-number), you increase the amount of the depth of field. An f-stop of 8, a common f-number used to achieve a reasonably good DOF, will be greater than that which uses an f-stop of 2.8.

FIGURE A2-2 Focal length set at 14 mm; aperture set at f/7.1.

There are times when too much DOF becomes distracting and confuses the point of focus in a photograph. When shooting portraits or a still life, or doing macro photography, use a shallow DOF so that the subject is the focus for the viewer. To achieve a shallow DOF, increase the f-stop (decrease the f-number) and either move closer to the subject if using a wide-angle lens, or zoom to a larger focal length to compress the space between the foreground and the background.

FIGURE A2-3 Focal length set at 14 mm; aperture set at f/2.8.

Framing and Composition

The frame one chooses has a tremendous effect on how a photograph is experienced. Don't always adopt the obvious frame: the better one understands how we, as a society, expect the visual world to be represented, the better one is, as a photographer, to engage his or her audience by contradicting these expectations. As I tell my students, "Make the abstract obvious!"

Horizontal Framing

Horizontal framing is the most common framing choice, because it represents how a photographer sees the world. As such, this style of framing provides a certain sense of stability and balance.

FIGURE A2-4 Horizontal framing.

Vertical Framing

I tend to use vertical rather than horizontal framing because I like to create tension by constricting the viewer's perception of the subject. Vertical photographs also tend to be more dramatic because the height of the shot is greater than its width, which works against the viewer's subconscious desire for visual balance.

FIGURE A2-5 Vertical framing.

Canted Framing

Canted or *angled framing* creates emotional and psychological tension. This technique follows a tactic developed by filmmakers who shoot the protagonist at angles that imply to the audience that all is not right with the hero, or with the situation he or she is in.

FIGURE A2-6 Canted framing.

Cropping

Henri Cartier-Bresson, the renowned photojournalist, did not believe in cropping photographs; he believed a photographer should be able to frame a shot from the outset, thus eliminating the need for later cropping. I agree with Mr. Bresson—one should not always rely on cropping to fix a poorly composed shot.

FIGURE A2-7 The power of cropping a photograph to tighten its point of focus or heighten the visual narrative cannot be overlooked.

Lighting

It is readily apparent that without light there is no photography. Yet knowing how to get the right amount of light for a properly exposed photograph is not all there is to understand about photography, digital or otherwise. Entire books have been written on how to use and manipulate light to achieve magnificent results; this section is limited to a few basics.

Natural Light

There are two types of natural light: *outside* and *inside*. Outside light tends to be diffused: even in the brightest sunlight, this light bounces off and is reflected through various surfaces and elements in the air. Humidity, albeit invisible to the naked eye, can filter sunlight in such a way that colors appear softened. Additionally, certain times of the day yield different lighting conditions based on the sun's position in the sky. The phrase "the golden hour" refers to either dawn or dusk, when color temperatures are often at their coolest. Midday is usually when sunlight is at its whitest. Natural light includes daylight and cloudy.

(A)

FIGURES A2-8, A, B   Photo 8A was taken at midday, with the sun directly above the subject, while photo 8B was taken at late afternoon, with the sun behind the subjects.

(B)

Artificial Light

Artificial light can be any source of illumination that is not from a natural source—a lamp, a candle, a neon sign, and so forth. Each source of artificial light has its own color temperature, which can add a certain cast to a photograph, providing emotional or psychological depth to the visual narrative—or ruining it. Generally, artificial light breaks down into the following categories:

- Tungsten: the typical incandescent bulbs in lamps. The color cast is usually warm, leaning more toward yellow or red.

- Fluorescent: cool light with either a green or blue cast.

FIGURES A2-9, A–C In all three photos artificial light is used to emphasize to the subject matter.

Flashes

There are two types of flashes, *built-in* and *external*. A built-in flash is most common with point-and-shoot and zoom-lens reflex (ZLR) cameras; some digital single-lens reflex (DSLR) cameras offer the convenience of a built-in flash. The camera generally correlates the burst of a built-in flash unit to the lighting conditions, but even at its best, built-in flashes tend to be overpowering and overexpose a shot. External flashes are added on to a camera or set up within the shooting space. They can be set according to the conditions of the environment and allow the photographer to execute more control than internal flashes.

Studio light

Studio lights can be tungsten or halogen, strobes or continuous light. In all cases, studio lights allow for the most flexibility and creative control. A simple studio lighting setup would consist of two *key lights* and perhaps a fill light, as well as a paper or cloth backdrop. You can add reflecting umbrellas to each light to soften the intensity of light falling on your subject, or a *softbox* which further diffuses the light to provide more even illumination.

Widely Used Applications and Formats Chart

Recommended specifications.

PROGRAM	WIDELY USED FILE FORMATS	MEDIA OUTPUT*	TYPICAL SIZES**	COLOR MODES TO USE***
Adobe Photoshop and Fireworks (raster graphics for print projects and Web pages)	.psd for design .tif for print .eps for print .pdf for print or document management .tga for video/TV .jpg for Web (photos or graphics—use this for any image) .gif for Web (for flat graphics only) In Photoshop, always save a .psd file with layers for future editing. The .png format can also be used for layered Web design files. In Fireworks, always save a .png file with layers for future editing.	Print Web graphics & Web Page layouts Broadcast Digital video Mobile Resolutions: Print projects: 300–350 ppi Web and broadcast projects: 72 ppi Always design to final output size.	Print (measured in inches): 8.5 × 11 8.5 × 14 11 × 17 Web (measured in pixels): Web banner: 240 × 320 Web or video/TV: 640 × 480 800 × 600 550 × 400 720 × 540 720 × 480 1280 × 720 Mobile device sizes vary. Projects can be of any size.	Use RGB for print graphics during initial design, then convert to CMYK. RGB for Web graphics. Use RGB for .jpg files. Use Web-safe index color for .gif files and Web backgrounds that must appear the same in all browsers. Use CMYK for print graphics (.in .tif or .eps format). As a final step, convert all print documents to CMYK before saving them in .tif or. eps format. Never use CMYK for Web graphics. Never use RGB for print graphics.

PROGRAM	WIDELY USED FILE FORMATS	MEDIA OUTPUT*	TYPICAL SIZES**	COLOR MODES TO USE***
Adobe Illustrator (vector graphics and layouts in Illustrator)	.ai for design .eps for print Exports: .tif for print .jpg for Web (photos or graphics—use this for any image) .gif for Web (for flat graphics only) Always save an .ai file with editable text before creating outlines for future editing. Open .ai files and .eps files in Photoshop or Fireworks and rasterize them into bitmapped images for the Web. Vector files cannot be placed on a Web site unless they are rasterized.	Print Web graphics and Web page layouts Broadcast Digital video Mobile Resolutions: Print projects: 300–350 ppi Web and broadcast projects: 72 ppi Always design to final output size.	Print (*measured in inches*):8.5×11 8.5×14 11×17 Web (*measured in pixels*): Web banner: 240×320 Web or video/TV: 640×480 800×600 550×400 720×540 720×480 1280×720 Mobile sizes vary. Projects can be of any size.	Use CMYK or Pantone colors for print design. Use RGB for Web design Use RGB for .jpg files. Use Web-safe index colors for .gif files and Web backgrounds that must appear the same in all browsers. Use CMYK and Pantone swatches for print graphics (one to four colors). As a final step, convert all print documents to CMYK before saving as them in .eps format. Use Pantone spot colors plus black for two-color work such as logos, cards, and letterheads. Never Use CMYK for Web graphics. Never Use RGB for print graphics.
Adobe InDesign (page layouts)	.idd for design .idd or .pdf for print Exports: .tif or .eps for print .jpg for Web (Avoid exporting graphics from a page layout program.) *Always save an .idd with all fonts and graphics for future editing.	Print Resolutions: Print projects: 300–350 ppi	Print (*measured in inches*): 8.5×11 8.5×14 11×17 24×36 Projects can be of any size.	Use CMYK and Pantone swatches for print graphics (one to four colors). Make sure all type and placed graphics are CMYK or Pantone spot color before final output.

PROGRAM	WIDELY USED FILE FORMATS	MEDIA OUTPUT*	TYPICAL SIZES**	COLOR MODES TO USE***
Adobe Dreamweaver (Web pages and sites)	.html for basic Web pages (proprietary format) .css for style sheets	Web Mobile Web and broadcast projects: 72 ppi Always design to final output size.	Web (*measured in pixels*): Web banner: 728×90 Web banner or pop-up: 240×320 Web page or pop-up: 640×480 Web page: 800×600 550×400 720×540 720×480 1280×720 Mobile sizes vary. Projects can be of any size.	All inserted graphics must be RGB or Web-safe index color (in .jpg or .gif format). All browser-based text should be Web-safe index color. Never use CMYK for Web graphics.
Adobe Flash (Web pages, Web sites, and motion graphics/ animations)	The proprietary format for Flash is .fla. Other formats include .swf, .flv, .avi, and .mov. Use .png or .tga for frame-by-frame output for broadcast. Always save an .fla file with layers for future editing.	Web Broadcast Digital video Mobile Web and broadcast projects: 72 ppi Always design to final output size.	(*Measured in pixels*): Web: 240×320 800×600 550×400 Web, NTSC: 640×480 NTSC D1: 720×486 NTSC D1 square: 720×540 NTSC DV widescreen: 720×480 1280×720 (HDTV) Mobile sizes vary. Projects can be of any size.	RGB Web-safe index color

*Projects can be repurposed only if they go from high resolution to low resolution output (from print to Web; **Projects can be created at many different custom sizes; the information given provides standards and starting points for pages and many projects; ***Projects that are printed on a printing press or deployed to a Web server must be in the proper color mode; otherwise, they will not output correctly.